ME AS HER AGAIN

NANCY AGABIAN

aunt lute books   SAN FRANCISCO

Aunt Lute Books
P.O. Box 410687
San Francisco, CA 94141
www.auntlute.com

Cover design: Amy Woloszyn
Text design: dendesign

Senior Editor: Joan Pinkvoss
Managing Editor: Shay Brawn
Production: Noelle de la Paz, Riah Gouvea, Soma Nath, Ladi Youssefi

This book was funded in part by a grant from the National Endowment for the Arts.

Library of Congress Cataloging-in-Publication Data

Agabian, Nancy, 1968-
  Me as her again : true stories of an Armenian daughter / Nancy Agabian.
    p. cm.
  Includes bibliographical references.
  ISBN 978-1-879960-79-4 (alk. paper)
  1. Agabian, Nancy, 1968- 2. Authors, American--20th century--Biography.
  3. Armenian Americans--Biography. 4. Armenians--Biography. I. Title.

PS3551.G33Z46 2008
818'.6--dc22
                                2008035560

Printed in the U.S.A. on acid-free paper

10 9 8 7 6 5 4 3 2 1

Table of Contents

Nonfiction Advisory

Me as her again is a memoir of my Armenian family's role in my life; it attempts to tell a story about the collective inheritance of trauma and denial. In order to construct a plot for this book, I had to invent some version of myself as a character in the act of looking back. Accordingly, early chapters are told from the perspective of a twenty-three-year old me, living in Los Angeles and writing poetry, remembering events in her childhood as though solving a riddle. Obviously, memories of childhood are relayed as stories, and because many of them are not so vividly remembered, the filled in details and dialogue form a type of fiction.

Because of the manipulation of memories and my desire to protect my family, I could have called this book a novel. But that would belie, among other experiences, the truth of my grandmother's oral history tape and its translation as described. Still, it should be understood that the accounts here are from my point of view and don't represent an objective truth. The depictions of my friends and family members weren't drawn to represent their full wondrous selves, but to tell my story. *So, Armenian gossips and busybodies beware:* if you happen to know my family members and believe they are as described in this memoir, you will come down on the wrong side of fiction versus non-fiction. They are lovely people and don't deserve to be judged as they appear in this text.

Granted, most readers expect that a book labeled "memoir" deals with such issues of craft, and they understand that the nature of memory itself is selective and creative. Due to the recent hyperbolic mistrust of memoirs in the U.S., however, I feel the need to confess that I did not fabricate any characters or stories from scratch. Although I took the creative liberty to compress time, to change the chronological order of a few events, and to compose a couple of minor characters based on two or three real people in order to streamline the story, everything in this book is based on memories, journal entries and researched and reported information.

So you, as reader, might be best served to let go of labels and accept this book as a blend of fiction and nonfiction: a true story.

ME AS HER AGAIN

My Grandmother's Letter
to an Armenologist on Mars

27 Oliver Street
Watertown, MA 02081

Miss Nancy Agabian
549 Venice Way, Apt #2
Venice, CA 90291

Sept. 23, 1992

Dear Nancy:

I'm still worrying about you. I'm still trying to find out what you're doing and when you're going to come back. I'm very lonesome, I'd like to see you shortly (short laugh). Now I have to make up my mind what I'm going to do. I'm still here - I'm worrying, I'd like to go home, you know, they won't take me there. And when you come back I have to decide with you. I'm waiting for you. I hafta - I think they gonna send me to the old age home and I don't want to go.

You have something important to do over there? Don't worry about the job - any time you can find a job around here. Well, Nancy, I don't know how much I hafta say it but ah, but, but, but, you have steady work? I have a lot to say but can't tell you in the le tter. When I see you we talk about everything.

Love,

Zanik

"No more - we're not making a newspaper you know"

typed by your brother on Aunt Mel's circa 1962 Smith-Corona Electric typewriter (salmon-colored)

8:40 pm

Enclosures:
1) $20.00
2) photograph

In the enclosed photo, Zanik is standing in the driveway, in front of her daughter's Reliant K station wagon, as if about to leave. She's wearing a navy t-shirt tucked in, which collects her drooping boobs at the waistline, a striped blue and white skirt, pantyhose, and white sneakers. A big white jacket and sizable white clutch purse complete the ensemble. Her white hair is short, but not too neat, hands are curved inward, hanging in front of her, gnarled. Sun is dappling off the green leaves in the background and onto the driveway cement. Roughly eighty-seven, she's looking at the camera openly but not smiling, with some slight question on her face: Who are you? or What do you see? or Why am I important? or You didn't cut off my head again, did you?

Judging by the way my brother was so delighted by the make, year and color of the machine, I'm guessing it was my grandmother's idea to bring out the typewriter. They would have eaten dinner, always at 6 P.M., and then after the news and coffee and dessert, she would have summoned him for a special project. She needed someone to help her write because she did not know how, and she must not have trusted my aunts. As they sat at the dining room table, she dictated, and Leo transcribed practically exactly, knowing that I would hear her old country accent and understand her words and the spaces in between—the way she starts out so confidently, gives a short laugh, questions herself, then, perhaps at his prodding to write a postscript, gives him some old-lady sass about wordiness with her newspaper remark.

Lately, I had received several letters from my dad and my aunts, reporting that my grandmother was obsessively asking them every day to take her back to her house in Oxford, out near Worcester, Massachusetts. Grammy lived there from the time she married at sixteen until her late sixties. She was born in an Ottoman Anatolian village where she lived till she was ten, then marched to Syria while watching her family die along the way. She somehow wound up in an orphanage where an older brother found her and brought her to America. It wasn't too surprising why she would be attached to the house in Oxford, a space of stability after a childhood disrupted by horror. It was where she became a woman, where she raised her family. But she was driving them crazy now with her pleas to go back; she was insistent and had practically nothing else on her mind. No one in the family believed that she would be happy there, alone, on her own; but she was sure she would like it better than being dumped in a nursing home.

Grammy wouldn't have understood why I was in California, so I never bothered answering her letter. I had told her a few times what my job was, but my job sucked, and I hadn't disclosed the real reason for my self-imposed exile—to get as far away from my family as possible. Now she wanted me to help her, but how could I? Valerie, my older sister, had pondered living out in Oxford with her, but I never entertained the idea—what else would be there, besides Grammy?

It was a fluke that I was even in California at all. Throughout college I had been plotting my mode of escape from my family, which required defying a longstanding Agabian tradition of adult children living with their parents: my three never-married aunts rooming with Grammy, and closer to home, my older brother Leo cramped out in his childhood bedroom. Somehow, I finagled a position at a Hollywood TV studio through an Armenian internship program, which met my parents' approval; they must have thought that it would have led to a good job, at least for a year or two, at which point I would move back to the Boston area. But something didn't sit right with my mother, for the morning that I was set to leave, she came into my bedroom and whispered, "You can't go."

I turned over in bed and saw her standing above me. Her dark brown eyes were wide, and her pale pink lips looked naked without her usual coat of mauve frosted lipstick. A few pin curls were clipped tightly to her head, revealing a delicate white scalp.

"What?" I asked, still groggy.

"You can't drive to California. It's too dangerous. We'll buy you a plane ticket."

The brown of her nipples floated ominously beneath her thin cotton floral nightie. My mother couldn't tolerate people leaving her, a trait so intrinsic that I wouldn't be able to question the reason till years later.

"No, I've made plans to drive and I'm going to drive." My friend Alisa was sleeping downstairs in the den. Months before, we had decided to drive across the country with my father's five-year-old Toyota Camry, which he had promised me for graduating with honors. It didn't seem fair to drastically change our plans last minute. "What am I supposed to tell Alisa?"

"Tell her she can take the bus. You don't have to be afraid of her." Throughout my childhood and adolescence, Mumma had often assumed I was taking action only because another person was pressuring me, which by now drove me totally crazy.

I started raising my voice. "What will I drive once I'm in L.A.?"

"We'll give you money to rent a car. You can't drive all the way across the country. You'll get into an accident," she insisted.

I was a lousy driver, it was true. And now that the day of my departure had arrived, I *was* pretty scared.

But I was more afraid that if I didn't assert myself now, I'd never leave my mother. Flinging off the sheets, like a character on a nighttime soap opera, I announced, "I'm leaving and you can't stop me!" and pushed past her to prepare for departure.

As my parents and brother looked on, I backed the packed Camry out of the driveway. *To California!*, I thought as I reversed into the telephone pole across the street from our house. Leo burst out laughing, Daddy arched his neck to see if there was any damage, and Mumma frowned. *Don't stop now!* I put the automatic transmission in D for Drive, pulled forward and waved. They all waved back and soon the split-level home of my childhood was gone from view.

At the stop sign at the bottom of the street, I broke into tears and sobbed to my friend, "I'm leaving everything behind!"

It was quite a drive through northern New England, with trees so lush and green they looked edible, then west towards Minnesota where I dropped off Alisa. I caravanned with some other friends through Wyoming, encountering the dome of the sky for the very first time. We made it through tornado-like weather in the Dakotas and a snowstorm near Yellowstone. Utah was repressive and Vegas was depressing. But it wasn't until I stepped out of my car at a rest stop in the desert that I felt everything change. I was terrified of the future, but I felt an unexplainable sense of belonging, as the pebbles crunched under my feet and the dry sun beat sharply on my black hair.

Now, two years later, I lived in Venice, California, and I was pretty depressed. Once I was far away from my home, I hadn't really known how to make a life, how to make friends, how to make food, how to do anything. If it hadn't been for Bee, my friend and roommate, I would have totally been at a loss; she had learned to cook all kinds of things from her mother, tacos and lasagna.

When we first moved in together, it was after the internship and I was unemployed, looking desperately for a job. I interviewed to be an art framer at a place with the deceptive name "Special Children's School" that was really a daycare center for mentally retarded grownups. My interviewer was taking me on a tour of the art studios when we encountered a middle-aged, six-foot tall Special Child wearing grey chinos and a navy blue v-neck sweater; he accused me of stealing his picture, then told me I was mean. I bawled on my way home in the car, but when I told Bee the story, she cracked up.

The truth was she could laugh because her life was pretty pathetic too. The only work she had found was taking photos of kids at soccer games, hoping a parent would buy. Things changed fast, though, and she was getting a real job and buying a car. We still lived together, two years later, but so much had changed between us that I actually missed those times now, missed all our shared misery. One night, back then, we were getting stoned on the floor with some Cheetos when our neighbor stopped by our open door to shoot the shit, told us she was an extra on the Keanu Reeves-Patrick Swayze surfing-FBI movie. She was blond and wearing a bikini top; I tried not to look at her boobs. Her roommate, also blond and built, pulled up on his motorcycle and she hopped on: they were going up to Malibu to watch the sunset. In contrast, Bee was wearing a pair of boxer shorts with the fly wide open and I was in my pair of pajama bottoms with period stains on the butt.

Fortunately, I found an escape from this reality. In a small tower room of Beyond Baroque Literary Arts Center, housed in the old Venice Town Hall, a grand, Spanish building, I attended a multicultural poetry workshop for women—young, old, rich, poor, lesbian, straight, bi, black, Latino, white. Hearing their words and absorbing the experimentation of poetry somehow made me feel like I had a story: all of what I had left behind. I spent nights filling pages with stream of consciousness, working my past and problems through the art filter. There was some meaning to be found.

One of the exercises we were given was to write your earliest memory. Mine was of a solitary experience apart from my family, a hospital visit when I was three years old. A nurse was reading me a picture book, a story about the number one. This **1** was red, an anthropomorphized character with eyes, a nose and a mouth. He happens to be lonesome, so he puts on a porkpie hat and hits the road. He runs into a green **1** and a blue **1** bobbing on a seesaw. When he asks to join them, they decline; a seesaw only works with two.

Little red **1** takes to the road again and comes across two yellow **1**s swinging a jump rope and an orange **1** jumping. He is informed that his presence isn't welcomed here either. As **1** encounters other systems of digits in increasing numerical order, he is repeatedly told that if he joins them, he will ruin whatever good thing they've got going. It seems unfair, especially in the case of nine multicolored **1**s having a party, drinking punch and playing pin the tail on the donkey, while **1** stands by himself in a corner, forlorn. Incensed, I looked up at the nurse for corroboration. She was wearing a white dress and a white nurse hat and she smiled down at me and I loved her.

"Ready?" she asked cheerfully.

I nodded my head.

She turned the page to reveal a big red zero in the middle of the spread. **0** is obviously a girl, with eyelashes and full lips drawn into the vast open space of her middle. **1** has finally met his match, his true fate, his place in the chaotic world of numerals. Together he and **0** form the number **10**. It is a happy day. The End.

My mother and my grandmother told me the rest of the story, when I was a little older, five or six. According to Mumma, I was three and a half when I became so sick with a fever that she had to take me to Dr. Edmund, one of only two pediatricians in our small town of Walpole. He informed her that I had a virus, and there was nothing to do except fill me with fluids and let me get better. The next day I seemed worse, unable to eat and listless, so my mother called the doctor with her concerns. Unimpressed, he told my mother, "You have to be a patient *nurse,* Mrs. Agabian."

Mumma could not lift me, I was so limp with sickness, so Daddy carried me to the station wagon. There was no time to find a sitter, so my brother and sister came with us. Valerie was ten and watched over Leo, who was eight, in the waiting room of Children's Hospital in Boston.

The doctors thought my condition was more serious than a virus and prescribed penicillin. Ingested back at home, it made my skin erupt with hives and closed my throat. Over the phone, the hospital told my mother to take me to the nearest doctor because I was having an allergic reaction and needed an adrenaline shot immediately.

"You shouldn't have brought her to Children's," Dr. Edmund reprimanded my parents as they bustled into his office. "This could leave a bad mark on my record."

"I don't care about your reputation, Dr. Edmund!" my mother snapped, her dark hair frantically pulled up, wisps in her face. "This is my daughter and she's number one!"

Edmund administered the shot, and my parents took me back to Children's Hospital. I was admitted to the ward and tested for spinal meningitis, children's arthritis, and rheumatic fever. "We didn't know what was wrong with you," Mumma told me. "We were all very worried."

"Really?" I asked. As a child, I loved hearing that everyone was consumed with angst that I might have died—it made me seem so special. Mumma said a prominent doctor at the hospital took over my case, gave me strong doses of antibiotics and watchfully waited. He talked about my condition with the residents, young men who asked me for kisses. I imagined that I must have been pretty irresistible, approaching death's door with a mysterious affliction.

"You were cryin'," Grammy told me. "Cry, cry, cryin'! I was so upset." While she and Aunties were visiting, two nurses arrived to insert an intravenous tube into my arm and closed the curtain around my bed. They ran into some difficulty finding a vein, and I screamed in agony. Grammy couldn't take it; she clutched her pocketbook tighter and yelled in Armenian for my aunts to do something. Auntie Mel was a nurse and explained that I was in no real danger, but Grammy didn't care. The sound of her precious granddaughter in pain was more than she could bear. "I wanted to push open the curtain," Grammy said. But just as she was about to, it was clacked aside by the nurses to reveal a clear plastic apparatus sticking out of my tiny arm, my mass of black hair messed up, tears smudging my baby face.

Mumma said my condition eventually improved within a couple of days. Everyone shrugged their shoulders and surmised it was an undiagnosed streptococcal infection gone awry. Talk about an anticlimactic ending; after all that melodramatic buildup, you'd think I would have had a really scary disease. I'd never heard of anyone losing their life to strep throat.

The Children's Hospital episode provided my earliest memory, one that I would recall throughout my childhood, adolescence, young adulthood. But I didn't remember the frantic trips to the medics, or my mother yelling that I was number one, or anyone in my family visiting or worrying or fighting for me; those were the stories of my mother and my grandmother. *My* story was of feeling alone, of the white nurse reading to me about the little red **1** who repeatedly found he didn't belong, wherever he went. I had a book, a story I could attach myself to, an escape route, and all I could do was identify. The strongest memory for me was **1**'s elation when he met **0**.

Hoping that the nurse might have given the book to me, I would periodically search for it all over our house, hoping to find that **0**. But she never turned up. I loved her absence and the feeling it left me with: the melancholy state of being misunderstood and alone. It was my story, a script, as the psychiatrists like to say—not so original, but one that I could relive repeatedly.

I also recognize that the yarns spun expressly by my mother and grandmother, in which they are heroines protecting something so special and fragile, are interwoven with mine; they are infused into the earliest memory, imbedding the story with a paradox, with more meaning: theirs and ours.

People don't want me to tell the rest of our stories. It's not because anything very scandalous or controversial happens. There are stories here of the bisexual, the queer, the transgendered, the outsider, the oppressed, the depressed, the victim, the survivor, the denied, the denier, the forgotten, and the remembered; but fundamentally, this is a mother-daughter-grandmother story. By now, 2008, the book market in America has been flooded for years with the autobiographies of un-famous people. Everyone feels the need to tell a life story, in our age, as an act of catharsis and/or social justice. The average reading audience has little attention for the memoir of the ordinary person making a phenomenon out of a personal struggle; the only true stories that get noticed anymore are those that contain specious details, so that the authors can get thrown to the lions. But sometimes you have to forget your time and place—stories can last forever, and you never know who will find them. Armenians have lived for eons, across the planet, and, despite their fears of not existing, it is likely that they'll be around for ages more in order to figure out their problems. Undoubtedly, they are going to need additional reading material. In the meantime, reader, while this story waits to be found by future generations of cloned Armenian colonies or Armenologists on Mars, you are welcome to escape or identify.

For a while, I too didn't want to hear these stories of the Armenians; I didn't want to be their special little one. Now I tell my life in order to sort out the yarns of the others, those mothers, to look closely at our threads of loss and longing and leaving, braided together, an emotional timeline of similar but different histories passing one another, over and under and around—bound. This is a story of what was left behind, what passed down, and how all that history pressed itself into bodies and minds as a life unwound.

PART I

1. CLEAN TO DIRTY

I was naked, sitting on a white enamel stool with a black rubber, grooved seat in the middle of my grandmother's bathtub. Grammy turned on the tap; when the water steamed, she filled an empty, quart-sized Colombo Yogurt container. I was wondering what she was going to do with it when she dumped it over my head.

"Wah!" I yelped.

Hot water flowed over me and collected in the crease between my shut legs, making me feel sick to my stomach. I was not used to bathing like this, wet skin in open air; at home, Mumma filled the tub with a few inches of placid warm water before letting me sit in it. Shivering now, I began to cry as Grammy soaped a rough white washcloth with Ivory, scoured my skin, and told me to shush. Then she filled up the yogurt container and doused me again. I cried some more but Grammy persisted. She poured Johnson's Baby Shampoo into her hand and scrubbed my head, hard. I could feel her fingers, her trimmed fingernails, press right into my skull. "Lotta hair," she said under her breath. "Just like me, when I was little." I looked up at her hair, which was short and gray and waved around her face, but then she pushed my head down and deftly poured several pails of water, one after the other, over my hair to rinse. Bitter suds ran between my eyes and spilled into my mouth. "Please stop Grammy, no more!" I spit.

"Almost done," she insisted. Normally, she was gentle with me, adoring even, so her treatment now seemed all the more harsh. The worst part was the anticipation, not knowing if another deluge was coming while water continued to filter through my thick long hair. All I could do was wait for it to be over.

And it stopped: as Grammy was washing my feet, she noticed the black birthmark in the middle of the sole of my left foot. She scrubbed it, and when it wouldn't go away, she brought it closer to her eyes to examine. "Magic Marker," she said under her breath, rubbing harder.

"No Grammy, it's a birthmark," I told her.

"I don't tink so," she said, shaking her head. My grandmother had been tricked before by the accoutrements of the 1970s child. Once she had seen my brother and me eating white Tic Tacs and had screamed, "Ruth's pills! Why are you taking Ruth's pills?" not believing they were mints until my aunt had compared her blood pressure medication to a confiscated Tic Tac in the palm of Grammy's hand.

My grandmother kept scrubbing at my birthmark; there was no way she would allow dirt to trick her. There was no way she would allow Magic Marker to soil her granddaughter's sole. But it wouldn't go away.

She stared at the mark as if she couldn't believe it. "Huh," she said, finally giving up. She dried me off and kissed the bottom of my foot. "Birtmark," she said in her scratchy voice, her wobbly old accent. She laughed. We both understood that I had somehow won.

———

Memories like these streamed out of me late at night, my light on in my peachy pink bedroom, the rubber tree's thick and full leaves pressing against my window. Sometimes I could hear the bus screech to a stop below on Venice Boulevard. There had been a reading at Beyond Baroque and I tried to stick around to talk to people but I couldn't, so I came home.

My hand scribbled columns of words over the lined paper in a little Japanese notebook. Bee had provided me with a constant supply. She worked at the L.A. bureau of a Japanese newspaper, over in Little Tokyo, and instead of the narrow spiral notebooks I'd seen in the stationery store with REPORTER'S NOTEBOOK printed on the cover, the Japanese reporters preferred these theme notebooks, around twenty pages stapled together, the cover a sheet of card stock with some specks of dust swirling through it. They reminded me of the homemade books I put together as a little kid with my father's special appraisal paper and a piece of construction stock for a cover, in which I would write and illustrate with my crayons the exploits of ducks and frogs.

As a young student I loved reading and got good grades in English. When I went to Wellesley, though, I didn't think I could write. So many of the girls went to private schools, where the English education was far better than what the underfunded Walpole public school system could provide. After flunking out of my parents' choice of architecture, I declared an art major; I wasn't sure I was very good at art either, but at the time artists represented free and cool individuality which I aspired to. During my junior year I started to insert words into my drawings and paintings. Recently I had been taping butcher paper to my bedroom wall next to a mirror, getting naked and drawing life-sized charcoal self-portraits: again the words appeared. I scrawled them on the paper, sometimes smearing them. Even though I was incorporating more and more words into my work, I understood that writers weren't artists. Writers are writers. Painters, sculptors, dancers, filmmakers, photographers, singers, musicians: all artists. They have talent with a very specific skill. Writers work to hone a medium that we all work with every day, and they try very hard to make that medium clear, understandable. They don't smear their words. They are serious and scholarly with their time alone with pen and ink or typewriter and all the words in their heads, all the books they read. I never got the sense that people like Charlotte

Brontë and her tubercular sisters were smoking dope and experiencing all they could of a full, free, corset-less life; instead, they occupied themselves with their little books in their dark and dingy house on the heath cliff.

So in my little Japanese books, I engaged in an artistic process: I wasn't a writer, I was an artist, just moving words around on a page, instead of lines and colors. It was funny that most of what I wrote involved my family, since they too were a medium that I worked with every day. They were gone from view, which helped, because now I could just move them around in my brain, remembering what they had said to me, trying to see them a little more clearly. It got confusing when they called me on the phone and reminded me they were alive, across the continent, waiting for me to come home. "The earth cracks over there!" Grammy once wailed into my ear. She never called me on her own; Aunt Mel would say hello, ask me how I was doing, and then Grammy would break in on the extension to tell me to come home. Mel would then pass her phone to Ruth, and Agnes would get on eventually.

No one I had ever known had three never-married aunts. Make that two, or even one. If the Brontës had lived today, they would have been freaks. Spinsterhood, celibacy—not exactly modern American ideals. In their three-story Victorian house, the aunts each had their own room, the way my friends in Walpole with multiple siblings had their own bedrooms. But were grownups, professional working women, really supposed to live this way? To be fair, nothing about their housing arrangement seemed strange when I was little. It was only later, as a teen, when I started to project myself into the future and imagine my life as an adult, that it seemed completely unacceptable.

In general, I loved visiting them as a kid, for they spoiled me, but it could be a bit treacherous at times, like my bathing experience. Just a child, I didn't have the awareness to explain to my grandmother that we weren't back in the old country and that we did indeed possess indoor running water. Usually I would get sent to her with my siblings, when my parents went to one of my father's appraisal conferences in the summer. But when my brother and sister started going to camp, I wound up there by myself.

One time, I woke up in the middle of the night to hear my grandmother snoring, and I had no idea what to do. Lying on the sofa bed, under a clean white sheet safety-pinned to a *yoghan,* I propped myself up and turned around to look at her. In the dim light, high atop two box springs and a mattress, I could make out the mound of her body, heaving with each snore. The task was to rouse her so she would stop. I shifted in the sofa bed to creak the springs. She didn't wake. I cleared my throat loudly; still she snored. Finally, I grabbed a bobby pin off her bureau and threw it across the room; it made a *tink* loud enough to startle her. As she fell back asleep, she stopped snoring… for about five minutes.

There was no choice but to call her name. "Grammy," I said. The word cracked open the night in a preternatural, embarrassing way. "Grammy," I said again.

"*Eench?*" she asked.

"You're snoring," I informed her.

She didn't respond.

"You're snoring," I said again. She shifted in her bed, fell back asleep and picked up where she left off.

I thought of my grandmother's facial features, of her small eyes covered by deep eyelids; her arched, thin eyebrows that she dabbed with Vaseline to keep neat; her high, wide cheekbones; her thin lips covering strong white teeth. And her nose. The skin between her eyes bunched around the bridge, the middle was thick and the end was a pointed bulb: a snoring instrument. The noise was never going to stop, and I was never going to sleep. I wanted to sleep.

So I padded over the shag carpeting in the hallway and peered into Auntie Mel's pink room with the frilly curtains. It was quiet inside.

Nudging Mel in her big brass bed, I whispered, "Can I sleep with you?"

"Is anything wrong, sweetheart?" she mumbled.

"Grammy is snoring."

Mel slid her tall, wide body over and I scooched under her quilt. It was only a matter of time before she also started sawing wood, though not as loud as Grammy: her nose wasn't as big. I gazed at decorative cut glass bottles filled with colored water that served as bookends for her novels (*The Carpetbaggers; Coffee, Tea, or Me?),* wondering what to do.

Maybe Auntie Agnes would be less apt to snore. In an old photo album, I had seen black and white pictures of her, the middle of her face X'd out with a #2 pencil. "That fool Agnes, she doesn't want anyone to see her old *keet,*" Aunt Ruth had said. Agnes' nose had been fixed.

I approached her open door and saw her round body gently swelling with heavy breathing. Since snoring seemed imminent, I paused at her closet door, where there was a poster of a leotard-clad lady demonstrating various exercises. Agnes' paintings of ancient Armenian ruins hung on the walls, and knick knacks from her worldly travels were displayed on her bureau, but naturally this ridiculous chart of the lady exercising intrigued me the most. I was studying her womanly curves just as Agnes startled me with a few quick snorts.

Auntie Ruth's room was located at the end of a long hallway at the back of the house. Her room was the least remarkable, in contrast to Mel's sexy pink frills and Agnes' world exploratorium. Ruth was the youngest, the most no-nonsense, the one who made the minor repairs and cooked many of the meals. She probably didn't have time to deck out her room to represent her personality. The walls were painted blue, and there were no distinguishing interior decorating details. There was also no snoring. I climbed into her bed and fell asleep.

In the morning I explained the situation. "You had quite a night," Ruth laughed in her deep, lispy voice, her sloping eyes filled with sleep. "You silly goose." Ruth sometimes seemed like a kid too, since she was littler than Mel and Agnes, and she went sledding with me and Valerie and Leo in the wintertime, and she often wound up at the kiddie table during holiday dinners.

"Why don't you snore?" I asked. Ruth had a sizable nose.

"I don't know, but you tell your grandmother and aunts that they were snoring," she said tersely. "They won't believe me."

"No," Grammy said when I informed her of her nocturnal concert. "I don't snore." She put on her bathrobe and disappeared down the stairs.

I crawled back into the sofa bed and relished the moment of stretching out, alone and tired, beneath the *yoghan:* I had survived. The sun shone through the leaves of the gingko tree by the window, and I fell back to sleep like a big girl.

"Good morning *poopooleeg!*" Grammy called as I entered the kitchen. She was standing by the stove, still in her bathrobe, which shrouded her large breasts and stooped shoulders. "*Eench guzes?* What you want for breakfast?"

"A bubble egg, please."

The aunts were sitting in the breakfast nook. Jam, butter, string cheese and a basket of *choreg*s were set up neatly on the yellow enamel table.

"What happened last night, Nansay?" Aunt Mel asked. She had a Boston accent like the other aunts but added a lilt of sophistication to it whenever she said any word ending in y: the aural equivalent of one of the frills in her room. She was the oldest aunt, and she operated with an air of authority, like she was taking care of not just her patients at the V.A. hospital but her family too. "I woke up this morning and you were gone."

"You were snoring," I said as I sat down across from her.

"No, Nansay," she said, shaking her head solemnly, wearing a fresh layer of pink makeup and a white nurse's cap atop her short, silver-streaked hair. "I don't snore." Mel had a vulnerable side, too.

"You heard her Mel!" Auntie Ruth retorted, thrusting her chin out, her kinky black hair coiffed into a tight sphere, matching her black knit turtleneck, the mod, Mary Tyler Moore, career-girl look. Ruth often pointed out when people were being stupid or making mistakes, a know-it-all. "Why would Nancy lie?"

"Mel can't accept that she snores," Auntie Agnes said quietly. The most even-natured aunt, often cheerful and chatty, she was wearing a huge turquoise pendant, nestled atop her big bosom. She turned to look down at me with her wide-set eyes. "She's like that about other things, too," she stage whispered.

"Oh shut up, Agnes," Ruth said. "You're one to talk. You're the worst snorer of all."

"I know I snore; who cares," she chimed in a high voice. "Does it make me a bad person?" Even as a child I got the sense that Agnes had a wider world view than the other aunts. Of course it had to do with her travels, of which she would occasionally give us a slide show in the living room. She was also a painter with a studio on the vacant third floor, shelves lined with massive art books, a table covered in gems, semi-precious stones and a soldering gun to create her chunky jewelry. My brother and I would sometimes escape there during family gatherings to listen to her Frank Sinatra albums, to follow the progress of her current painting, to bang or pluck one of her exotic instruments from Peru or India. She was always going out to some cultural event, the symphony or a jazz concert or a gallery opening, with one of her single girlfriends, and then, she was always telling you about these events, and about anything she read or thought, even when you stopped listening. The other aunties seemed to resent her, both for the activities and her broadcast of them, and she would passively point out their flaws in response. Though they had different personalities, the aunties were all wrapped up in the same game of self-defense.

"Enough!" Grammy shouted from across the kitchen. She hobbled towards us with my egg over easy, yelling quickly in Armenian. Here was their puppet master, an unlikely little old lady.

"Oh, Ma, you really know how to hurt me, don't you?" Mel bellowed. She was up now, putting her dish by the sink.

"What did Grammy say?" I asked.

"She said we snore because we're heavy," Agnes said. "That has nothing to do with it, Ma."

"Razmouhi don't snore. I don't snore. Melineh and Aghavni snore because they're too fat," Grammy said.

"Ma!" Mel exploded, screaming at Grammy in Armenian. Among the foreign words, I thought I heard "Weight Watchers." Sometimes when she screamed her voice would go incredibly low, a growl through her nose. As suddenly as she had blown up, she stopped, halted her breath in resignation and shook her head at the floor, as if she didn't know what had happened to her life. Slinging her pocketbook over her shoulder, she said, "I'll see you later, Nansay. Give your Aunt Mel a kiss." I shook my head no. She was scaring me.

"No?" Mel said. "I'm so disappointed in you, Nansay. I'll get another niece if you don't come over here right now and give your Aunt Mel a kiss."

Standing up from my chair, I placed my lips gently on her antiseptic, powdered face. She squeezed me hard before walking out the door. A moment later, the other aunts departed, Ruth to a good government job working in the federal milk agency, and Agnes to the illustration department of an engineering firm. I watched their heads bobbing down the back steps past the kitchen window.

Suddenly the house was quiet. I ate my egg and Grammy watched. She buttered a piece of toast for me.

My mother once told me that my grandfather Jacob, who died before I was born, really wanted boys, in accordance with the outdated old country tradition, the whole worker-in-the-field theory: a girl you eventually lost to the family she married into, but a boy could muscle in the harvest and carry on your name. Jacob was ten years older than Grammy, who was about seventeen when they started having babies: Mel came first, then Agnes, then Auntie Sherrie, who lived on Long Island with Uncle Tony and my cousins, and then Ruth. Finally Grammy had a boy, my father, and Jacob said she could stop having babies.

With all those girls growing up under one roof in rural Massachusetts, you'd think there must have been all kinds of intrigue, not like that of the tormented Brontës, with their dark secrets and vows of revenge, but more like the March sisters in *Little Women:* Amy marrying Laurie when everyone knew Jo was supposed to wind up with him, but it was okay because then Jo met that old guy, an intellectual like the author's dad, a Transcendentalist. Why did the aunties remain so single? I imagined it was because, unlike a Transcendentalist, an Armenian may not have been so appealing; it was the only possibility my grandparents allowed, though.

My mother would inform me, when I was a bit older, that Mel had once fallen in love with one of her patients at the V.A. hospital; he was a paraplegic she would bring around in a special van equipped to load and unload a wheelchair. Grammy had said she would disown her if she married him, so Mel didn't. Grammy had also threatened to disown Sherrie if she married Tony because he was Italian, but Sherrie married him anyway. Agnes had a couple of Armenian boyfriends when she was young, but Mumma said she probably talked their ears off, so she didn't marry either. Ruth never had a boyfriend, it seemed.

In 1969, a year after I was born, the aunties all found themselves with jobs in Boston, and Grammy was a widow, so they pooled their money and bought a house in nearby Watertown. At the time of this particular visit, in 1975, Grammy was seventy, and the aunts were in their late forties and early fifties.

As I said earlier, at the time, I didn't think it odd that they lived together. It was fun to be around so many ladies and their beauty processes:

Ruth's Dippity-do smeared into her rollers, Mel's endless shades of bright pink lipstick, and Agnes' Queen Helene Mint Julep Masque which made her look like a Martian. It was like a pajama party, except for when they yelled and screamed.

Mel was the worst for sure, followed by Grammy and Ruth. Agnes wouldn't let her temper flare out of control, but she was often the target of someone else's rage, so she would have to fight back. When the outbursts happened, often without warning, I could feel myself swallow something hard, like a peach pit. I wasn't really scared, more in shock, even though it happened repeatedly. I didn't hate them for it, or want to run away even; there was something so compelling about a hefty, menopausal lady completely losing her cool. And of course I didn't question it. I can't say it was like watching TV, but there was some safety, perhaps a voyeur aspect to the drama, knowing that they would never cause me bodily harm or draw me directly into their craziness. But I had swallowed some of it.

During the day, while the aunts were at work, Grammy cleaned the house. She hung the wash on the clothesline so that the sheets smelled nice. Hand-crocheted doilies covered the tables, which Grammy expertly dusted. She vacuumed the Oriental rugs in the den and dining room and the white shag carpeting in the living room and parlor.

When she finished cleaning, Grammy joined me in the dark, wood-paneled den for games of Gin Rummy and Go Fish. She taught me how to crochet, to twirl yarn around a hook in order to make a bookworm, while she watched *The Young and the Restless*. When *Sesame Street* came on, she switched the channel and pulled out a pad of paper and a pencil from a side table. As the show progressed, she practiced her English letters. I turned around to look at her from my spot on the Oriental rug. "I learn too," she said shyly.

Grammy didn't drive. Holding hands, we walked down to the Woolworth's in Watertown Square, where she bought me a toy jewelry set of necklace, earrings and bracelet, the plastic garnet birthstone reminding me of the pomegranate seeds we ate the afternoon before.

As we walked home, Grammy told me that when she was young she wore a whole armful of gold bracelets. She gestured to her elbow to show how many. "But we sold to get on the boat to America. Beautiful gold. Tsk tsk," she said through her teeth. "The family I worked for, the Arabs that saved me, they paid me. Tree, four, five bracelets a year."

When we got home, I sat on the floor in front of her on the sofa and she spoke some more.

"They cleaned me, the Arabs. I had lice, swollen feet, dirty, dirty, dirty. From all the walkin'. The dust. Nowhere to rest." Grammy paused and looked at her hands in her lap. Then all of a sudden her scratchy voice became louder. "Walk, walk, walkin', the Turks make us walk, and then we can't walk anymore." She shook her head. "One morning, I'm sleeping with my sister, her arms around me, and she won't get up." Grammy wrapped her arms around herself. "'Wake up! Wake up!'" Grammy wailed. "Her arms were so heavy. I couldn't move them. She never woke up."

Head down, I pulled at the band at the end of one of my braids, yellow elastic stuck and ugly between blunt ends of black hair.

"And then this man," she started again, looking determined, "this man grabbed me. He shook me…" She clutched the air, her voice rising. "How would you like it if that happened to you? If a person did that to you?" She wasn't looking at me anymore. She was interrogating the wall as if the scary man were looming there on the wood paneling, hanging there like one of Aunt Agnes' paintings.

After the aunts came home from work, we had dinner with them at six o'clock prompt. Grammy made salty pilaf, roast chicken with crisp skin, and a salad dripping with oil and vinegar. She served me more of everything as soon as my plate emptied. When I finished the seconds, she spooned thirds onto my plate.

"Grammy, I can't eat any more," I protested.

"Eat!" Grammy said. "You're too skinny!"

"Ma, leave her alone!" Aunt Mel intervened. "Didn't you hear her? She's full!"

"Ahccch," Grammy said, waving her hand at Mel like she was a fly. "She tinks she's the big boss."

After dinner we watched TV in the den until Grammy said it was time for my bath.

"No!" I said. "I don't like how you do it."

Mel was reading the newspaper. She put it down.

"What's wrong with how I do it?" Grammy asked.

"I don't like how you pour the water over my head with a Colombo Yogurt container."

"Nansay," Mel intervened. "Why don't you take a shower instead?"

"I've never taken a shower before."

"You're seven years old and your mother hasn't taught you to take a shower? What's wrong with her? C'mon, I'll help you. You'll like it—it's the grownup way to wash."

Mel led me upstairs to the bathroom that the aunts shared. As I removed my clothes, she turned on the shower to make sure the water was temperate, and then she opened the sliding glass door to let me in. A moment later she hopped inside, surprising me. I had never seen a naked woman before. Mumma never got nude, and Valerie was still just a girl. Mel had big white breasts and brown jiggly-eye nipples. Even scarier was the black curly bush between her legs.

It was 1975, the sexual revolution in full tilt, coinciding with a wide scale back-to-nature ethic evidenced by Euell Gibbons, an old lumberjack who ate tree bark on TV in order to hawk Grape-Nuts; in parts of the U.S., there probably were families doing their household chores entirely in the buff. What was so weird about an aunt, and a nurse at that, helping a little girl to take a shower? All I can say is that I was dumbstruck. Everyone in my family covered their bodies, from bathroom to bedroom; even at the beach none of us were comfortable exposing so much skin. We just weren't the type of people who could be blasé about our bodies. So why was my aunt now revealing herself to me? Perhaps she wanted to break me from our modesty, or perhaps it was all done in innocence.

But I felt differently. "What's wrong, Nansay?" Mel asked, handing me a bar of Ivory and a washcloth. I didn't answer and rubbed the soap into the towel, a rain of water stinging my eyes.

Nervously shifting from foot to foot in the kitchen, I stood by my suitcase, dreading the ritual of kissing and hugging Grammy, Mel, Ruth and Agnes goodbye. Their mouths were sharp when I kissed them, the perfume and close body contact suffocating.

I hugged Grammy last. Her breath smelled slightly of string cheese, her skin of warm Vaseline, a sad look in her eyes. "Let her stay a few more days," she said to my father.

"No, Ma," he laughed, "her mother misses her." I looked at his five o'clock shadow, dark sideburns, and cigar. The week of separation made it seem as if he were a stranger and my aunts and Grammy were actually my family.

When I got home, I noticed my mother looked odd too—smaller, thinner and younger than my aunts. "Welcome home, sweetheart," she said in a smooth, soft voice. "Did you have a good time at your grandmother's house?"

I told her that I did. I showed her my birthstone set.

"Did your aunts or grandmother say anything bad about me?"

I told her they didn't, choosing not to relay Mel's criticism that she hadn't taught me to shower.

"Are you sure? They didn't say anything about our messy house?"

I shook my head.

Mumma went on, "You know there's four of them and only one of me. Heaven forbid if you kids help out around here. They only take care of you a few days a year. What right do they have to come over here and judge me?"

Grammy and Aunties would occasionally drop by our house unannounced with a box of Dunkin' Donuts. The doorbell would ring: "Jesus, it's his *mother!* Clean up the house quick!" Mumma would command.

Scattering, we would grab our belongings and throw them into our rooms. Daddy would open the door, and as they entered, the aunts and Grammy would look disapprovingly at the dust on the mantle or the piles of newspapers on the footrest. When she was feeling especially brazen, Ruth would sneak up to our bedrooms and announce that she was mortified by our slovenliness.

"Do me a favor, please, and don't tell them anything about me," Mumma said.

I trudged up our narrow staircase to my room, which was still the way I left it—bed unmade and inside-out clothes stomped on the floor. I put down my suitcase, filled with clothes that Grammy had washed, hung out to dry, and neatly folded.

After a while I stopped taking baths because they were for babies; instead, I took showers. Mumma didn't seem to mind, but once school started she insisted that if I went out after taking a shower, my body temperature would plummet and my immune defenses would disengage. "I'll give you three days," she would caution. "In three days, you're going to get sick, and then who's going to have to take care of you? I will, that's who."

I showered every two or three days partly to avoid her wrath, but also because I felt sick to my stomach whenever I took off my clothes. I'd be fine while inside our narrow shower, overcrowded with shampoo bottles, but once I jumped out, I'd feel queasy until wrapped inside a big towel.

One day Mumma brought home from CVS a spray-on shampoo called Psssssst. "You can use this on your hair so you won't catch a cold," she said. Pushing the aerosol button triggered a load of white powder that covered your hair like a layer of artificial snow. Then you rubbed it in to absorb the oil secreted by your scalp. Come winter I heeded Mumma's advice, showering just once a week and using the Psssssst when my hair got greasy.

Sometimes when Leo was using the Psssssst, he would totally overdo it, hogging the bathroom while he sprayed an even coat of the chemical concoction over his thick, bushy black hair. Then he'd emerge from a cloud of noxious gas, his hair whitened like an old lady's, and proceed to entertain us with an imitation of "Mama," a campy old crone played by Vicki Lawrence on *The Carol Burnett Show*. Mama lived with her middle-aged daughter Eunice and they constantly argued, drawling anger in Southern accents. Often Mama criticized her daughter until Eunice pitched a mental fit. Naturally, we thought they were hilarious.

Leo would stand in front of the fireplace, on the brick ledge that acted as a stage for the living room, assuming his character. "Eunice!" he yelled, "You're gonna lose on *The Gong Show!* There's no way your whiny voice can get past the gong!"

I ran onto the stage and joined him, taking my part as Eunice, screaming, "Oh yeah, Mama, I'll show you. I'm gonna follow my dream!" Then I sang, *"Feelins, whoah whoah whoah feelins, whoah whoah whoah feelins, agin in ma heart."* Leo gonged me, using the fireplace pitchfork against the grill. I stood frozen, the way Eunice had on TV, looking completely bewildered, like I didn't know what had happened to my life.

2. AMERICAN SCHOOL

Two blond women, sisters I surmised, in sunhats and jeans, crouched down to look at my blanket. I was sitting with my back to the beach, which felt like the edge of the earth. Trying not to appear as if they were my first customers and that my very existence depended on their purchase, I busied myself with arranging the merchandise. One sister tried on a crocheted hat with three horns, and the other picked up the plastic astronaut men attached to blue marble earrings. "Yikes Jewelry," the latter read from the card upon which the earrings were mounted, "dedicated to the memory of Karen Carpenter, who sang, 'Rainy days and Mondays always make me feel even more anorexic.'" She laughed and I cringed; as I had been making them, I'd never imagined that people would actually read the cards out loud, and now the Karen Carpenter line sounded callous.

"Thanks," the sisters said, standing up. "You have great stuff!"

I smiled up at them. *Well, why didn't you buy anything then?*

This morning I had gingerly set up my blanket in order to sell the items I had made over the last few weeks in order to keep from getting dejected about not having a decent job. I'd made the jewelry with a bunch of fittings that Auntie Agnes had given to me, and the hats with the crochet skills I'd picked up from Grammy. My spot was at a calmer part of the Venice Boardwalk, several blocks from the Legalize Hemp stand, the guy who juggled chainsaws, and the black midget quadriplegic dancing atop a skateboard. It seemed like a fun and easy way to make a few extra bucks, but I'd never taken into consideration that I would have to be a salesperson.

I was ignoring more customers when Bee appeared, wearing sunglasses and a red bandanna tied over her short dark hair. She cracked up at the sight of me in my paint-splotched purple sweater, sandwiched between the Salvadoran kid smearing seascapes onto dishes with his fingers and the black guy in a gas mask spray painting trippy posters of the solar system.

"Hey, how's it going?" Bee called.

"Okay," I peeped.

The customers instinctively turned towards Bee, a laid back Latina who meshed well with the boardwalk. She said hello to practically anybody, even the midget when he scooted past. She had been the same in college, friendly to the point of absurdity with even the biggest social outcasts in the dorm. Now propping her sunglasses on top of her head, she crouched down and asked whoever was there, "Aren't these great earrings? Nancy made them herself. She's very talented." Then she patted me on the back with a thud.

"Yes, they are great," one lady said. "How much are they?"

"Ten dollars," I said.

The lady looked uncertain. "But if you buy two pairs she'll give them to you for fifteen," Bee chimed in.

The lady bought two pairs and the other potential customers whose eye contact I had been avoiding coughed up their money too. By the end of the day I'd made two hundred dollars and thought I had it made, but the next day a pair of cops darted up on their bikes and asked me if I had a vendor's permit. They let me off with a warning, but told me if they caught me permit-less again, I would be fined. I didn't have the five hundred dollars for the permit, so I stayed in my spot, and when I saw a cop coming, I would scoop up my blanket and make a break for the apartment, catch my breath and try to get my nerve back to set up again.

I was doing my best to think of all this as a quirky story to tell my grandchildren later and not as a pretty pathetic existence for a college graduate. On certain days, though, like when Tibby asked me how I was doing, I completely crumbled.

Never in my life had I imagined that I would know someone named Tibby, but at Wellesley the stereotype of ridiculous preppy names turned out to be true. She was in L.A. for a Teach For America conference, the organization she had been working for since graduation; now she was teaching a sixth grade class at a school in Harlem, where kids passed through metal detectors when they walked through the door.

Daddy thought Teach For America, a new, privately funded enterprise, was ultimately a right-wing plot, asking recent graduates of prominent colleges, unqualified in childhood education, to manage a classroom with little training, instead of pressing the government to invest more money into the schools. I couldn't say that I didn't agree with him, but I had applied for Teach For America my senior year because I needed a job and vaguely wanted to help people. The application process made me so nervous that I got sick to my stomach a day before the sample lesson and wound up in the infirmary. I somehow roused myself out of there and donned a green wool suit that my mother used to wear; she had even advised me on what my sample lesson would be. The magic suit helped me get through the ordeal without totally embarrassing myself, but I wasn't nearly as perky and together as Tibby had been. I made it to the waitlist, but later declined, deciding I wasn't ready to teach.

Now, a year later, here was Tibby wearing sunglasses and drinking iced tea at a Venice Beach cafe with Bee and me and a few other friends from college. Tibby had been plying us with stories of teaching in Harlem, and I was fascinated with details like the lack of chalk and the way the kids called her "Teacher." All of a sudden, when she probably got nervous that she'd been dominating the conversation, she looked at me, who had been quietly listening most of the afternoon, and asked, "So Nancy, what are you up to?"

Everyone turned to look at me. How could my activities, selling jewelry illegally on the boardwalk and painting pottery for eight dollars an hour, compare with the noble act of serving America's underprivileged children? I couldn't even pay my rent; my parents mailed me checks to cover it.

"Nothing," I said. "I'm doing nothing."

"That's not true," Bee tried to prompt me. "Tell them about your jewelry company!"

I sat there silent, about to cry. I couldn't even tell Bee to keep her mouth shut, or assure people I was fine. Eventually, I'm not sure how, the conversation moved off of my inappropriate reaction.

But it wasn't long until I was back at the same cafe, with Bee and a few friends, to celebrate the first poetry reading I had ever done. At the end of a twelve-week session, the workshop invited friends and family to Beyond Baroque and we held a reading. When my name was called, I walked to the podium and followed the instructions the teacher had given me earlier, to see the manifestation of each word in my mind and to relive the experience that had propelled me to write in the first place. I couldn't see anyone in particular because of the lights shining in my eyes, but I could feel them: a sympathetic black force that heaved with laughter from time to time. When I was done, everyone cheered.

It always seemed to be this way. I flunked architecture by giving the impression with my shyness that I didn't care about it, but to my art professors I was a standout student. Even when I was a little kid I experienced a polarity of existence, excelling in one area and completely flopping in another.

———

My third grade teacher, Ms. Duffy, was the first teacher to make me feel really special. Though well-meaning, she inadvertently set me up for many a disappointment later in life by blowing up my ego as a teacher's pet.

Thus, Ms. Duffy was still special in my mind. I remembered that she changed her name from Mrs. to Ms. during the Christmas break of third grade; it was hard to get a handle on the modification at first, but I soon figured out that Ms. was just Miss with a "z" at the end: Miz Duffy. Some kids never got the hang of it, though. One rainy afternoon, Carl DiGiorno asked her, "Do we have indoor recess today Mrs. Duffy?"

Ms. Duffy smiled. "What did you call me?" she reminded him.

"I mean, Miss Duffy?"

"It's *Miz* Duffy. *Miz.* Repeat after me: *Mizzzz* Duffy."

"*Mizzzz*...es Duffy?"

Ms. Duffy sighed. "Yes, we have indoor recess today."

I was proud that I never had to be corrected on Ms. Duffy's name, never let a Mrs. slip. I also knew that Ms. was a women's lib thing. Mumma had explained to me that Ms. was the equivalent of Mr., that some women felt they should have the same right as men to use a form of address separate from their marital status. To me, it made her seem ultramodern, the effect enhanced when Ms. Duffy showed up one morning with her thin, light brown hair in tight, frizzy ringlets covering her head. She'd gotten a perm, also termed an "afro" in Walpole. Perm-mania was sweeping the suburbs in the mid '70s, but Ms. Duffy hadn't seemed the type to jump on the afro bandwagon. Then again, she hadn't appeared to be a women's libber, like *Maude* on TV, either.

One Friday afternoon in spring, Ms. Duffy passed back the results from the standardized tests that our class had taken a month earlier. I looked down at the dot-matrix printed scores, a 99 appearing after each test: Reading Comprehension, Grammar, Math and Science. Ms. Duffy announced to the class with her shrill Boston accent, in a slow, teacherly way, "Class, Nancy scored higher than ninety-nine percent of all the children who took this test in America." Glancing up, I found all eyes on me and I blushed. Later, when I was leaving to go home, Ms. Duffy gave me a hug in the hallway and whispered, "I'm so proud of you, Nancy." Her purple velour turtleneck felt even softer than it looked, causing a wave of embarrassment to wash over my face and chest.

Fluttering out of the school, I made my way down the street, past the boxy Colonials, Cape Cods and split-levels, clutching the scores in my hand. I strode across our grassy yard in a diagonal path and rang the front doorbell. Mumma swung open the door.

"Hello sweetie," she said. She was wearing a green sweater vest with long costume jewelry beads, her straight hair styled into bouncy curls like a kid's drawing.

"Mumma, I got all ninety-nines on my scores! Ms. Duffy announced it to the class and everything." I shoved the scores at her.

"All ninety-nines!" Mumma excitedly screeched. "Well of course. You are a very smart girl."

I heard the stomping of feet from the cellar stairs and Daddy bounded through his office door. A self-employed industrial appraiser, he worked out of an office in our basement. "Who's a very smart girl?" he asked, smoking a cigar and leaning towards me, revealing the yellow collar of his white undershirt.

"Get away from her with that thing," Mumma said, waving smoke from my face. "Is that how you treat your daughter who got ninety-nines? Mrs. Duffy announced it to the class."

"It's *Miz* Duffy," I corrected her.

"Oh, pardon me, *Miz* Duffy."

I watched as my father took his wallet out of his back pocket and rifled through the bills, drawing out a five. "Good work, Nance," he said, smiling as he placed it in my palm. *Wow,* I thought, staring into Lincoln's face.

"Okay, sweetie, you need to hurry up and get ready for Armenian school," Mumma said.

Oh no. No no no no no no no. In my eagerness to scoop up all the positive attention I could get for my scores, I had forgotten that today was Friday. "What? You mean I have to go? After I got all ninety-nines on the SRA? Shouldn't we celebrate?"

"We can celebrate afterwards. We'll go to Celo's." It was a family restaurant that we frequented after Armenian school.

My brother had been sitting silently on the couch in the living room this whole time, overhearing us talking in the lower level of the foyer. Leo now punctuated my dismay, aptly calling out, "Sap!"

Before I officially attended Armenian school at the Sts. Sahag and Mesrob Armenian Apostolic Church, I used to accompany my mother and siblings on the half-hour trek down to Providence every Friday afternoon. Mumma would drop off my siblings at church, located in a neighborhood of decrepit triple deckers, and then we would swing by Newport Creamery, located in the white Apex department store that was shaped like a pyramid in Pawtucket. Mumma would visit with friends over frappés and fries sprinkled with vinegar, and I would look up from my coloring book to watch the dark-haired, bright-lipsticked ladies, with names like Dolores and Lillian, gab about the old days in Cranston.

An hour and a half later we would drive down Jefferson Avenue towards Valerie and Leonard, slouching with their friends in the parking lot, Armenian school books coolly slung under their arms. They would climb into the car jabbering about some kind of hijinks. Leo once stuck his head out his classroom door and saw Diggin Arlene, the Superintendent, standing in the hallway oblivious to the fact that it was 5:30 and time for Armenian school to end. "Ring the bell," he said in a monotone and shut the door.

A moment later Diggin Arlene burst into the room, thundering, "I'll ring the bell when I, and only I, feel it's time!" Mumma yelled at Leo for being insubordinate, but I wished I could have been there to witness such shenanigans.

Now with my older siblings long graduated, I sat alone in the car with Mumma as we barreled down Route 95, dreading my solo Armenian school attendance. Or should I say tardiness. We hit traffic and I walked into the church hall a half-hour later, greeted by six closed doors. I could hear muffled lessons as I walked toward the far end of the hall, to the last door on the right. *Here we go,* I thought, slowly opening it.

"Parev," Miss Lu said, smiling. I quietly slunk to an empty seat and smiled back.

Miss Lu was wearing black. As usual. It was understood that she was in mourning, but it wasn't clear to me who had died. I assumed she was a widow, but I wondered why, if she were so devoted to a dead husband to wear black every day, did she call herself Miss Lu, and not Mrs. Her-married-last-name-ian? (Most Armenian names end in "ian," which I was told in Armenian school meant "the family of.") Or if she were never married, who besides a husband would she mourn in such a dedicated way?

Miss Lu was my aunts' age. Her nose was round and bumpy and her smile was impish. *"Eench bes es?"* she asked. How are you?

"Shad lav," I replied by rote. Very good.

"Eenchoo oosh es?" she asked.

I had no idea what she was saying. I didn't know the words, I didn't know any of the stupid Armenian words with the *ch, sh* and *oo* sounds. I sat quietly, hoping to be left alone.

"Eenchoo oosh es?" she asked again, looking at me patiently. Shushan, Maral, Seta and Gary waited for an answer too; they all spoke Armenian more fluently than I.

Aunties insisted that Valerie, Leonard and I would learn the language if our parents simply conversed in Armenian at the dinner table. Mumma and Daddy had tried it a couple of times, but it was a hassle. Even they stumbled over the language, improvising the word for fish sticks—*tsoog* stick*ereh*— and laughing. The only words we regularly used were those too embarrassing to say in English: *vardeek* for underpants, *voor* for butt, and *betkeran* for bathroom. I obviously came from an Armenian-challenged household, but I didn't take this into account as I silently watched my classmates fiddle with their pencils; Shushan sighed.

"She's asking you why you're late," Seta finally informed me.

How am I going to answer that? I thought.

It wasn't that I was completely inept at Armenian: I knew the thirty-eight letters of the alphabet (some looked like English characters: "u" was an s sound and "n" was a v sound) and how they were invented by St. Mesrob, one of the namesakes of our church, in 404 A.D. in order to write the Bible in Armenian. I could read anything put in front of me; I could memorize vocabulary words such as *aclor* (rooster), *nareenj* (orange), and *gosheeg* (shoe). But I didn't know how to put together a sentence. I couldn't speak.

"*Eenchoo oosh es?*" Miss Lu asked one more time.

"There was a traffic jam," I finally blurted out.

"Okay," Miss Lu said. "How do you say that?" she asked the class. Maral answered with a sentence that seemed to have far more Armenian syllables than the English version.

"*Abrees,*" Miss Lu answered.

Then to me she said, "You come here on time next week, okay?"

"Okay," I nodded. Miss Lu must have forgotten the conversation I had with her, which I seemed to have every year at Armenian school. Someone, either a teacher or student, would invariably ask, "Why do you always come late?"

"Because I come from Massachusetts," I would say.

"Why don't you go to an Armenian school in Massachusetts?"

"Because even though this one is in Rhode Island, it's closer."

"Where do you live?"

"Walpole."

"Is that near Watertown?"

"No."

"Is that near Worcester?"

"No."

"Are there Armenians there?"

"Not really."

"Why do you live there?"

"I don't know," I sighed. Apparently Armenians only lived in cities, like Watertown and Worcester, where there was a sizable Armenian population; I had no idea why we lived where we did. In Walpole, when I had to explain to my friends why I couldn't play after school on Friday afternoons, I was met with a similar kind of confusion, for no one had ever heard of Armenia. Everyone in Walpole, it seemed, was either Irish, Italian or Polish. And Catholic.

"You have to go to what kind of school?" they would ask.

"Armenian," I would say, waiting for the inevitable interrogation.

"What's that?"

"That's what I am. The same way you're Irish. I'm Armenian."

"Arabian?"

"No, ARMENIAN."

"So, where is—?"

"Armenia. It's near Russia."

"How come I never heard of it?"

"Because it's a part of the Soviet Union."

"So you're a Commie?"

"No."

"Are you Catholic?"

"No."

"What religion are you?"

"Armenian Apostolic."

"Is that Jewish?" This seemed to be the most crucial question to answer correctly, for it was asked with an air of suspicion.

"No, it's Christian," I retorted.

"But you're not Catholic?"

"No."

"Are you sure?"

"Yes," I sighed.

And hence the polarity of existence began, as I became accustomed to being misunderstood, explanations barely helping my case. A typical cross-cultural American experience, as I would later discover in the women's multicultural poetry workshop: the feeling of never fully being yourself, in both the predominantly white world and in the traditional ethnic community of your family.

I might have found a way to bridge the Walpolian and Armenian worlds, if I had used the tools my teachers tried to give me. Every year at Sts. Sahag and Mesrob we watched a filmstrip that informed us of our heritage. We would file into the faux wood-paneled Harry Hovanessian Media Center and one kid would man the filmstrip projector while Diggin Arlene would play the accompanying audio tape. "Armenia, Land of Pride!" a man's voice would boom into the room. The first frame of the filmstrip showed a map of Armenia with the words "Land of Pride" superimposed onto it. Then the tape recorder gave a long beep, a signal for the kid to manually turn to the next frame, a picture of an ark.

"There is a legend," the man's voice announced, "that Armenians are descendants of Noah—" the tape beeped again, and a photograph of a mountain slid onto the screen, "—who landed on Mt. Ararat in Armenia."

The filmstrip then highlighted the kingdom of Dikran the Great during the first century B.C., his empire of Armenia covering a part of the Middle East as large as modern Great Britain, beep. It flashed Armenian illuminated manuscript depictions of Thaddeus and Bartholomew, bearded and heavy-lidded Apostles who brought Christianity to Armenians, beep, and stated that Armenia was the first nation to convert to Christianity in 301 A.D., beep.

Then, due to invasions of more populous peoples such as Persians, Arabs, and Turks in the following ages, Armenian lands shifted and changed. The map of Armenia became smaller, beep, and then smaller, beep, and then still smaller, beep, until it disappeared.

And then the filmstrip depicted the massacres of Armenians that happened in 1915. Our ancestors had been killed by Turks, driven from their native homeland in mass deportations through the desert. Some Turks gave Armenians the opportunity to stay alive if they converted from Christianity to Islam, but Armenians preferred to die rather than give up their faith. The perpetrators denied what happened, and the Turkish government still hasn't acknowledged what their predecessors did, and we should all be angry about that and never forget. The filmstrip represented all this with a black and white blurry photograph of skinny orphans, and then beep, an aerial view of thousands of orphans.

Those orphans reminded me of a story Grammy had once told me. She hadn't recognized her older brother when he suddenly appeared at the dormitory, because he was wearing a big Russian hat and soldier's uniform. It dawned on me that Grammy had been one of the thousands of skinny children, shrouded in white and orphaned by the massacres.

I didn't have too much time to ponder this though, because the filmstrip continued, explaining that after the massacres, the eastern provinces of historical Armenia became an independent nation for only two years following World War I, but faltered during a war with Turkey and soon succumbed to become a republic of the Soviet Union,[1] beep.

And then the voice on the filmstrip stated that despite the horrors inflicted upon them, Armenians have become very successful in America, like the billionaire Kirk Krikorian, and Alex Manoogian who invented the Delta faucet that pivoted on a ball joint, and Garo Yepremian the placekicker for the Miami Dolphins, and Mike Connors of television's *Mannix* and finally, Cher, in a white, Bob Mackie-designed, Native American get-up, seated atop a white horse. Beep.

So I had all this information at my disposal whenever I was questioned in Walpole about my ethnicity. But the map of Armenia getting smaller was depressing, and so were the massacres. And who had heard of any of the successful Armenians? The only one vaguely recognizable to the average ten-year-old was Cher, but everyone insisted she was an Indian.

I just wanted to be something simple that everyone had heard of, like Irish, Italian or Polish. I didn't want to be different, to have to explain myself.

So I couldn't speak.

At around 4:30, a knock came on Miss Lu's door. She opened it a few inches and a hand stuck a red plastic basket filled with Little Debbies into the room. I was relieved. Sometimes apples were thrust upon us.

After snack time, we often adjourned to the auditorium to learn Armenian songs. It was the only activity I liked since the words were easy to learn, written with English letters on large cards for us to follow along, like the bouncing ball cartoons.

---

[1] Aremenia was a republic of the Soviet Union until 1991, when it gained independence.

But today, Diggin Carol, who was the fifth grade teacher, knocked on our door and announced that she needed three more girls for a dance she was choreographing for the upcoming *Hantes*.

Shushan, Maral, Seta and I marched into the auditorium behind her. We stood in the darkening room while the late afternoon sky seeped into the narrow windows, reflecting off the black and beige checkerboard linoleum floor. Diggin Carol wore her hair in a huge bouffant—it was dyed a light coral color in the front and dark brown in the back.

"Okay girls," she said. "In this dance, we need you to be very graceful, like swans. You're going to walk across the auditorium, and I want you to extend your arms," she raised her arms out to her side, making a T, "and wave them." Diggin Carol let her elbows relax and she undulated her fingers, hands and wrists, carrying the wave up to her shoulders. Her arms looked like the wings of a bird.

"Diggin Carol," I asked, "Are we supposed to look like a swan flying?"

Diggin Carol stopped her movement and looked at me.

"What did you call me?" she asked.

"Diggin Carol?"

"No, honey, it's not 'Diggin.' That sounds horrible. Who taught you that?"

I didn't know what to say. *Deegeen* was a term of respect the kids used to address the teachers at Armenian school, with the exception of Miss Lu. But Leo and I had corrupted the pronunciation of Dee-*geen* to the gruffer sounding Diggin in order to more effectively make fun of the Armenian school teachers. Diggin was also reminiscent of TV beatnik speech we heard on *Bewitched* and *I Dream of Jeannie:* "Dig that crazy sound," and "Can you dig it?"

"Look honey," Diggin Carol said to my befuddlement. "It's not a short *i* sound. It's a long *e*. So it's Dee-*geen*. Dee-*geen*," she said, "Repeat after me."

"Di-*geen*," I said. I caught Shushan smirking at Maral.

"Close enough. Let's dance, shall we?"

The four of us walked around in a circle while Diggin Carol inspected us and hummed some music. I tried my best to gracefully wave my arms the way she had. But my movements weren't fluid like those of the other girls.

"Very good, *shad lav*," Diggin Carol said.

We went back to class. A half-hour later, a knock came on Miss Lu's door and a hand shoved three costumes on hangers into the room. Safety-pinned to each was a piece of scrap paper with a name in block letters: MARAL on one, SHUSHAN on another and SETA on the third.

I hadn't made the cut. I wanted to cry and I didn't know why. It was one less thing for me to worry about, and I hated Armenian school, so what did it matter?

I had worn the same costume for the *Hantes* last year, when there was no tryout, when every girl danced. The veil was an elastic band attached by a lady volunteer to a piece of sheer white fabric, which fell around the head like long hair. Around the bottom rim of the headband, little gold coins were sewn to dangle delicately over the forehead. There were gold satin palazzo pants that came to the ground or your shins, depending on your height, and a little maroon velvet vest with gold trim. I had loved wearing the whole ensemble, especially the veil. But now I consoled myself that it was an old, ugly costume.

Last year, as we were traveling home up Route 95, I had shown the costume to Leo. He had placed my veil on his head and wrapped the sheer fabric across his nose, waving giddily at unsuspecting New England drivers. I thought of Leo's big black eyes shining from behind the veil and how he'd been transformed. *My brother was prettier in that costume than you will ever be*, I thought as I looked at my classmates. Seta had frizzy brown hair and wore grey braces on her buck teeth. Shushan was stocky and her wide face reminded me of the monster in *Where the Wild Things Are*. Puny Maral, with her bowl cut and big nose, resembled Ringo Starr. I became more depressed the more I critiqued the girls' appearances. With my dark skin, bare trace of a moustache, and greasy black hair, I looked more like them, I realized, than my pretty brother, than the fair-haired Ms. Duffy in Walpole.

At about 5:15, Superintendent Diggin Arlene came to Miss Lu's door and announced that all the classes were gathering in the sixth grade room for a brief meeting before leaving. Over fifty kids and several teachers crowded into the room, and Diggin Arlene informed us that she had just received the results of the standardized Armenian test that we had taken three months before. "I'm very disappointed with all of you," she said. "Your average score was the worst of all the Armenian schools in America. You all need to dedicate yourselves more urgently to the Armenian language." She frowned; her large round eyes and lack of chin resembled Olive Oyl's countenance.

Diggin Arlene passed back an exam to the top-scoring student, who received a 75, then announced each person's score until she got to 50. I watched as kids received their substandard papers, hanging their heads low. When she got to the last exam, she handed it to me and gave me a look of pure disdain.

I glanced down at the paper to see, handwritten in red pen, the number 7.

"Our culture has survived for over two thousand years," Diggin Arlene lectured. "Our people have suffered countless hardships and still we've persevered. Your parents send you to this school so that the flame of Mother Armenia can be kept alive. There is little hope if you kids don't learn the language. Your ancestors are crying right now, I can tell you that. They're crying."

I didn't know about my ancestors, but I was about to have a nervous breakdown. Mercifully, my mother was on time to pick me up. "Do you want to go to Celo's to celebrate your test?" she asked.

I didn't know how she found out about the seven, and I couldn't believe she would joke about it until it dawned on me that she was talking about the SRA test. It was hard to believe that a few hours before, Ms. Duffy had hugged me for winning what was surely just the first in a string of countless honors leading up to the Nobel Prize.

Clearly, I was a complete failure at being Armenian. Though I could reject my identity by making fun of it and by refusing to learn the language, and I could embrace the white world by following all the rules and excelling at American school, I would still look different to everyone in Walpole, I would still have the label of my last name, and I would still come to learn that my grandmother's stories were never acknowledged.

"Or do you want to go home?" Mumma asked as I was struck dumb by the polarity of existence.

"Home," I said, and we traveled up Route 95, away from the Armenians, in silence.

3. WONDER GIRL

On the first day of the Beyond Baroque workshop, I was nervous that I had left my headlights on. Ever the good student, I picked out a spot at the long table next to the teacher, Rita. She wore her black hair in a long braid with a headband framing her face, and she was nervously arranging her pile of materials which had already been arranged, book on top of book, pen and keys on the side—I instantly liked her. "Do I have time to check if I left my lights on?" I asked her.

She looked at me with both eyes and told me, "Yes."

When I returned, Rita began the class by setting up an altar with a candle and asked the class if there was anything we wanted to light it to. Then she said, "I am lighting this candle to honor..." and held the match to the wick, "the truth," or "insanity," or "understanding," or "flowers," or whatever people suggested. *Cheesy New Age crap*, I thought. But as the weeks progressed, I came to discover Rita was the opposite of cheesy—quite fierce, in fact, as a poet and a sensitive teacher. She explained to us on the first day, "This is a multicultural workshop. Which means that no culture is dominant and everyone's voice is equal."

One week, she asked each of us to speak about our racial, ethnic, and class backgrounds in order to discuss our experience with racism. Lily, a blond, frizzy-haired German visual artist, lamented, "I come from the most anal retentive race of people on the face of the earth." Maria, a young, hip poet and a Latina proclaimed, "My family has been here for generations and yet white Anglos always have to ask me where I'm from." Ellie, a lesbian from Westchester who recently graduated from Brown and nannied for a famous actor's kids admitted, "My town was so homogeneous, that just being tall made me feel different."

When it was my turn, I said "I'm Armenian and I grew up in a mostly white town, and I remember when I was in high school, I was looking into my bedroom mirror with a few of my friends, and I was surprised at how dark I was next to them. I mean, I had known I was darker, but I guess I somehow thought that I looked more like them, like these people I looked at every day. And I was so ashamed."

I hadn't thought of this memory since the event had actually happened; the realization of the racial dimension formulated as I described it to the workshop. It was probably because no one had ever asked me before what it was like to be different. And yet there were many instances in Walpole when I received messages that I was a stranger, but they were covert signals, in codes I barely knew how to break.

One day a U.S. military plane crashed on Paradise Island, a tiny, sovereign, secret nation inhabited solely by Amazons who wore white togas and lip gloss. There was a cute, unconscious guy inside of the plane; the name on his uniform badge read "Steve Trevor." Deciding they must return Steve Trevor to America, the tribe held a vote and chose Princess Diana, the eldest daughter of Queen Hippolyta, to perform the task. This wasn't surprising: Princess Diana was a brunette, which meant she was smart. Before departing, she put on powerful, bulletproof bracelets and changed into a new outfit: red, blue, gold, and skimpy, with a tight, strapless bodice that revealed her cleavage. She flew to Washington D.C. in her invisible plane, dropped off Steve with government officials, and then used her otherworldly powers to round up some criminals. In order to protect the sanctity of her Amazon clan back home, Princess Diana never revealed her identity, so the government officials dubbed her Wonder Woman.

Princess Diana decided to remain in the United States because she was in love with Steve Trevor. She pulled her hair into a bun, donned a high-necked dress and extra large glasses, changed her name to Diana Prince, and found a job as Steve's secretary. Diana Prince never pursued Steve but kept her love to herself—it was enough just to be around him. When she needed to help him with a case, she surreptitiously twirled in a circle, transforming into Wonder Woman to save his life. Boldly confident in her boobalicious outfit, she saw the awe in Steve's eyes, but she never took advantage of him.

As a nine-year-old in front of the tube, I intuitively understood that her abstention from Steve's affection wasn't just a precaution against blowing her cover. She wanted Steve to love her true self, but her sexy Wonder Woman persona didn't represent all of it—she was also a loving, watchful assistant and a dutiful immigrant daughter.

Nevertheless, it drove me crazy that Wonder Woman couldn't just jump Steve and kiss him, her ample boobs sticking straight out at the fully clothed weaker human she secretly adored. I wanted to kiss so bad, I didn't care about the risks. *Just kiss, just kiss,* I thought as I watched, trying to will the characters to the demands of my desire.

One day in September, Karen and Danielle came over to my house after school and, when they thought I wasn't looking, deposited most of my seashell collection into their underpants. Dirty blond and suntanned, Karen and Danielle were the same age as me and lived in my neighborhood. They were best friends, and I was their subordinate friend; they often made fun of me for having a moustache. After inviting me down to Karen's house, they immediately disappeared into her bedroom closet to remove the shells from their hiding places; I could hear them clinking. "Here's *our* collection," Danielle said, opening the door and holding out a shoebox of my shells.

I was pissed, but I couldn't say the words, "you stole my shells," because if I did, it would mean that Karen and Danielle were bad. Karen and Danielle thought they were good. Who was I to argue? They were the same age as me and lived in my neighborhood. They were girls, and I was a girl, and I was supposed to be like them, but I had failed: I was not dirty blond nor suntanned; moreover, I possessed a moustache. So I went home, ceding that my shells were gone forever.

An hour or so later, Karen and Danielle showed up at my front door, shells in their cupped hands, looking remorseful.

"These are yours," Karen said, glancing downward. "We took them."

"We're sorry," Danielle said, smiling slyly.

I sensed they didn't really care about my feelings. They just wanted to be good girls who told the truth.

"That's okay," I said, taking my shells back. "Thank you."

A few weeks later, I was walking home from school and saw the driveway was empty of cars. *Maybe someone's home? Val or Leo?* I rang the doorbell and no one came. I rang it once more, then jammed on it a million times. *Locked out? Not again.* I twisted the doorknob in vain and slammed my shoulder against the door with all my strength. "Stupid door!" I muttered under my breath before giving up.

This is all Mumma's fault, I thought.

She wasn't home because she was either teaching as a substitute teacher or as a docent at a local art museum. Before she had me, Val and Leo, my mother had been a second grade teacher. She told me how smart she'd been not to wear her wedding ring on interviews because if principals had known she was married they might have thought she'd be having children soon, and then they wouldn't have hired her. But she was married for five years before she had kids and the money she saved from her salary paid for half our house.

I wanted Mumma to be like the other moms in Walpole who made it their only business to mom, but she said she had a mind and that she wasn't going to just clean all day long. So sometimes she wouldn't be home to let me in after school, and she didn't give me a key either. What if I dropped it and a robber found it? "Then we would be done for," she said.

I walked around the back to see if the bathroom window was open. There were holes in the screen that I could force my fingers through to release the hatches and wriggle in. But the storm window had been pushed down and the screen up. I threw my books on the ground in disgust. There was nowhere else for me to go now but the woods.

I stomped through our back yard, past the hutch of Charlotte and Thumper, our pet rabbits who had died the year before. They had wandered away from their pen when four big dogs, who we'd never seen in the neighborhood before, had emerged from the woods, ripped through our yard, tore Charlotte and Thumper apart, and then disappeared back into the woods. The rabbit hutch, now weather-beaten and warped, stood at the back edge of our property line, in memoriam.

Just beyond it was the path that led to the field, and a few paces along it, a patch of Lady Slippers, an endangered flower illegal to pick. Their protected status made seem even more beautiful: two pink organs, resembling slippers, hung in midair from a thick green stem. If you plucked one, you would have destroyed the chance for it to grow back again next year.

Dark and quiet, the woods were. I scanned the oaks, maples, birches and pines, to see if anyone else was out here. There were paths from the back yards of each house on our street that wended through the trees to a nearby field. Everyone said that the Indians had made the paths, but I wasn't so sure —the Indians seemed way too cool to have actually lived in our neighborhood. I thought teenagers were responsible; I often found their deserted lairs under the pine trees: fire rings and faded Bud cans and waterlogged cigarette packs and rusted bottlecaps. You could feel their presence, less extinct than Indians and Lady Slippers and pet rabbits.

Spotting a fallen oak branch that was leaning against a small birch tree,

I sat down under it, feeling the cold damp through my corduroy pants. The wind calmly rustled the dead leaves, the sun was low but still warm, but I couldn't completely relax. Anything could happen out here in the wild. Kids bigger than me rode minibikes in a nearby field. None of them was out today—I didn't hear their buzzing motors. But it wouldn't be out of the ordinary for a big kid to pass through the woods and decide to bully a little kid hiding under a branch. Danielle had once told me that in the woods behind the Fergus' house, two houses up from mine, a gang of boys had tied up Annie Leach and pulled her pants down.

Detecting some dead, sizable branches nearby, I stood up to gather them and leaned them against the birch tree to make the beginnings of a fort for protection. Slowly I assembled a makeshift structure, a slightly round shelter. As I crawled inside, I couldn't believe I'd made such a cozy place.

I stayed there a while, not quite knowing what to do with myself, until I heard the distinct sound of Mumma yelling. Then I heard my father's voice, even louder than Mumma's, yelling too. I couldn't make out the words as I made my way home, but they were arguing as usual.

The next few afternoons, whether anyone was at home to let me in or not, I spent in my fort. Because I could do whatever I wanted, I took the opportunity to partake in the forbidden—playing with matches. With a book snatched from Daddy's fishbowl of matches, I struck a stick, watching it burn down to my thumb and forefinger, nearly singeing my nails before I blew it out. I lit another match and held the flame to a leaf, which disappeared into a filigree of veins. Trying my hand at twigs, I soon found myself tending a mini campfire. I spent hours in the fort, gazing into the flames, snapping and smoky. The fire was totally wild, but it was mine. All mine. No one else's.

As they watched the flames gain momentum, Karen and Danielle's mouths fell open. The low sunlight dappled through the leaves and shone on their dirty blond hair as they tentatively fed the fire with twigs.

It was too good to keep to myself. I had to show *somebody*.

When it was getting dark, our mothers called us home, and we stomped on the flames with our feet.

"Let's become a club," Karen said. "We'll meet here tomorrow with more matches."

Our club convened a few times, creating fires together on intermittent afternoons, until one day when I was fleeing a lockout, I went to the fort by myself.

It was gone. All the branches cracked on the ground. I prodded the wreckage with my foot in disbelief and then ran to Karen's house; I found her and Danielle in the basement planning a dance routine to one of her parents' old 45s—"Splish Splash."

"The fort's gone!" I told them.

"Yeah," Karen said. "We took it down."

"What? Why?"

"It was too dangerous to light matches in there with those dried branches," Karen said.

"We could have gone up in smoke," said Danielle.

I was struck with embarrassment that I didn't have enough sense to realize the fort was a fire hazard. Karen and Danielle were right. And I was wrong. Still, they hadn't even told me first, and I was the one who had built it, who had made it mine.

About three feet of snow fell that year, during the blizzard of '78, muffling the danger and allure of the woods with a thick white blanket. Snowmobiles zoomed through the field, but walking through the woods was not so easy. It was more fun to sled down the street. I also found a way to carve a fort into the six-foot-tall snow banks that the plow had deposited in front of our house.

When spring came round, I found myself playing with Meg and Polly, who were two years younger than me. Karen's little sister Meg looked exactly like her but she was smaller and wore her ashy hair in two stubby, melancholy ponytails. Polly, a tiny mouse of a girl, lived next door to Meg. The two operated as a team, the same way Karen and Danielle did, only they were the nice, put-upon version. With my two long Armenian braids woven by my mother, I was the only girl in our neighborhood who operated as a free agent.

It was a relief to hang out with the littler kids. I explained to them that picking Lady Slippers was against the law. I showed them how to suck on the ends of the tall sweet grass that grew in the field. I demonstrated how to hold a buttercup under someone's chin to see if she liked butter. We picked dandelions, purple clover flowers and the wheaty-looking weeds that weren't wheat. And when we ran into Karen and Danielle, we snubbed them. "What are you guys doing?" they asked suspiciously, ready to judge us.

"M.Y.O.B.," Meg said. Mind Your Own Business. Ms. Duffy had taught it to us and I had taught it to Meg. Karen and Danielle looked at me as though I had betrayed them. "C'mon," I said to Meg and Polly, "let's go to the field."

In the middle of the field there was a large island of trees that the minibikes used as a lap. Ridden by boys who lived on the other side of the field, the minibikes were evil; we made it a game to get chased by them. You just had to stand in the field and a boy would zoom after you for a second, then zip off and pop a wheelie.

We were being pursued by a troop of minibikes when one of them chased me towards the island of trees, so I leapt into it. As I hit the ground, a branch gouged my cheek. The bike stopped, backed up, and the rider lifted his helmet's visor. He had red hair and his face was freckled.

"Are you okay?" he asked, looking concerned.

I nodded my head and ran for Meg and Polly who were hiding at our rendezvous point, the creek behind Meg's house.

"What happened?" Polly asked.

I didn't tell them the boy stopped to see if I was okay; it would have wrecked our game of good and evil. "The minibike was chasing me, so I ran into the woods to escape!"

"Oh my God, you're bleeding!" Meg cried.

Acutely aware of the Band-Aid Meg's mom had stretched over my cheek, I looked out the window of the yellow and green flower wallpapered bedroom that Meg shared with Karen. The sun was hovering just above the tops of the trees—it would be a while before my mother would call me home for dinner, so I suggested to Meg that we play Wonder Woman. "You can be Steve Trevor," I said and twirled in a circle to transform myself. We pretended to catch bad guys, but it was only a matter of time before I informed her that we were to make out.

We spent a lot of time on the carpet hugging each other, rolling to and fro. Then we slowed down, and for the first time I felt my heart squash under the force of someone else's weight. It was a wild sensation, like being swallowed up, but not. Meg's skin was soft on my face and the sugar-chemical scent of Johnson's in her hair tickled the back of my throat. We were breathing hard but we must have been pretend-kissing because at one point Meg said, "Okay, now let's really kiss," so we put our mouths on each other's. Kissing turned out to be more exciting than I expected. I got lost in the wetness of Meg's mouth and forgot that we were playing Wonder Woman. The most intimate I felt, though, was when she locked the bedroom door so that Karen wouldn't be able to interrupt us.

We never played Wonder Woman again, probably for the fear of being discovered. It didn't matter, though; my desire had been relieved. If Wonder Woman kissed Steve, all her true selves would be seen: the watchful observer, the dutiful immigrant daughter and the superstar. In those kisses, such liberation seemed to rub off on me—I felt an opening, an acceptance. But unfortunately, in reality, it was all just make-believe.

4. HARD AND SOFT

Dr. Smith was a lewd old dude, making double entendres and coming on to unsuspecting women left and right. The crowd was laughing, but I found it all a bit unnerving.

Somehow I had convinced Bee to come with me to the Shrine Auditorium for this science fiction convention. As we wandered the halls, we spotted many regular folks dressed as Spock and Stormtroopers. Bee was delighted to encounter a subculture of Trekkies and *Star Wars* geeks and she went into reporter/social anthropologist mode, talking to anybody. But the convention itself was of secondary interest to me; I wasn't a sci-fi fan, but I had read that Jonathan Harris, who played Dr. Zachary Smith on the TV show *Lost in Space,* would be making a special appearance.

The truth was that I had partially moved to L.A. because I was drawn to Hollywood; I nurtured a secret fantasy that I might somehow become an actress and famous. Since I had arrived several months before, I had made a couple of exciting star sightings: Drew Barrymore and Anjelica Huston. But something about seeing Dr. Smith, a figure from my childhood, in the flesh, was so much more mind-boggling than running into your regular everyday movie star.

My brother had been fascinated with Dr. Smith, the sniveling, persnickety stowaway that always botched the Robinson family's plans to return to planet Earth. Whenever he appeared on the screen, Leo went a little crazy. "Dr. Smith, Dr. Smith!" he yelled and jumped up and down. The guy was really good at insulting the family robot, which, as he explained from the stage, was mostly unscripted; he used to dream up the verbal abuses late at night. The robot was at the convention too, down on the floor, and I had stood in front of it, marveling at its phony lights and buzzers. A manifestation of an idea, albeit a dumb one, which flickered over a screen and took up space in my brain, was actually dreamed up by some TV producer and created in the prop department. And then an actor would spend nights thinking up how to insult it? For some reason, I was really drawn to this loss: the stupid meaningless reality contrasted to impressionable childhood naiveté.

"You bubble-headed booby," Dr. Smith now yelled at the robot, which had been propped up by the stage. He then proceeded to make sexual allusions about the boobies of the female cast members and winked at women who asked questions from the audience. I had assumed he was gay and now couldn't figure out whether he was just an oversexed old man who happened to be effeminate, or he was putting on some kind of closet act.

There was another mystery too: why my brother had been so obsessed with him. I suspect old Zach Smith provided some comic relief to my brother, an unathletic boy in our hypermasculine town where jocks reigned supreme; Smith was cast in an ultimately powerful and prominent role. It must have been appealing to my brother to witness a figure who could fuck things up so badly for the status quo, which on the show was represented by a straightlaced hunk of a father and his humorless butch pal, Major Don West.

There was something familiar about Dr. Smith as well: my father was funny, but he could also be the villain, though not as dramatic and silly as Dr. Smith. Daddy was also unpredictable; you never knew how he was going to react. What you thought might make him laugh would piss him off, and vice versa.

Once, he completely disappeared during a visit to Horseneck Beach. "What do you think happened to Daddy?" I had asked my mother. It was five o'clock and starting to get cold; people around us were packing up their coolers and beach chairs to go home. Daddy had taken off down the beach a couple of hours before. He had floated on his back with the tide and body-surfed the waves, and then he lay on his old Army blanket to dry off. It was weird for him to take a walk since he always made fun of Mumma for never swimming, just strolling along the water's edge to dip her feet in.

"I don't know what's happened to him," Mumma said. "He's trying to upset me, that's what he's trying to do."

My parents had fought earlier that morning, as we were preparing to head out. It started like any other pre-day-trip conflict, with Daddy irritated at Mumma for leaving the house too late and bringing too much stuff, fruit and jackets, but then all of a sudden he bellowed, "You can't always have everything your own fuckin' way!"

My father's everyday repertoire of swears included *son of a bitch, god damn it,* and *bullshit,* but rarely the f-word, and his normal voice range was rather high—my friends often mistook him for my mother when he answered the phone. So Daddy's deep-throated cursing was super scary, causing my adrenaline to rush. "Hurry up, Nance," Val had prodded me. I finished buckling my sandal and turned the corner to Leo's bedroom to check his reaction.

"What are you looking at, spoiled brat?" he sneered, so I ran down the stairs.

Mumma responded to Daddy's outburst with a stony, angry silence. The car ride down to Horseneck was excruciatingly quiet. After we all visited the bathhouses to change, they still weren't speaking; Val and Leo went swimming with Dad, and I dug a hole in the sand while Mumma, in her floppy hat and owl-eye sunglasses, flipped through her *Redbook.* When it was time for lunch, Daddy brought back hot dogs and potato chips from the concession, but Mumma and Daddy were still silent to each other.

My parents usually forgot what caused their fights, but sometimes it took a while for them to quit remembering. Once, two weeks had passed before one night, when I was unable to sleep, I nervously called Mumma from my bed and asked her if she and Daddy were going to get a divorce. The room was dark and the light in the hallway was shining behind her, so I couldn't see her face. "No, we're not going to get a divorce," she said softly. A day or so later they were speaking.

The sky was turning purple when Daddy finally reappeared, trudging through the sand to the blanket. Dried salt water had matted down the hair on his body, including his combover, which was flattened to the wrong side of his head. When he was in his bathing suit, you could really get a good look at the permanent ridge in the middle of his belly, indented from years of wearing his belt cinched too tight; Grammy had initiated the practice when she dressed him as a little boy. He wasn't wearing glasses, which made his small eyes and square face look more open and soft.

"Where have you been?" Mumma demanded. "You wanted to worry us? Is that it?"

"Oh, did you miss me *geeneeg?*" Daddy said in a pinched baby voice. He was obviously in a better mood. He tried to hug Mumma but she pulled away. "Oh no, don't think you can hug me after what you did."

Daddy wiped his nose on a towel. "Okay, are you guys ready to go?" he asked as if nothing had ever happened.

"Once upon a time there were three little girls who went to the police academy. And they were each assigned very hazardous duties. But I took them away from all that. And now they work for *me*. My name..." Leo paused, "is *Charlie.*" We were in his room, on his bed, and he was pushing the RECORD and PLAY buttons on the tape recorder.

I sang the *Charlie's Angels* theme song and Leo joined in. "Duh, nuh nuh..." we sang. Then Leo made the sound of an explosion with his mouth.

I took my role as Bosley. "Angelsth, Charlie hasth a new asthignment for you."

"What is it, Bosley?" Leo asked as Sabrina, one of the Angels.

"Hold on, let me get him on the sthpeakerphone," I said.

"Hello Angels," Leo said, now Charlie with a low voice. "I have an assignment for you. You need to find Damien Roth."

Leo and I had lost interest in *Lost in Space* and were now distracted by Aaron Spelling's latest pop TV machination. During the fourth season, former Angel Jill Munroe returns to wreak havoc on Charles Townsend Associates detective agency because Farrah Fawcett-Majors, the actress who played Jill, was contractually obligated to do a few more episodes after quitting prematurely a previous season. The Angels are dismayed to find that Jill has taken up with one Damien Roth, a dashing James Bond-ish diamond thief. After a heist, Jill and Damien flee to Diablo Island, and the Angels follow in hot pursuit to the location of Roth's secret lair, also a habitat to man-eating cougars.

"Are there any dangerous elements on Diablo Island, Bosley?" Leo as Charlie asked.

"Uh, no Charlie, uh, not that I know of," I said, trying to act like Bosley acting evasive.

"Bosley! I demand to know what is on that island with my Angels!"

"Catsth, Charlie. Big…catsth."

We broke into laughter and then immediately tried to suppress it so as not to be heard on the tape, which made us laugh even more. Leo pushed the STOP button and we fell apart. We just couldn't get over Bosley's lisp. It was too much. It was so *faggy*. Backed by a crescendo in the soundtrack, the "Catsth, big catsth" moment was obviously intended to be dramatic during the telecast, but Bosley's sibilate referral to the cougars as cats rendered it hilarious. We had to recreate it on tape. And rewind it and listen to it.

"It's too funny," I gasped in between laughs. "I'm gonna die."

"Let's play it again," Leo said giggling.

"No, I can't breathe." I was on the floor in a fetal curl, my stomach aching with each convulsion.

My brother pushed REWIND. The anticipation of hearing the segment made him lose it and he fell to the floor, doubled over like me.

There were moments when I lost control of the laughter so badly that I thought I was going to suffocate. But after my stomach relaxed and I could breathe again, my brain and body felt great. We laughed the same way rock stars got so addicted to drugs they nearly OD'd. Our drug of choice just happened to be making fun of faggy people.

A fag was a guy with limp wrists. He ran and threw like a girl. He pranced around easily excited. He liked the color pink. More significantly, he liked other guys.

Fags lived in San Francisco, a fact I had deduced from watching Norman Lear sitcoms, but most of my knowledge about them was dispensed at recess. If anyone exhibited any signs of fagginess, a bigger kid was always there to identify it as such. "You *fag!*" a big kid would yell at a little kid. But no one really believed the little kid liked other guys—he was just *acting* faggy. Girls could act faggy. Sometimes we even called our moms fags. "Faggy" was used interchangeably with "gay" or "queer," but they all meant the same thing. They were used to describe any behavior that was flamboyant or silly or dorky or soft.

Maybe it was an aspect of working-class culture that required a certain toughness in order to survive, or the result of traditional small-town Catholic/Protestant homophobia, but sensitivity and gentleness were not acceptable characteristics in either boys or girls in Walpole. Multiple times during the day I was ridiculed for my calm voice and slow way of speaking.

In any case, Leo and I adopted the standard rubric of fagginess for judging Bosley. The guy was a pansy because of his lisp. He also displayed certain facial expressions that were really gay. In the opening credits there was a shot of him at his desk, swiveling in his chair, offering a gift to the Angels. Here was another side of softness, in contrast to Dr. Zachary Smith's cowardly antics. With his shoulders hunched and ruffling his suit, Bosley glanced up with a bashful, sweet self-consciousness akin to a little kid. This kind of vulnerability, in a portly middle-aged man, was simply not acceptable.

So we created wild absurdities about Bosley in order to make up for the cognitive dissonance. Above his right eyebrow, there appeared a sizable mole that we surmised he had a habit of squeezing, like a teen to a pimple. With the contents, Bosley made a "zit juice" martini, a lethal concoction. Sabrina offered one to Damien Roth on our tape recorder and it instantly killed him.

"I ain't eatin' those peas," Leo said to Mumma. He was imitating Bum Phillips again.

"You sure as hell are going to eat those peas or you won't watch the game," Daddy said.

It was Monday night and the Houston Oilers were playing. My brother was a big fan of this underdog NFL team, led by head coach Phillips, a bespectacled old coot in a cowboy hat. Leo covered the eagle and tri-cornered hat wallpaper of his bedroom with powder blue banners of oil rigs, and while he watched the game, he wore a black cowboy hat, procured during a visit to Knott's Berry Farm. He had even mail-ordered pencils personalized with some of his favorite players' names: Earl Campbell, Dan Pastorini and Curley Culp.

I had a habit of chewing on pencils and found it especially satisfying to drive Leo crazy by engraving teeth marks around a gold embossed *BUM PHILLIPS*. As I stood in front of the TV gnawing, Leo grabbed the specimen out of my mouth. The paint was peeling and the six facets were hardly distinguishable—a misshapen twig. "Don't chew on my pencils!" he yelled and pounded me on the arm.

"Ow!" I cried as the impact hit my bone. His punches had been getting much harder lately.

"Stop that!" Mumma intervened. "You're going to give her a bruise and bruises can turn into cancer!" My mother's carcinogenic claim seemed dubious to me, even at the age of ten. I was simultaneously glad she was defending me and unnerved that I might someday contract a terminal disease. "Do you want to give your sister cancer?!" she screeched.

"Yes!" Leo said.

Daddy came upstairs from the basement to investigate. "Leonard hit me!" I told him. "He's going to give me cancer!"

"Don't hit her again," Daddy said. He pounded Leo on the arm the way Leo had pounded me. Leo flinched and his cowboy hat fell off.

"Stop it, Tip!" Mumma cried.

"That's right," Daddy yelled. "Let him do whatever he wants. Just keep coddling him!"

"This is all her fault," Leo said, pointing at me. "She takes my things and ruins them!"

"Son of a bitch!" Daddy yelled. "Who do you think you're talking to like that?" He grabbed the broom behind the kitchen door. Hunched over and red-faced, a stocky man in a short sleeve shirt, bell bottom polyester pants and wire-rimmed glasses, Dad bolted for Leo. I hated to see my father this mad, but for some reason, I felt the urge to laugh. I couldn't though, it would only make him more angry. So I silently rooted for Leo, nervously giggling and making a break for it.

Every time I passed through the kitchen to get a snack, I could hear my brother and his new junior high school friend, who had come over for the first time, laughing hysterically on the back porch. Mumma had instructed me to leave Leo and Will alone, but as I was assembling my third English muffin pizza for the toaster oven, I couldn't take it any longer. "What are you laughing about?" I asked, swinging open the door to the porch.

"The Dicks," Will answered.

"What?" I asked.

"Dick Jones. Tricky Dick O'Reilly." Leo was laughing nervously.

"Who are they?"

Will looked around for a minute, considering whether to tell me. He must've regarded my brother's laughter as permission, because he responded, "Well, according to Leo, they're *lovers!*"

My brother cackled out of control, while Will explained to me that the Dicks were teachers at East Junior High. One time they had allegedly emerged from the bathroom together, looking as if they had been engaged in some sort of lascivious behavior.

Leo later pointed out the Dicks at the EJH Open House, but they didn't seem so faggy to me. Tricky Dick O'Reilly was an older man with a crew cut who barked as he discussed with parents how he taught Earth Science. Dick Jones, his younger supervisor, wore big aviator glasses, an overgrown "dry look" haircut, and an untucked poly/cotton button down shirt.

But I soon discovered that it was hilarious to imagine two people of the same sex, who weren't necessarily faggy, as a couple.

I conjured up a tape recorder story about Diggin Arlene and Diggin Carol. Inspired by the cocktails I'd seen on the lido deck of *The Love Boat*, I imagined the women getting drunk on non-alcoholic piña coladas and retreating to the Boston View Motel over on Route 1.

Advice columnist Ann Landers captivated us with her huge bouffant and the quirky way she spoke out the side of her mouth on *The Hollywood Squares*. Equally fascinating was Toppie Smellie, an old lady with pointy cat eye glasses and a shock of white hair, who drawled on the Oven Fry coated chicken ads: "I can describe this fried chicken in two words: Mm-mmm." It only made sense to couple the crones inside of a baby grand piano.

My brother, Will and I made fun of just about anyone by imagining them in homosexual assignations in odd places. For some reason, heterosexual trysts just weren't very humorous.

This was a lesson I learned in more detail when I discovered a dirty magazine in my parents' top dresser drawer. It wasn't a *Playboy*. It was small, the size of a *Reader's Digest,* with black and white pictures of naked people. When my parents weren't home, I took it out of their top drawer and furtively spied a picture of a naked man lying on top of a naked lady on top of a hospital gurney. The man's dark hair was parted neatly on the side and the woman's blond hairdo was separated into messy locks that revealed dark roots. This was a naughty picture; my stomach dissolved as I looked at the man's slightly raised bum. After a few seconds, I shoved the magazine back into the dresser.

Leo caught me slamming the drawer and opened it up. "Well, well, well, what do we have here?" he asked, as if he were a villain on *Get Smart*. He pulled out the magazine and flipped through it, examining the pictures. Then he smiled sinisterly, his big teeth showing. "Oh, you're in big trouble now."

"You're not gonna tell Mumma and Daddy are you?"

"I will if you keep stealing my pencils."

"I never stole your stupid pencils, I just chewed on them!"

"Oh, you little spoiled brat. Talk to me that way some more and I *will* tell them."

"Oh yeah, well I'll tell them that you…"

"Yes?"

"That you…"

"Go on."

I had nothing, so I lashed out with my fists. Soon I was being pummeled.

"Valerie!" I screamed as I got thwacked in the back. "VALERIE!" Leo pounded harder as my older sister who was seventeen, and therefore huge, tore into my parents' bedroom. My skinny brother straightened and started for the safety of the bathroom with its lockable doors, but he didn't make it in time. Valerie grabbed him by his striped shirt, lay a big hard blow on his arm and bellowed, "STOP HITTING HER!"

"Oww," my brother whined, rubbing his arm. "I didn't hit her *that* hard."

"You did too!" I snapped. "You big liar."

"You did too!" he mocked. *"You big liar!"* Before my sister could wallop him again, he ran down to the den to watch *Gilligan's Island.* After a while, I went down to join him.

Obviously, a lot of escapism was going on at the time, and not just on our parts. Fantasy TV shows involving magic or the supernatural, featuring witches, genies and ghosts, were de rigueur. Sitcoms employed highly unlikely scenarios, like hillbillies living in Beverly Hills, and an unusual cross section of folks (sexy movie star, farm girl, wealthy old blue bloods) getting stranded on a deserted isle. These were the years before the faux socially conscious TV movies of the week. Later, in the Eighties, Farrah Fawcett, a.k.a. Charlie's prodigal Angel, gets beaten up by her spouse, her famous hairdo finally mussed, looking like a bruised and bleeding peach in *The Burning Bed.* A boyfriend once told me, a first-generation ethnic himself, that he thought my brother and I were so fascinated by '70s TV not just because we needed to be entertained, but because we constantly lived in cultural contrast—we subconsciously got something about America that Americans didn't.

So what happened when we watched ourselves? Every once in a while, the whole family gathered in the basement, settling onto benches covered in aqua and ochre vinyl cushions, a hanging lamp covered with brown glass baubles hovering above us. My father set up a collapsible screen between his desk and the filing cabinets, then signaled to Leo when to turn out the lights. As the projector ticked and whirred, running the Super 8 images my father had captured years before, we saw characters we recognized, and some complete strangers. Mumma provided the commentary.

"This must be Stacy and Markar's wedding," she said. "Oh my God, that's Lucy. Isn't that Lucy, Tip? Look at how young she looks." Lucy, a relative on my father's side, was svelte in a fuchsia suit, but the last time I saw her at Sts. Sahag and Mesrob, she was a bit stocky with a double chin. Grammy and Aunties also appeared slim in their wedding outfits. "You've all turned into pigasauruses," Leo noted.

There were some shaky shots of the Catholicos, the patriarch of the Armenian Apostolic Church, wearing a long white beard and a black, nearly dunce-like pointed hat, entering the Cambridge church during a rare visit from then Soviet Armenia. In the parking lot afterwards, my brother and I appeared in the backwards seat of our station wagon. I was wearing a yellow dress and smiling sweetly next to Leo in a jacket and bow tie, grimacing and jabbing a pink plastic sword at the camera. Daddy froze the frame.

"Things don't change much," he said to Leo, who now had braces on his teeth and a thick bushy head of black hair, like a cushion.

"Ha ha," my brother grimaced.

At the end of the screening, Leonard put himself in charge of labeling the contents of each reel. I watched as he titled the one of the Catholicos, "The Big Cheese from Etchmiadzin." The reel of Stacy and Markar's wedding he titled, "Pigasauruses." He was applying satire techniques, picked up from *MAD Magazine,* to our own family.

Daddy packed up the projector and screen and headed upstairs. He heard me giggling and sternly warned my brother, "Do that right, *please.*"

There was one reel that was gray and plastic, not white like the rest. "What's this?" I asked Leonard and he held it up to the light. In the squares of film we could see a tiny naked lady. "Oh!" I said. Leo quickly rewound the reel and put it back in the box, unlabeled.

The next time my parents went out for the evening and Val launched a marathon conversation on the phone in the basement with her boyfriend, Leo set up the screen and projector in my parents' bedroom. He and I sat at the edge of their bed and watched the title bleed onto the screen:

Gorgeous August

Then we watched August stroll into the frame.

"Oh my god!" I cried.

"Shut up," Leo said stonily.

The naked lady looked a little like Auntie Mel had in the shower, but she was thinner and younger with a brunette, bouffant hairdo. She sat on the arm of a sofa and smiled. For a while. Her skin was white, her nipples a dark gray and her boobs big and bouncy, jiggling quietly as she shifted on the arm of the sofa. Sitting. Smiling. Talking. We couldn't hear her; there was no sound.

"What is she doing?" I asked my brother.

"Shut up," he said again, his arms folded across his chest.

A moment later, August stood by a lamp and spoke to someone off-camera. She seemed awfully chatty for a person who was naked in a living room. After walking away from the lamp, she sat in an easy chair, crossing her legs. She bounced the top leg, playfully. I counted to twenty. The End.

The film wasn't much of a turn-on; I found my parents' dirty magazine more exciting than August.

"If you tell Mumma and Daddy about this I'll kill you," Leo said, quickly putting everything away.

"I won't tell," I promised.

I looked around my parents' bedroom, at my father's shoe shine box and shoes lined up by the bed, at my mother's stack of books—*Your Erroneous Zones, Please Don't Eat the Daisies, The Women's Room*—on her nightstand. I was pretty sure the movie was Daddy's. Maybe he watched it as a stag film at his bachelor party like on *Happy Days*.

As my brother shoved the projector and screen into their closet, my eye was drawn to my mother's wedding picture on the wall. It was a professional black and white studio shot of her in her wedding dress. She was smiling with her full lips, her skin perfectly smooth and her dark eyes glossy. She didn't look like Gorgeous August, who was supposed to be sexy. She also didn't look like the Mumma I knew, who yelled at us and screamed at Daddy. I couldn't imagine who she was then, mild and in love.

Daddy would often get so overtaken with affection he would suddenly hug you from behind and smack a kiss right on your ear. When he did it to Mumma, she would scream "Go away!" and struggle out of his embrace. Sometimes, I heard them at night in the next room, Mumma telling him "no" in a stern, irritated voice.

"You've been chewing my pencils again!" Leo yelled and smacked me hard on the arm.

"Ow!" I yelled. "I'm telling!" We were in the den, and I could hear Daddy's steps up the basement stairs towards the door.

"You little spoiled brat, if you say one word, I'll tell him about the dirty magazine."

"What's going on in here?" Daddy boomed into the room.

"Leo hit me!"

"What did I tell you?" Daddy asked Leo.

"Wait a minute," Leo said. "She's not so innocent—"

"G.A." I blurted out.

Leo looked at me, stunned.

"If you say another word I'm going to tell about G.A." I said to Leo.

"You're bluffing," he whispered.

"Try me," I taunted Leo.

"I don't know what's going on here, but you're not to touch her again, do you understand?" Daddy asked.

"Yes," Leo grumbled.

I gloated over my victory for about twenty-four hours, until we were home alone one evening and Leo came at me, pushing hard. "That's for that G.A. stunt you pulled, you spoiled brat." I fell onto the Oriental rug in the living room and he thrashed at me. "Who are you going to call for help now?" I tried hitting him, but I didn't stand a chance.

What makes him think he can do this? He was always going to punch and pound me. Always.

"I'm not going to take this anymore!" I suddenly screeched.

I must have startled Leo, because he laughed hysterically.

"You can't beat me up all the time!" Somehow, I got on top of him, pinning his arms down. "No, no, no!" I shook my head, turning mental. Tears and saliva flung over the Oriental rug; I couldn't feel my brain anymore. The more I lost it, the more Leo laughed. He was cracking up so badly, he was unable to defend himself. "Stop it! It's too funny!" he pleaded.

As I struck him, my arms pounded through flesh to solid bone. I was surprised that it hurt really bad, worse than being punched, but I kept at it, bruising him and me. My brother still couldn't stop laughing, though silently now, his body convulsing between hard and soft.

PART II

5. SHAKESPEARIAN

"Would you wear a dildo and fuck your boyfriend in the ass?" It was after hours at the workshop, and somehow the topic turned to sex. Poetry students who were becoming more than acquaintances were suddenly talking about sex toys. Since I had no experience, I had absolutely nothing to say, which kept me in a constant state of painful blushing. I wanted to lose my virginity just so that I wouldn't feel like a freak, but I was afraid of sex. Bee had told me she had once been fucked by a guy, a friend from high school, who had transformed into an animal and pummeled her like a jackhammer. The prospect of having sex with a woman wasn't any more comforting since I didn't exactly know what happened there. So I completely shut down during the post-workshop bull session, hoping no one would notice how innocent I was.

Later, a bunch of us were lingering by the bulletin board in the lobby and noticed a sign for an upcoming performance: "The Sting Dreams." It wasn't quite clear what the show would be, but I'd had a huge crush on Sting throughout my adolescence, first during his stint in The Police and then later in his pseudo-jazz solo career. I was curious.

"The Sting Dreams?" Ellie asked. She was the tall blond lesbian from Brown. I watched as she read the flyer. "Is anyone going to this performance?"

No one responded. "I'm kind of interested," I said.

"I'll go," Ellie said, "if anyone wants to meet me here."

"I will," I told her. A few other women pronounced that they might come too.

When Friday night rolled around, Ellie and I were the only ones from the group who were in the audience. The stage was a black box, and the set was a bed; a woman wearing a flowing peignoir held a microphone and announced all the dreams she'd had about Sting. I can't recall if there was a point to the whole thing.

Afterwards, Ellie and I went out for coffee. It turned out we knew people in common at Wellesley and Brown. She had moved to L.A. around the same time I did and was trying to break into sitcom writing. She had grown up in Westchester, so her East Coast-ness felt very familiar to me in this foreign Californian world. Here was a potential new friend.

But I was cautious. Over the next few weeks, we hung out after the workshop. One night, while giving me a ride home, she was complaining about someone in the workshop, and I found myself unable to say anything for fear of saying the wrong thing; I felt myself emotionally squirming. Over the phone I told Alisa, who had driven across the country with me in what seemed years ago, that I wasn't so sure about this new friend.

"You need to give people a chance, Nancy," she said.

I had been noticing, over the last few years, that friendship meant more to me than it did for other people. I fell hard for friends, becoming dependent on them, the way one might for a romantic partner, investing time and thought and care and a lot of my identity too—everything, practically, but sex. So if things went wrong, my world fell apart. My caution didn't have so much to do with Ellie, but with historical circumstances, starting with the first best friend I ever made, when I was twelve years old.

—◆—

"My parents aren't going to let me go," Emine said while we were sitting on top of the jungle gym at recess. She hung her head down and her shoulder-length, shiny black hair swung from the barrettes that were clipped behind each of her ears.

"Why not?" I asked her.

"They just won't," she said, her eyebrows furrowed. "Do you think your parents will let you go?"

"I'm pretty sure. They let Valerie and Leonard." It was a tradition for Bird School sixth graders to take a weeklong trip to Maine in the spring. Our teacher Mr. Fields had just given us permission slips for our parents to sign.

That evening, Emine called me on the phone after she had shown the slip to her parents. "They won't let me go because they don't think boys and girls should stay overnight together."

"I don't get it. We'll be in different rooms from the boys."

"That doesn't matter," she sighed. "They just don't think it's right."

"Ask Fields to talk to them," I suggested. "You have to go!" I couldn't imagine going to Maine without my best friend.

Emine had moved to Walpole several months before. Mr. Fields, with his Brylcreemed hair, yellow short sleeve shirt and khaki chinos, had introduced her to the class, explaining, "Emine and her family moved to America four years ago. She's Turkish."

An alarm had blared in my head. I knew what Turkish was. It belonged to the realm of Armenian school. As in "Turkish people killed Armenian people." My stomach turned. I didn't want to hate the new girl, but I felt I had to after what the Turks had done to us. But every year in school on Martin Luther King, Jr. Day, we learned that hating people for being of a certain race, without really knowing them, was morally wrong.

Over the next few weeks, I realized that Emine and I had a lot in common. She was smart and liked school. She had black hair and brown eyes and the same skin color as me. Turkish was foreign in Walpole, the same way Armenian was, and Emine wasn't Catholic either. Emine's curiosity and wonderment of Walpole, of everything I had long before resigned to not question, was a revelation. I nearly cried when she asked, "So what do they do at CCD[2] anyway?"

It wasn't long before we became friends. Now, when I found myself not fitting in, I had someone to keep me company. I also took pride in serving as Emine's cultural emissary. I taught her the words to the songs in the movie *Grease* (though Mumma had not let me view the PG-rated feature), lent her my copies of the dirtiest Judy Blume books, and informed her what the words "pisser," "wicked" and "scumbucket" meant. But I was stumped when she asked me about the word "rape."

"I hear it on the news," she said. "I asked my parents but they won't tell me."

"I think it's when a woman gets mugged," I told Emine. "I think a man gets mugged and a woman gets raped." She nodded, her face still a question mark.

I would have asked my big sister Valerie, but by this time she was going to college all the way out in Worcester. The next time the six o'clock news announced that it had happened to a woman in Brookline, I queried my parents. Daddy looked over his newspaper and across the living room to Mumma in her chair.

"You don't need to know," she said solemnly.

As I waved out the bus window to Emine standing in the Bird parking lot, I tried not to look too disappointed. She waved back, her thin lips caught between an angry frown and a resigned smile. Emine took my advice and had Fields explain to her parents that we would be chaperoned the whole time in Maine, with girls and boys in separate sleeping rooms, but to no avail. Her parents held firm to their belief.

"What's her parents' problem anyway?" Danielle asked.

"My father said it was because of their religion," Karen said.

"It sounds like a stupid religion," Danielle said.

I wanted to defend Emine, but I couldn't deny that I thought her religion was stupid: Turks had killed Armenians because of it. It was also nice to not be the weirdo for once.

In Maine I took nature walks led by a hippie counselor named Ben. My feet got wet in the bog, and I made tea out of rose hips. One morning I woke up at 5 A.M. to watch the sun rise over the ocean. Jeff Lacey and Carl DiGiorno tried to visit Colleen Easton and Suzette Poiron in our room,

---

[2] Confraternity of Christian Doctrine, or confirmation classes. I didn't know what the letters stood for or the purpose, just that all the Catholic kids had to go to CCD every Wednesday after school.

but they got caught scrambling up the gutter to our window.

When I returned, I told Emine every detail of the trip. Her eyes turned sad, and then blank, as I told her about the excitement she'd missed. I was going to console her by saying the trip would have been much better if she'd been there, but I didn't.

"Nancy, did you get a letter from school for me?" Mumma asked. "About a lecture at the high school?"

A notice about a menstruation assembly, co-sponsored by the town of Walpole and Kotex Brand feminine products, was given to all the sixth grade girls to bring home.

"Yes," I said hesitantly.

"Why didn't you show it to me?"

I had thought she wouldn't want to go. When I was eight, I had pointed to her soft pack of feminine napkins and asked what they were. "I'll tell you when you're older," she had said sheepishly. Reading the Judy Blume classic on menstruation, *Are You There God? It's Me, Margaret*, helped to fill in the details.

"I don't know," I answered.

"Do you still have it? It's important."

So I showed her the slip, and on the designated weeknight, we went to the high school and entered the noisy, gargantuan auditorium filled with the female population of Walpole.

There was a group of girls from Bird. "Where's Emine?" they asked.

"Her mom didn't want to come," I said. Their faces seemed eager for more information, so I continued. "She threw the notice into the trash." The girls gasped.

I peered back at my own mother, small and smiling next to the other moms, sitting several rows behind us. *At least our mothers are "normal,"* I thought. In this heavily Catholic town, where parents were still preaching chastity till marriage and that contraception was a sin, our moms were probably just as ill-equipped as Emine's mom to address a procreational bodily function. But they were able at least to accomplish the minimum, accompanying us to the assembly while Kotex representatives did the dirty work. Soon, some women in business suits appeared with a nurse in a white coat to pass out pamphlets and samples. Giggling commenced. Giggling ceased and it was over.

"Well, now you're prepared," Mumma said in the car, driving home.

A month or so later, I noticed some pink watercolor stains in my underwear. I shyly called Mumma into the bathroom and showed her. "Oh, you're going to get your period," she said, smiling tentatively. "Let's see if you get it by morning."

Nothing showed up in my underpants the next day. "You should take your napkins to school, just in case," Dr. Agabian advised.

I went off to school, sans pads, unable to accept that I would soon have to wear a napkin between my legs to sop up blood. Already I was growing embarrassing little tits, hair was sprouting everywhere and my nose enlarged and acquired a bump. Couldn't nature reverse its course so that I could be little and simple again?

At school, we were taking the SRA tests. Normally I loved filling in empty ovals with graphite, the intense quiet of the classroom, the possibility of scoring in the ninety-ninth percentile. But now I was anxious, super-vigilant of any wetness down there. When I felt something moist during the middle of the math portion, I went to the bathroom and saw on the crotch of my underpants a bright red spot.

I wanted to cry. Instead, I stuffed a bunch of toilet paper in my pants and went back to class.

Unfortunately, Emine didn't show up for school that day, and I really needed to confide in someone. Annie Leach seemed like a safe choice. She was a tomboy, uninterested in anything remotely girly, so I didn't think she would get hysterical. At recess, I whispered in her ear, "Don't tell anyone. I got my period!"

She just looked at me, wide-eyed.

After school, I trudged home and went to the bathroom. The toilet paper in my panties had traveled up my butt, and my underwear was stained with an even larger splotch which had bled to the inside of my jeans. I pasted a pad into the crotch of a clean *vardeek* and wearily updated my mother.

"Have you had any cramps?" she asked.

"Yes," I said.

"Well, I'll give you a Tylenol and that should help." She spoke to me gently and smiled at me funny. I was glad there was a medical component that she could focus on, because I would have hated for her to get mushy on me.

Auntie Mel would ask me later, while I was staying over at Grammy's house, what my first period was like. "So your mumma explained everything to you about it?"

"Yes," I said tersely. I was too embarrassed to talk about the personal details of my menses, but I was also hoping to circumvent any criticism she might have of my mother.

"That's good, Nancy," she said gently, "because, you know, your grammy never told me anything. So when I got it, I was really frightened." She blinked and I noticed how long her lashes were. "I thought I was dying."

After the Tylenol kicked in, I called Emine to tell her the news. "I feel awful," I told her.

"Really?" she asked with a lot of enthusiasm, like my parents had just given me a new bike.

"Yes, and I came in last in the six-hundred-yard dash." Of course we had to be doing the Presidential Physical Fitness Test in gym that day.

"Oh well. But now you have your *period!* I wish I had mine," she said longingly.

What's her problem? I thought. I didn't have time to explain to Emine that bleeding out of one's vagina was definitely not cool, so I told her the homework and got off the phone.

The next day I wore my bright red Levi's corduroys. I thought if I leaked, their red color would hide the blood.

At school, Mr. Fields was having trouble looking me in the eye. More girls said hi to me than usual. Emine noticed the changes too. "I think people know," she said at lunch, leaning over her cafeteria tray.

"Did you tell anyone?" I whispered.

"No! Did you?" Emine asked.

I tracked down Annie at recess. "I didn't really get what you were talking about," she said. "So I asked Danielle about it."

Annie didn't read Judy Blume (or books in general, for that matter), and she didn't bring notices to her mother, since they usually meant she was in trouble, so she had missed the menstruation assembly. She didn't know what a period was, so she had asked Danielle, one of the dirty blond girls who stole my seashells and tore down my fort, now the biggest loudmouth at school.

Everyone knew I was a disgusting pubescent. Everyone knew, and I was wearing red pants.

Mrs. Saddler wore her red hair swirled up in a bun. One morning in October, she announced the honor roll for the seventh grade at East Junior High. I didn't hear my alphabetically-privileged name at the beginning of the list. *How could I not get on the honor roll?* I thought. All I had done was study since I started junior high, my only friend Emine. When Saddler was done reading names, she gazed at me expectantly. I nervously adjusted the strap of my too-big bra, a yellow-armpitted one of my sister's that she'd left behind when she went to college. My burgeoning boobs had outgrown undershirts, but I was too ashamed to alert Mumma and get mixed up with the salesladies in the Bradlees lingerie department. "There was one student in the seventh grade who made high honors," Mrs. Saddler said. "She received straight A's in every subject, and she's in our homeroom—Nancy Agabian."

Oh my God, I thought. *Really?*

The bell rang and I met Emine in the hallway. "You got on high honors!" she enthused, her dark doe eyes narrowing behind thick lashes. They'd announced it in her homeroom too.

"Oh my God, you got all A's?" Kristy Door asked while we were rotating on the volleyball court during gym. She was the most popular girl in school and her lips glistened with an excessive application of Kissing Potion. "What do you do, like, study all day?"

I didn't know what to say. I shrugged at Emine.

"Hey, you must really be a geek," Jeff Lacey said as he approached in the hall, "to get all A's." Once when we were in fifth, Jeff and I had played Girls Chase the Boys at recess and I missed tagging him, so he called, "Miss me, miss me, now you gotta kiss me." I had noted it in my diary. Now he was popular and wore a plaid shirt over a t-shirt, cords and work boots. As he passed by, he shouted "LOSAH!" making an L out of his thumb and forefinger and branding it to his forehead.

"I guess it's not so great to get all A's in junior high," Emine surmised.

When Emine and I tramped into her house after school, her mom was sitting on a stool, watching *Guiding Light* on the TV in the kitchen. The dark brown roots in her honey blond hair and her designer jeans made her look younger than Mumma and most of the moms I knew in Walpole. She smiled at me, and her eyes narrowed like her daughter's as she spoke to Emine in Turkish and gave her some Hostess Cup Cakes.

We walked down the hall to Emine's room. Her house was built from the exact same blueprint as many other homes in Walpole: no matter who you were visiting, you knew precisely where the bathroom was. But the decor differed: Oriental rugs covered the floors, like the ones in our house, and a blue and white glass eye hung on the wall in the living room—Auntie Agnes had one like it dangling from her rear-view mirror; she said it was an evil eye to ward off curses.

Outside her bedroom door, we ran into Emine's brother Temel, who would never say hi to me. He was fifteen and his body was developed with a big round butt and a bulging crotch. I tried not to look at these parts whenever he came near, but I always failed. As he spoke to Emine in Turkish, completely ignoring me, I wondered if he hated me because I was Armenian or because I stared at his man-area.

Emine and I plopped down on her lemon-colored wall-to-wall carpet and looked at the new issue of *Seventeen*.

"It says here that your hair only grows a half inch per month! It's gonna take forever for my hair to grow out!" I lamented.

"Here's a facial we could try," Emine said. "My skin is so scummy."

I flipped to a page with photographs of three girls in leotards, one fat, one thin and one muscular, with scientific terms labeling their body types. I said, "I think I'm an endomorph," the scientific word for fat girl. I had reckoned that Emine was an ectomorph (skinny girl), but before I could tell her she flipped to Brooke Shields' description of her first kiss, which was an ad for Love's Baby Soft, a pink-colored perfume that came in a bottle shaped like a phallus.

"Is there anyone you like?" Emine asked.

Mister Rogers, Donny Osmond, Peter Brady, Davy Jones of The Monkees, and George Harrison of The Beatles, had been objects of my crushes from the time I was four until I was ten. In the fifth grade, I had started to like real boys: Jeff Lacey who was tall and blond, Carl DiGiorno with the intense blue eyes and Timothy Connors, my next door neighbor with whom I shared a penchant for *Peanuts*.

But in sixth grade, when girls started to pursue boys, I hadn't thought I was pretty enough for any boy to like me. And then Emine moved to town and became my best friend. I had never had a best friend before.

"Well, of course, I still like Jeff Lacey," I told Emine.

"What are you going to do about it?" she asked eagerly.

I stared at Emine. Jeff had just called me a "losah" and was obviously way out of my league—everyone knew he liked Kristy Door. I was satisfied with my elaborate daydreams of Jeff and me forming a rock band together, composing and performing love songs for each other. In reality, he, Timothy and Carl would walk home from school and holler at me, "Hey Arabian, your camel's double parked."

"I don't know," I told her.

I was walking home quickly from Emine's through the woods, via one of the many paths I had recently discovered. My trail blazing had been motivated by news of a bald man with shoe polish on his head who had grabbed Shawna Love and threatened her with a hypodermic needle. Shawna lived up the street and was a year older than me. She was on her way home from school on the shortcut path through the woods when the man assaulted her. Luckily she was able to scream and run away. Strangely, no one was alarmed enough to actually do anything about this information: either the townsfolk shrugged off the story of Shawna as just a rumor, and/or they were not so sensitive, in the early Eighties, to the abductions of minors, for we all kept using the same path as the shortest route to school.

A few days after I'd heard the story, I was trudging home and heard footsteps behind me. Terrified, I ran to the end of the path where it met the street and waited to see who it was. I could make out the shape of a person, then a boy's jostling walk, then my neighbor Timothy Connors. I let out a deep breath.

"Timothy, I thought you were the man who grabbed Shawna."

"Aaah Nancy! I'm Mr. Shiny Shoe Head!" he had mocked, waving his hands in the air.

Since then, I had found dozens of alternate routes through the woods. I felt proud whenever I led Emine on a new shortcut.

But now my head and eyes tensed as I walked through the woods alone. I couldn't help imagining the scary man coated in navy blue Kiwi that came in a tin, the kind Daddy kept in his wooden shoeshine box by the side of his bed. The color contrasted with the man's bloodshot eyes, watching me from behind the cover of trees. I quickened my pace as I visualized him crouching in the woods nearby, ready to brandish a deadly needle. Faster and faster I strode until I could see the glimmer of lights from our house. Almost safe. Stopping in my tracks, I looked all around, into the vertical layers of trees and leaves and the quiet spaces between them that went on forever. I let the terror invade my bloodstream, it bore down on me like a drug.

I ran. I booked it outta there as fast as I could, my book bag bouncing against my leg.

"Did you have dinner at Emine's house?" Mumma asked.

I threw my book bag on the floor in the foyer. "Uh, they don't eat dinner," I said.

"What do you mean they don't eat dinner?"

"They eat snacks."

"Snacks!" Mumma exclaimed.

"Snacks!" Leo echoed. "Like what? Doritos and Fritos?"

"Yeah, basically."

"Oh my God!" Mumma said.

When Emine came over for my thirteenth birthday party a couple of months later, Mumma prepared chicken and pilaf and *fasoolyah* and my father's oil and vinegar iceberg salad. We consumed Hood ice cream and a Betty Crocker cake for dessert. The next morning Emine called to tell me she had fainted after she arrived home.

"Oh, that's terrible," Mumma said.

"They're going to think you poisoned her," Daddy said. I had to admit it seemed suspicious. None of us were sick, and Emine had never fainted before.

"What's the big deal? She just isn't used to not eating snacks," Leo joked.

Mumma called Emine's parents to find out how she was doing and told them what she had served her.

"Her father was very nice," she said.

"Well, I tell you one thing. They're never going to let her come over to this house again," Daddy said.

One Saturday morning, I was eating Life cereal in the kitchen when Uncle Joseph said, "Nancy, I hear you have a friend who's Turkish." Sometimes my mother's bachelor brother worked late at his job in Boston, so he'd spend the night on our sofa if he was too tired to make the drive back to his home in Cranston, Rhode Island. He was looking at me now with the same big eyes as Mumma's. "You know what the Turks did to us, right?"

"Yes," I replied quietly, though it had been a while since I'd had to hear about it at Armenian school. I was to have graduated at the end of sixth grade, but Diggin Arlene decided to add on an extra year to my sentence. The seventh grade teacher was from Soviet Armenia and had insisted we learn noun declensions, an advanced form of Armenian school torture. I had complained so much to my mother that she gave up and stopped making me go.

"You know what they did and you're still friends with her?" Uncle Joseph asked. "Imagine that." He shook his head like I had let him down, let all the Armenians down.

But Emine hadn't killed Armenians, I reasoned. Her family, with the exception of Temel, were always kind to me. They also never asked me about my religion, and Emine never talked about hers. She didn't seem to practice it, with the exception of her parents' enforced rule to not go to Maine, and looking back on it now, that seemed more cultural.

Our friendship made sense to me, our parents didn't actively oppose it, and the kids in Walpole (as well as the teachers, most likely) had no idea that Emine and I came from enemy ethnic groups. But now my uncle was reminding me of the obvious, of the Romeo and Juliet situation she and I were in.

One afternoon, Emine and I were doing homework in her dining room, by the sliding glass door that led to the deck at the back of her house. We were sprawled out on the olive shag carpeting and sun was streaming through the window. Emine lay on her side, facing me, and I noticed the curve of her hip. She was wearing dark blue jeans and a fuzzy brown velour top. I thought about how messed up and gay I would be if I wanted to kiss her. Then I tried really hard, as hard as I could, to wipe it out of my mind.

"In study hall, Jimmy Sweeney asked if I use a vibrator. Do you know what it is?" Emine asked.

I didn't. Jimmy Sweeney was a druggie, so I suspected it was something nasty.

"Then he asked me if there was hair on my head. When I said yes, he laughed. Do you get it?"

"I think he was asking if you have hair, you know, down there," I told Emine.

"Oh," she said. I could tell by the way she said it that she liked him.

We were spending a Friday afternoon in her basement, eating Cheetos and watching *The Benny Hill Show,* which Emine had recently discovered. She cackled when Benny squeezed a pregnant lady's boob into his tea. "He's so funny!" she said, as I rolled my eyes. I had seen just about every episode two years before and was no longer amused.

After the show, she said, "I have an idea. Let's write wishes that we want for each other to come true. And then we'll give them to each other."

"Okay," I said. *I hope your mom and dad get less strict,* I wrote. Lately Emine had been complaining about her parents, how her brother never fought with them about their stupid rules and how she had to challenge them in order to go to pool parties or the Showcase Cinema in Dedham.

I wish for you to get a makeover so that Jeff Lacey will like you, Emine wrote.

"Thanks," I said and put the stinging wish into my pocket.

"Do you want to do it now?" she asked. "It will be fun."

I was curious as to what she had in mind, so I followed her upstairs to her bedroom and for the next hour she curled my hair with a curling iron, spread blush on my cheeks and applied eye shadow to my lids. I held my breath as I felt hers lightly gracing my cheek. "Let's go over to the mirror," she finally said. "But wait, you have to close your eyes." Emine led me by my arm and sat me down in the chair in front of her bureau. "There's just one more thing I have to do," she said. I felt her tie something around my head. "Okay, now open them."

Emine's face was smiling above mine in the mirror. She was wearing a blue headband across her forehead and I was wearing a red one. They were the kind Olivia Newton-John sported—braided with gilded thread.

"What do you think?" she asked.

"It's okay," I told her.

"Do you like it?"

"Yes, I like it," I lied. "It's great."

The makeup and hair were fine, but the headband was too much. I looked like a sleazy Indian maiden. A nice Armenian girl masquerading as a slut. It just wasn't right; she didn't get it. On my way home through the woods, I ripped off the headband, threw it on the ground and stomped it into the dirt.

Emine stepped out of her mother's car, decked out in her headband, tight jeans and light blue heels. It was spring, and she and I had slowly been drifting apart. I wanted to be little and simple, so I started hanging out with other girls who liked to take walks in the woods, and gradually saw Emine less and less. But she had called me and asked me to go to the Town Fair with her; she had never been. I wouldn't normally consider going, since mainly little kids and their parents went. But I kind of missed her, so I said yes.

It was a sunny Saturday in Walpole Center. I noticed that Emine had just done her makeup and her hair was freshly curled and bouncy. She didn't look like a girl anymore, but a glamorous person on TV. She wanted some attention, obviously. Dumpy in comparison, I was wearing shorts and sneakers.

We watched the high school marching band and the Walpole veterans parade down Main Street, ate barbecued chicken and corn on the cob at a church picnic, and silently roamed around the square, looking at craft booths with crocheted toilet paper covers.

I could tell Emine was let down by the moment she had so prepared for, but I didn't console her. Instead, some part of me felt vindicated for being left behind. *Who does she think she is, to think some Walpole boy would like her, a Turk?*

It was the last time we spent as friends, and as we strolled together quietly, I thought about how much I hated her.

6. SISTERS AND DAUGHTERS

"C'mon, it'll be fun," Bee said. We were getting stoned on a Saturday night and she was trying to convince me to go to the movies. But my idea of fun didn't involve throwing myself into public with a paranoid-but-seemingly-heightened consciousness of how pathetically I functioned in the world.

"No," I told her.

"C'mon," she said again.

"No!"

"C'mon, why not?"

"I told you why not. I get paranoid."

"Please, it'll be fun. It will. Don't you want to have fun?"

"NO I DO NOT WANT TO HAVE FUN!" I yelled.

Bee laughed uncontrollably. Then she calmed down and wiped away the tears. "C'mon," she said again.

Bee and I had been spending so much time together that we had an unspoken rule that we were a team, that we could rely on each other as companions for Saturday night plans or when we needed to get a muffler replaced. Shop clerks often asked if we were sisters, since we both had dark hair, dark complexions and were approximately the same height. It didn't matter that our mannerisms were completely different: I would say something quietly and Bee would laugh loudly and slap me on the back so that I lunged forward, my eyes bugging out. But we obviously possessed a certain closeness, construed by strangers as the intimacy of family. We finished each other's sentences; we felt free telling each other there was spinach in our teeth; and most importantly, Bee annoyed me and I could yell at her, just as I did with my family.

The morning after Bee and I had seen *The Last of the Mohicans* stoned, I came home with a bag of I & Joy bagels.

"Yes!" Bee said. "You're the best."

"You're the one who should be buying *me* bagels after making me witness such gore. I'm Armenian, you know. That shit touches a nerve."

Bee spread some cream cheese on a bagel and asked, "Don't you think it's weird how well we get along?"

"No, because I don't think we get along," I half-teased.

She laughed. "Like, we do everything together, and I can't see living without you. Let's grow old together. Don't ever leave me," she pleaded.

A shy smile came over my lips. Silently, I made a bagel and tried my best not to let on how touched I was. I loved Bee. She helped me sell jewelry and made me tacos and laughed at me so much I took myself less seriously. As best as I could, I held onto this sweet feeling of being needed, protecting it like a bubble about to burst.

When I had been a kid, my mother sometimes needed me, especially after my brother and sister were away for college. I was just starting eighth grade when I was left alone with my parents, who seemed to be arguing more and more lately.

One afternoon, Daddy was rifling through the junk drawer in the kitchen. It was Saturday, and he was wearing his khaki pants with the housepaint stains. Becoming aggravated the more he searched through the drawer, he finally slammed it shut, yelling, "Jesus Christ, can there ever be any order in this goddamned house?!"

Mumma was lying on the couch, pale and tired, her slippered foot propped up on the back of the sofa. She was having her period, which she said was especially painful because she had a fibroid in her uterus. "What are you getting so upset about now?" she called out.

"Where are the screws I bought last week?"

"Is there any need to scream over a box of screws?" Mumma yelled. She pulled off the afghan Grammy had crocheted and shuffled towards the junk drawer.

"You think you're gonna find it in there?" Daddy yelled as she tinkered. "You need mental help, keeping a house like this. Look at that drawer, filled with junk." He nudged her out of the way with his elbow and picked out a teacup with no handle. "What are you saving *this* for?"

"That was my mother's!" Mumma grabbed the teacup and escaped into the living room.

Daddy followed her and yelled, "If you kept some order in this house, if you threw out some of the crap, maybe I'd be able to fix some things! No, you're off gallivanting around to museums, pissing away money. I can't get anything done in this pigsty!"

"I won't have you screaming at me like this when I'm not feeling well."

"So that's your excuse for this mess?"

The question both enraged and energized Mumma. "Oh, I'm supposed to be responsible for every little nook and cranny of this house?!" she yelled. "I am not a maid. Who says you can't clean too?"

My father's voice became low, slow and stern. "I have tried to throw out the junk, and you take a fit whenever—"

"You'll throw out everything in the house if I let you!" Mumma shrieked.

"You know you really have a problem. You really are sick."

"No. No," Mumma said, "I am not going to spend my entire day cleaning. I will not be a slave to this house." Then, muttering under her breath, she said, "You're just like your mother, backwards from the old country."

"CLEAN THE HOUSE! JUST CLEAN UP THE FUCKIN' HOUSE!" Daddy exploded.

Then he disappeared into the basement as Mumma mumbled, "You can't talk to me like that."

Before long, Mumma and I were traveling on the VFW Parkway, headed towards Boston. She still wasn't feeling well, but she didn't want to stay in the house with Daddy in a funk. "He's just like his mother," Mumma said. "Losing his temper like that. Is there any need to get so upset over a box of screws? His sisters are like that too; they scream about nothing. I never should have married him. I never should have."

"Daddy never lost his temper before you married him?" I asked, staring out the window.

"No, and neither did his mother. They were behaving themselves. I should divorce him and let him go live with his mother and sisters for a while, see how he likes that." I imagined Daddy sulking around the white shag carpeting at Grammy's house.

"Your parents didn't yell?" I asked Mumma.

"No! My mother was nothing like your grandmother. She was born in this country, and her parents arranged her marriage after she met my father just *once*, so of course it didn't work out. She never told me who I had to marry, and she always, always encouraged me to get an education so I could support myself. Maybe if she hadn't died, I wouldn't have married so young. But everyone was asking me, at twenty, why I was still single." Mumma shook her head with regret. We were in the Fenway now; she was looking for a parking spot.

"And your *grandmother!* After your father and I were married for just *one* year, she's asking if there's something wrong with me because we didn't have a baby. No, I was supposed to have children immediately, like this is the village and I'm to cook and clean all day long for her prince who can do no wrong. Backwards, I'm telling you. She used to scream at your grandfather, you know. He had to stay at our house a couple of times, she drove him so batty. Oh, there's a spot."

Mumma parallel parked the Plymouth Satellite and we walked to the Isabella Stewart Gardner Museum. She showed her Brockton Art Museum docent card to get us in for free, and we entered a turn-of-the-century mansion built around a central courtyard. The pamphlet said it was designed to look like a Venetian palazzo and that after her husband died, Isabella Stewart Gardner built the mansion as a museum and moved into the top floor, where she lived for twenty years till she died.

After Mumma and I strolled through the dark-paneled, velvet-upholstered rooms, gazing at the Renaissance and Baroque paintings that Mrs. Gardner had collected on her travels, we sat in the garden courtyard. The walls were a veiny pink and the air was still and warm. People spoke in hushed tones.

"What are those orange flowers?" I asked.

"Birds of paradise," Mumma said. Then she gasped. "Just look at those orchids. This is how it was when she lived here, you know. She must have had a full-time gardener. All that money she inherited from her father. It was before there was an income tax."

We walked past a painting by John Singer Sargent of a Spanish dancer. She seemed to be pointing towards the cafe. "Let's get a little something," Mumma said.

We sat at a tiny table, and once the waiter arrived with the little tin pot of hot water, tea bag and cup, I made my mother's tea for her. I dunked the bag in the hot water, and after it steeped, I placed it onto a teaspoon, wrapped the string around, pressed the paper tab against it and squeezed out the excess liquid. I stirred in sugar and poured the milk, which swirled, then stirred again to turn the tea a pinky-brown shade, the color of Mumma's lipstick when she sipped. I loved making her tea, watching the chemical process, and knowing that she would actually enjoy something that I made for her. In some small way, I felt like I was taking care of her, repaying her for all the sore throats she tended in me.

On the way home we rode in silence. I stared at the houses we were passing, at the grand old New England homes, catching glimpses of people through their windows, preppy-looking folks getting ready for dinner. They looked calm and stately and didn't appear to be screaming violently at each other.

My thoughts trailed back to Jacob, Grammy's husband, my grandfather. In a black and white photo documenting the building of our house, he stood next to a crew-cut Daddy on the unfinished roof, wearing a plaid shirt and holding a hammer. Jacob was the same size as Daddy, with a larger nose, small, intent irises, and curly gray hair. Unsmiling, he looked stern, yet wild.

I knew even less about Mumma's father, who had died when I was a year old. He'd owned a grocery store in Cranston—the freezer in our garage had come from his shop—and I saw in my parents' wedding album that he was bald, wore a bow tie, and his frown was oddly proud and distinguished.

Mumma talked most often about her mother, but I had seen a picture of her only once in my life. A few years before, she showed me and Leo some old photographs that she had pulled out from the depths of her bedroom closet. They were of her family at the beach.

"This is my mother," Mumma had said of a woman wearing a black dress. Her thick black hair was pulled behind her neck; her little face squinted into the camera.

"When did she die?" I asked.

"A long time ago. When I was nineteen, a little older than Valerie. And these are my grandparents."

A graying couple was sitting on a beach blanket in old-fashioned striped bloomer bathing suits. "They passed away not long after my mother," Mumma said. "My grandmother had a very hard time when my mother died. They say that's the greatest pain there is, to lose a child."

I couldn't even imagine how my mother would carry on if I or Val or Leo died; the thought was frightening.

She never brought those photos out again. It wouldn't be till years later that I reflected on how strange it was that she didn't have even one photo of her mother displayed in the house somewhere, considering the strong feelings she had for her. It was like she needed to keep her hidden away, and this, of course, made me feel all the more drawn to her memory.

I wished I could have known her myself, not just through Mumma. More than any of the dead grandparents, I imagined her as my ally, looking at me sympathetically from wherever she was, as I rode in the car with her daughter.

The Museum of Our National Heritage, the Danforth Museum of Art, the Wellesley College Art Museum, the Rose Art Museum of Brandeis University, the DeCordova Museum and Sculpture Park, the Institute of Contemporary Art, the Museum of Fine Arts, the Fogg and the Sackler, the JFK Library, The House of the Seven Gables, the Rhode Island School of Design Museum, the Newport Art Museum, and all the Newport mansions:

Marble House, The Elms, Chateau-sur-Mer, Rosecliff, and The Breakers.

I would spend the next few years of high school visiting such cultural institutions with my mom. I liked looking at the art, but sometimes I preferred to hang out with my friends.

"Oh no. I am not going to the museum with you in that weirdo outfit," Mumma said once as she opened the door to my bedroom. I was wearing my jean-jacket with a bleached design of a honeycomb on the back (in homage to Sting), a yellow vintage sweater from Mumma's cedar chest, a black velvet skirt, bright orange tights and black patent leather pumps. My hair was cut asymmetrically with one side short, one side long, and I used Jolen Creme Bleach, usually spread above my upper lip to vanish my moustache, to create an orange streak in my hair. I thought I looked pretty rad.

"My outfit is not 'weirdo' and I'm not going to the museum, anyway. I told Annie I would go to the mall with her today."

"You can go with Annie to the mall any time," Mumma said. "When else are you going to see Bill Viola's videos. He's internationally known!"

"But I told Annie—"

"And how are you going to get there?"

"We'll walk."

"No, you won't, I don't like the idea of you walking home in the dark."

"Are you kidding me? It's not dangerous to walk home from the mall. I've done it a million times!"

My mother tightened her lips, shook her head in disapproval and said, "Who's more important anyway, Annie or your mother?"

As we silently drove to the museum, I listened to the radio; Cyndi Lauper was singing "Time After Time" and I imagined that I was singing it with my pretend band. *If you're lost, you can look and you will find me, time after time,* I sang to Sting who was plucking his bass guitar and gazing at me lovingly. *If you fall, I will catch you, I'll be waiting, time after time.* The song ended and I had trouble finding another good one on Mumma's car radio. I sighed and collapsed into my seat.

"I don't like it when Annie's mad at me." She had sounded pretty pissed on the phone when I canceled.

"Nancy, you can't care so much about *what other people think.* That's what the docent educator told us. When you realize you're worrying about W.O.P.T., just stop."

I didn't understand how such an easily forgettable acronym could help me right now, so I stared out the window. The woods along the highway passed by fast. I caught an image of graffiti scrawled on a rock—"Marky loves Patty."

"Is there something wrong with me that I haven't gone out with a boy yet?" I asked.

"What do you mean 'something wrong'?"

"Well a lot of my friends have been dating, but I'm not and I'm sixteen. Maybe I'll end up like the aunties."

"Oh, Nancy, don't be silly. You have plenty of time to date. Besides, it's better to not be distracted. Just do well in school."

I looked into the landscape and sought out places that looked neat. Little gaps in the forest, patches of grass. I wanted to explore them, but I didn't know how I would ever find that little nook in the woods off Route 128 again.

Now that I could drive and explore, in the capital of car culture, the irony was that I didn't really want to. I preferred when Bee drove over the ten-lane highways. As we traveled to new and different parts of the sprawling city to run errands or just to explore, she told me more about her family: hers wasn't so perfect either. Her parents were young when they married and had been on-again, off-again for as long as Bee could remember, her parents trapped in an alcoholic/co-dependent arrangement. I flinched when she told me a story of her trying to pull her father off her mother as he sought to strangle her to death. But Bee always seemed much more grounded and stable than I. She had family in L.A., a young aunt with a newborn out in West Covina, who we had visited, and another aunt from the other side of the family who was a prominent local politician. I came along with Bee when she worked on her campaign for city councilperson. One morning we awoke at 6 A.M. and drove out to East L.A. to hang flyers on doorknobs. Here, there were no patches of grass, only little scrubby lawns, sickly palm trees, pit bulls chained to fences, and me and Bee trying to find our way through the endless gray of smog.

7. I.D.

There was a knock on the back door. I had just taken a shower and put on my underwear, so I wrapped a robe around myself. I wasn't expecting Jesse for another half-hour.

We had met a few weeks before at the open poetry reading series Jesse coordinated in a laundromat in Silver Lake. It was a Sunday afternoon in October, and I was too nervous to make small talk before the reading. So

Bee, in her brown suede jacket, with her brick red lipstick and long lashes, chatted people up while I hung behind her left shoulder. After I signed the list, we watched countless underground, unpublished poets with names like Reverend Al and Bowerbird Intelligentleman sputter such lines as "Off with the head of Mayor McCheese!" while Salvadoran moms looked on and hipster girls leaned into the industrial-sized washers.

I was one of only two women who read. The other was a woman my age who wore a big sun hat and read poems loaded with images of glass shards and spiders. When it was my turn, I read a poem about existential concerns, which used the word fuck half a dozen times, not to mention shit, cunt and dickhead. It was pretty dark:

> All I've got to say is
> this just better be
> a phase because I don't
> think I'm going to be
> able to go through
> life like this I'll die
> by the time I'm 30.
> I won't wanna stay.

Still, people laughed and clapped. They probably weren't responding to the near-suicidal message so much as my surprising presence—a meek girl uttering curse words in a low-key, deadpan manner.

Jesse approached me afterwards. "Hey that was great!" he said. A friendly, goateed, twenty-something Latino guy with greenish teeth, he struck up a conversation with me and Bee and took our number. He soon invited us to see El Vez, the Mexican Elvis, perform at Atlas Bar. Bee couldn't make it, so I had to tell her how at one point during the show, El Vez, wearing a mariachi outfit and an early-Elvis pompadour, jumped out of the audience, swiveled his hips, looked me in the eye and asked "Are you a virgin?"

Of course I was, so I found this completely mortifying. Gripping my chair during the rest of the concert, I decided that Jesse would be the candidate to rid me of my virginity. He was cute and small, his skinny brown arms poking out of his t-shirt, legs lost within baggy khakis. When I found myself dancing with him and Bee at a house party in Silver Lake last night, I made my move, whispering in his ear, "I like you!" He smiled, took me by the hand, and led me outside, down a narrow winding street to a niche within some bushes where he kissed me, slipping and sliding his lips over mine. I felt the breath rise out of my body. Jesse's eyes were closed and he resembled some kind of woodland animal—a mole or groundhog.

Bee eventually looked for us, calling our names by her car. We walked towards her holding hands, and he kissed me goodbye.

"Oh my God, what happened?" Bee asked as we drove away.

"I told Jesse I liked him and we made out."

"Way to go, little one!" Bee yelled. "I want to make out with someone!"

I smiled at her. It was nice that I was actually doing something without Bee, that I didn't need her for once.

"You're a little early. I'm not ready yet," I now told Jesse, standing at the back door while I clutched my robe closed. It was still our first date: we had met earlier in the day at the art museum, and now we were meeting up to go to the gallery opening of one of his friends.

"That's okay." He put his hands on my shoulders and pushed me against the counter, kissing me stridently. I liked the passion but not the powerlessness. Backing me onto the couch in the living room, he made out with me for a while before suggesting, "Should we go to your bedroom?"

"I'm not ready for that," I said.

"Nothing will happen. Just to be more comfortable." But once we landed, he placed my hand inside the slit of his shorts; his dick was huge. This was quite a surprise, considering his stick limbs and woodland animal demeanor.

Producing a condom, Jesse asked, "Do you want to make love?" which sounded so of place, like we weren't on my futon on the floor with my half-finished drawings on the wall, but on the lido deck of the *Love Boat*. I thought about telling him no, but then I thought, *What the fuck, let's get this over with and then I don't have to feel so much shame.*

And so he pumped into me for a while and it hurt like hell and I didn't tell him to stop. It was like Bee had said. They just go at you as if you don't exist.

In the following weeks, Jesse called all the shots, and I went along with them. We went to dance clubs and parties and saw poets read at the Onyx Café. He knew everyone everywhere we went, and when he introduced me, I smiled. We sometimes made out in his car on side streets since he lived with his parents. I met them once when we spent an evening watching a video in their living room; they were old and spoke Spanish to Jesse, telling him to teach me not to leave on lights in other rooms in order to conserve electricity. After that we went to see *My Own Private Idaho* in the movie theater and I could barely concentrate as we held hands, rubbing fingers and thumbs. Other times we just drove around town in Jesse's old Mercury with the top down. This was California living. But often when I turned to look at Jesse, I didn't know what to make of him, of the funny facial expressions he made in place of conversation. Boys were mysterious to me; I had actually never spent so much time with one.

As Jesse and I continued to cruise up and down boulevards, I was reminded of my sister, Valerie. One of her high school boyfriends drove a black Corvette, which he had custom painted with two white racing stripes down the center and "Valerie" in script by the passenger side door. Since I'd never had a boyfriend, most of my associations with dating came from my childhood memories of her. I tried to remember them in more detail, hoping that they would give me some clue of how to be a girlfriend, how to be a girl.

———

When she was a teenager, I had been in awe of Val. She was a DJ at the high school radio station, spinning AC/DC, Cheap Trick, and KISS; she talked on the phone for hours with friends who called her "Gabes"; she sported a short hairdo and had a string of boyfriends: a geeky WHS DJ who cheated on her, a shy, scruffy-mustachioed grill cook at Howard Johnson's where she worked as a waitress, and a cute, bowl-cut engineering student who drove that restored, black '64 Corvette. The summer before she started college, Val briefly went back to the DJ and broke up with the engineering student, why I could never understand, since the latter had forged her a spoon handle bracelet in his garage workshop. Seven years younger and prone to tattle as an attention-garnering technique, I wasn't exactly confidante material, so my sister revealed little to me about her life.

During recess one day in the sixth grade, Jennifer Rohner told me, "Your sister is Val Agabian? Oh, she's a bad girl. She did it with my brother's friend Stevie. Yeah, your sister is wild."

Her assessment of my sister made me recall an incident the year before, during a high school graduation party for three of my cousins, thrown by my aunts and grandmother. The house was filled with a cacophony of Boston, Providence, Long Island and Armenian accents. There were first cousins, second cousins once-removed, cousins who we called cousins but were really our aunts and uncles, and cousins who were the children of our godparents but were blood-related somehow though no one could untangle where and when the connection had started. Because of the massacres, our family tree had cut-off stumps and burned branches and new limbs grafted onto it, roots that poked up from the ground and vines from nearby trees that intertwined with the leaves.

I was the youngest kid, clamoring for attention by singing John Denver songs, which caused my cousins to avoid me en masse. Forced to hang out on the white carpet in the living room with the grownups, who were discussing how they were going to pay for tuition, I soon became bored and weaseled my way into a congregation of teens on the front porch.

"I'm not innocent," my cousin Jackie said.

"I'm not innocent," I echoed, thinking I'd stumbled into some sort of bragging game.

A couple of cousins laughed.

"Yes, you are," my sister said.

"No, I'm not," I replied. I was thinking of all the times I had lied.

"Yes, you are," Val insisted, pausing to make her point. "You are very innocent."

I looked at her: my sister was speaking with the kind of authority that only came from experience. Valerie probably wasn't innocent either, though I had no idea what this meant until Jennifer Rohner told me my sister was wild. I felt some sort of shame then, that my sister had hidden such a life from me, and some kind of pride. At that time, during my puberty red pants period, I was not even close to being popular, and my brother had an even nerdier reputation; our sister was the only one with a decent image in Walpole. Back in the sixth grade, an association with such a sibling might have meant there was hope for me yet.

Unfortunately, this turned out not to be true, as I spent junior high and high school always on the line somewhere between a smart, shy girl and a nerdy weirdo. And though I had many crushes, I never dated a boy. I wouldn't have traded Wellesley for any other school, but it did seem to have further stunted my social ease with guys, which didn't change till I moved to L.A.

Jesse and I were driving down the Pacific Coast Highway, back from a Mercury convention, when he told me, "I don't think we click."

"Oh?" I responded.

"Do you?"

It was true that I wasn't happy with the whole virginity-losing bit. I also didn't like that he didn't ask me questions about myself—that our conversations centered around whatever statements he made about the art we were seeing, the poetry we were hearing, the parties we were going to and the cars he owned. I was constantly trying not to be disturbed by the greenish hue of his teeth.

But still, I had a boyfriend. My first one. I wasn't about to give him up now, after two and a half weeks.

"I think we click," I said.

"My friends keep telling me that you're not my type. I think we should just be friends," Jesse said.

The next night, I went to a movie by myself, and there he was in line with another girl. She was blond and skinny and wore a lot of makeup. I recognized her as one of the girls who lounged on top of the washers at the laundromat while all the guys yelled their spoken word. Was this the type that his friends told him I was not? I wasn't sure who Jesse was rejecting— the passive virgin or the deadpan freak who cursed at the mic.

"He's stupid," Bee told me, but it wasn't much consolation. Now I would be back to hanging out with her on Saturday nights, and I would be faced again with my fears that I was too dependent on her, that I would turn into an old maid like my aunts, or, my other longstanding concern, that I was really gay.

My attractions for girls started with Emine, if not earlier with Meg, my Wonder Woman playmate, but I didn't really note them till later, when I was in my freshman year of high school, and my sister was in her second year of college.

One weekend Val showed up at our front door with her hair shaved to an eighth of an inch. Her head was a perfectly round, black fuzzball. She made us all feel it, and I remember that her hair felt rough when I rubbed in one direction, soft when I rubbed in the other. Mumma and Daddy didn't like it at all, especially since we were about to celebrate their twenty-fifth wedding anniversary; Grammy and Aunties had prepared a big party.

I suspected my parents had already been concerned that Val might pull some kind of stunt. The previous Easter, she had come home from school and announced to my parents that she'd broken up with her boyfriend and wanted to transfer out of Worcester Polytechnic because she was having trouble passing her classes. My parents were livid, insisting into the night that she stay at the school and finish what she started. When I went downstairs to the den in the morning to wake her up, I found a note, written on Daddy's yellow legal pad, on the sofa bed: *I went to EST. Love, Val.*

Erhard Seminars Training was a self-help/spiritual program that resembled a cult, infamous for degrading participants by calling them names and prohibiting them from peeing. My parents tried to retrieve Val from EST, because they thought it was, in Daddy's terms, "a load of bullshit," but Val somehow managed to complete the weekend training, which she'd paid for with a student loan. After the EST debacle, she returned to WPI, dropped out, transferred to UMass Amherst and moved to Northampton, where she'd been living the past few months.

I was in my bedroom preparing for the party, coiling my layered hair around a curling iron, working hard to reproduce a flippy wing on the left side of my head to match the one on the right, when Val bustled in. She bumped into me and the iron singed the top of my forehead. "Ow," I winced.

"Oh, 'scuse me, Nance," Val said brightly. She set her towel down on my bed and put on her bra and underwear, revealing bushy black hair growing under her arms.

"That's a nice dress," she said, looking at the purple polyester number that Mumma and I had selected from the clearance rack at TJ Maxx the week before. "Mumma's making me wear this dress to the party," she said. "What do you think?" It was straight out of my mother's closet. She wore it all the time. It was covered in white and black geometric shapes with buttons on the shoulders.

"It's queer," I told her.

She laughed. "Oh well," she said. "I have to wear something. Mumma's making me wear nylons too."

I watched Val wrangle with the pantyhose, stretching them over the black down on her legs. I had been shaving my shins for a couple of years; Mumma taught me not to shave my thighs or the hair would grow back too thick.

"Why did you shave your head?" I asked Val.

"Uh, cuz I felt like it?" she said.

"How come you don't feel like shaving your legs and armpits?" I asked.

"Because the boys want me to and I'm not gonna do anything the boys want me to do."

"What boys?" I asked.

"The boys in the media who objectify women and impose an unrealistic and dangerous standard of beauty on us."

"Oh," I said.

She watched me put on deodorant. "That stuff is bad for you, Nance," she said. "It's unnatural to stop your sweat glands. The boys invented it."

"Okay," I said and retreated downstairs. I was normally interested in anything Val wanted to teach me, like when I was five and she gave me multiplication lessons on the Mickey Mouse/Donald Duck chalkboard in the basement. But it was overwhelming to absorb all this new information, to figure out who she was *this* time.

The same cast of characters from the 1978 graduation party appeared at the 1982 anniversary fête. Like my parents, I was nervous as to how they would respond to Valerie's new hairdo. I felt safe in my dress and nylons and pumps and makeup. No one would criticize my appearance, copied from *Seventeen,* I didn't think. I looked over at Leo; in college, he had transformed into a preppy, and he now appeared reserved in his penny loafers and navy blazer with a crest on the pocket. We were on display, the 100 percent Armenian fruits of my parents' twenty-five year union.

From beneath the wings of my hair, I watched Valerie party. She removed her shoes and danced with her butt sticking out. As she boogied on the dance floor, she made the aunts, uncles and cousins feel her shaved head. The only one who refused was Grammy.

"The Arabs shaved my hair. I cried and cried! Why she wanna look like a worm?"

I knew my grandmother was talking about the Arab family who saved her, the ones she had told me cleaned her up, made her a servant and paid her with gold bracelets. I nodded my head gravely; she gave a short, sad laugh and squeezed my hand.

A few months later, my parents had the talk radio tuned up in their car. The topic was Reaganomics, and a caller was extolling the advantages of cutting taxes, limiting social services spending and sinking revenues into the military.

"You asshole," my father told the radio.

"These Republicans just want to get rid of all the policies that help the poor," Mumma said. "They're so greedy."

"This is all your fault, you know," Daddy said.

"How is it my fault that people are greedy?" she demanded.

"You should have disciplined her more as a child." We were on the Mass Turnpike to Amherst to visit Val so that my parents could talk some sense into her after she had failed most of her classes.

"I can't believe you're actually going to blame me."

"Someone has to take the blame," Daddy said, and Mumma didn't talk to him for the rest of the ride to Amherst.

When we picked up Val at 1126, the communal house she lived in, she hopped into the back seat with me, wearing overalls and a sweatshirt. "Hi Nerds!" she sang.

"Hello Valerie," my parents said, glancing back at her reservedly.

"That's where I work!" Val called out as we passed a grocery store called Price Chopper. "I get to take home free food sometimes. But right now I'm fasting to clean out my system—"

"You're not eating!?" my mother screeched, turning around, wide-eyed.

"What the hell are you doing wasting your time out here?" Daddy cut to the chase.

"I'm not wasting my time."

"You've flunked your classes. You're shitting on all the opportunities we've given you."

"Valerie, we're concerned about you," Mumma said. "If you don't graduate from college you have no future."

During lunch at a pseudo-Colonial restaurant, my parents laid into Val, insisting that she get serious and pull herself together: she needed to earn a college degree from a good school so she could find a good job to support herself. It was the same demand they screamed at me when they caught me doing my homework in front of *Entertainment Tonight*. I glanced over at Valerie; after being battered with parental concerns and veiled wishes all afternoon, she looked exhausted, melancholy.

When it was time to drop her off, Val asked if I could go inside to say goodbye. My parents agreed, looking at us askance as we walked down the dirt driveway to 1126's front door. Val opened it, revealing a marijuana-infused living room with high ceilings, Indian tapestries hung over tall windows, and an unmade mattress on the floor. I spied dreamcatchers on walls and a vase that I didn't realize was a bong on the coffee table.

One of her roommates, a girl with long, mossy brown hair, appeared out of nowhere. "How were the 'rents?" she asked.

"Not so good," Valerie said.

A bevy of roommates floated towards us. They were dressed sloppily in moldy-smelling clothes, like those of the druggie kids I sat next to on the bus to Walpole High. Each of them shook my hand and smiled when Val introduced me.

We walked up a narrow flight of stairs to her room and sat by her window, looking down on my parents' car. Valerie seemed forlorn, so I told her that I loved her. We never said stuff like that, the Agabians didn't, but I had seen families on TV say "I love you" all the time; I figured people must have said it in real life somewhere. "Oh, Nance," Val said, hugging me. "I love you too."

I ran down to my parents' car and they grilled me for information about 1126. "Give us the dirt," they said. "What's it like in there?"

I was about to tattle to them about the marijuana smell and the messy roommates and the dirty kitchen. But I stopped myself. I had identified with Val in her struggle with Mumma and Daddy, and my sister had taken me into her confidence. It was a new kind of closeness, one that I hadn't experienced with her, never mind anyone in my family.

"It's a nice house," I told my parents. "I don't understand what the big deal is."

In June, Val left 1126 and moved in with a friend named Carly in Northampton. That summer, they made frequent trips to a women's peace camp in upstate New York, living communally and protesting the development of nuclear weapons.

Val took a break in her activism to visit us in Walpole. She had taken to writing in a journal and carrying it with her everywhere. Once, when she got into a fight with my mother in Au Bon Pain, she wrote in large block letters FUCK YOU, but Mumma didn't notice as Valerie darkened the words over and over again.

One afternoon when no one was home, I came across the journal on the kitchen table, so I opened it. One line stood out: "Mumma and Daddy are freaking out because I'm a lesbian."

I didn't breathe. Here was the source of her changes lately. Valerie was gay. That was bad. Gay people were bad; everyone made fun of them. *I* made fun of them. They were so, so… queer. I didn't want anyone to know Valerie was queer.

I closed the journal and tried not to wonder if I was gay too. *No, I'm not. No, I probably am.* I spent most of my time with my friends who were girls. *But I've always liked guys,* I thought, reminding myself of my crushes. *Yes, but you've never dated one. And what does it matter anyway?* Valerie had been with several boyfriends and now I was reading that she was a lesbian.

Desperate, I turned to my mother's copy of *Our Bodies, Ourselves.* Mumma had referred me to it for detailed information about my period, and I had noticed there was a lesbian chapter. I turned to the page and stared at the title: "In Amerika They Call us Dykes." Too scared to read, I looked at the pictures instead. There was one of a woman wearing a floppy crocheted hat, a corduroy blazer over a waistcoat with a watch chain looping out of the pocket, an ascot around her neck. *You look like a nut.*

Another picture featured three smiling women. The one in the center was freckly and wearing a fedora. The two lesbians on either side wore jaunty newsboy caps, and they were darkly ethnic, with prominent noses, lips and eyes. They could have been sisters. *Are they sisters?* I stared at their faces a long time, trying to make an identification. Then I noticed that the woman in the center had her arms wrapped around the others' shoulders, each of her hands grasping a sister-breast.

I shut the book.

Then I opened it again.

The last photo in the chapter took up a page. Two women were on a bed near a window, one on top of the other. The one on top had messy curly hair that fell into her partner's face. They were beaming at each other, and I found myself caught by the beauty of the picture, in the calm, sleepy love it expressed. They didn't seem like such freaks.

Valerie went back to the peace camp, and as the days passed I calmed down and decided it was okay that she was gay. She was my sister and I would love her no matter who she was.

But I'm not gay, I told myself. I repeated it at night in my bed, inside my head, *I'm not gay, I'm not gay, I'm not gay…*

A little, dented Datsun pulled into our driveway. From my bedroom window I watched the car muffle to a stop as Valerie turned the ignition off. She hadn't done well at UMass, so my parents offered that Val could live at the house and commute to Wentworth, a technological college in Boston. Today was moving day.

There was a woman reclined in the passenger seat and an unidentified third person in the back. Valerie sprung out of the car and lugged a big army duffel out of the trunk, while the woman in the passenger seat opened her door and stumbled out; she was tall with ruddy skin and shaggy brown hair. She pushed her car seat forward and reached into the back seat and grabbed the third person, which was the armless torso of a naked female mannequin. The woman, who I now realized was Carly, put the torso on the ground and began to pry the mannequin's pink legs from the car. They caught on the seat belt, and Valerie laughed as Carly yanked on them repeatedly. For some reason this embarrassed me; I turned from the window, ran downstairs and waited as they walked up the flagstone path. When the bell rang I swung open the front door. "Hi Nance!" Valerie greeted, dropping her bag and hugging me. She introduced me to Carly, who had an Adam's apple and breasts. Carly shook my hand gently, said "Hi Nancy," in a strained low voice, and handed me the mannequin's legs. Then she went back outside to get the torso.

"Hi Valerie!" my mother called. She walked down the hallway stairs, beaming at my prodigal sister. As she approached, she looked at Val suspiciously, like she couldn't trust that this girl in ripped clothing was really her daughter.

Carly returned to the foyer with the torso, and my mother put on her gracious public persona, ignoring the vacant stare of the mannequin's plastic-lashed eyes. "You must be Carly!" she said.

"Hello, Mrs. Agabian," Carly said, revealing her masculine voice.

My mother continued to smile, but her eyes turned toward my sister in slight confusion. Carly handed my mother the torso. "Here's Val's new roommate," she said in a depressed timbre that didn't quite register as deadpan.

Mumma laughed nervously. "Please, come sit down," she said. Carly sleepwalked the five stairs up to the living room and slumped into a soft chair, exhausted.

My mother and I followed Valerie upstairs to her new room, which was my brother's old room, still covered with ye old Yankee wallpaper motifs—eagles and tri-cornered hats. It was cluttered with my brother's stuff, and the three of us plus the mannequin and the duffel barely fit.

Mumma closed the door. "Is there something wrong with Carly?" she whispered.

"Nothing's wrong with the Carly," Valerie said.

"She seems like a guy," I offered. My sister laughed.

"Yes, she seems like a *guy*," Mumma said, emphasizing the word as if it were a curse.

"She used to be a guy. Her name was Carl. Now she's Carly," Valerie replied.

My mother was speechless. Then incredulous. "You mean to tell me that she's a man?"

"No. I mean, yeah. I mean, she doesn't know."

"What do you mean she doesn't know?"

"She had an operation but she doesn't like the way the hormones make her feel anymore, so she went off them and now she's depressed; she thinks she made a mistake."

"Oh God," Mumma said, sitting on the bed. She shook her head and looked up at my sister with her big brown eyes, her lips pursed. "Is she on drugs now?" she asked.

"No! I just told you."

"She seems like she's on drugs, she can barely stand up."

"No, she's just tired. It's a long ride from Northampton."

Again my mother did the head shake, which seemed to say, *I did nothing wrong, I refuse to take the blame here.* In her carefully matched plaid pants and solid top, she suddenly didn't seem like Mumma anymore, but a forty-nine-year-old woman grasping for her identity, sinking on a sagging twin bed.

After a moment, she resurfaced. "Well, I'm not inviting...that person...to stay for dinner."

"Fine," my sister said. "You don't have to."

Mumma sulked out of the room. I watched Valerie assemble the mannequin on a chair.

"What's that?" I asked.

"It's my mannequin. Her name is Zonna," she said dejectedly.

"Like Donna with a Z?"

"Yeah, like Donna with a Z. I made it up. Do you like it?"

I didn't know if I liked it. Donna was a quintessential Walpole name; there were at least two Donnas in each high school class. The added Z now transformed it into something completely subversive. *Having a friend named Carly who used to be Carl isn't weird enough?* It didn't occur to me that Zonna sounded like my grandmother's name, Zanik.

"What's it for?" I asked.

"She's for decoration, like a doll. I'm going to dress her up and stuff. Isn't she neat?"

"I guess so," I said.

Valerie left the room and I followed. She tromped downstairs and sat down on the couch by Carly; I perched at the top of the steps.

"Did I cause a problem with your mom?" Carly asked my sister.

"No. No problem," Val said.

I stared at Carly's unisex hairdo and strong jaw. A person of neither sex wasn't common in Walpole in 1983. But it wasn't Carly's blurry gender that drew me in the most; rather, it was her whole deeply sad aura. Even my grandmother who had lost so much in the massacres didn't seem this bereft.

Carly noticed me on my perch at the top of the stairs. "Hello up there," she said.

"Hi," I yelled back.

"Nancy, come talk to Carly," my sister said.

I slowly descended the stairs and sat on the couch next to Valerie.

"How old are you?" Carly asked.

"Fifteen," I answered.

"Are you in high school?" she asked.

"Yeah."

"Do you like it?"

"No."

Carly and my sister laughed. For a long time. More than was warranted by my answer.

"Well, Val, I sure will miss you," Carly said. "I hope you get along with your mom."

I found myself drawn to Carly. She was gentle and there was something familiar to me about her sadness, about this person who didn't know who she was.

8. GIRL SCHOOL

The five of us squeezed into Bee's car to make the rounds of the girl bars. The Catch One, The Palms, Little Frida's and the mother of them all, Girl Bar. I didn't like Girl Bar; it was in a huge club, packed with lipstick lesbians, smoky, phony and loud. The Catch was in South Central and played old disco tunes to a mostly black and Latino crowd of ladies, The Palms was a smaller bar in West Hollywood that catered to the yuppie, mostly white gals, and Little Frida's was a late night cafe for everyone.

I wasn't looking to pick anybody up (and didn't have a clue how to do so), just happy to be with my friends. Liz, a bright Southern girl, was one of Ellie's college pals who had recently moved to L.A., also to try her luck writing sitcoms. Marianne was a funny character who had graduated from Wellesley a year after Bee and me. She had been one of the most popular girls on campus, now assigned to a school in L.A. with Teach For America. So suddenly, we had this little clique of friends.

It was almost like we were back in the dorm when Marianne and Liz moved into an apartment downstairs from mine and Bee's. Liz started to call the arrangement Melrose Place when we were always going back and forth, up and down the stairs. Marianne was quite the thespian, so there was always some impromptu play production going on—she had stock characters like Normahn, a luxury-loving gay European man, and Tilda, the alcoholic mom from The Main Line in Pennsylvania (where Marianne hailed from). I revived my John Denver imitation for Liz and Marianne, singing a medley of his hits while wearing a gingham shirt. I owned a long black wig I had bought on a lark; one night Ellie put it on while we were hanging out in my room. Liz walked in and didn't recognize Ellie for over an hour. She thought she was just some strange girl from the poetry workshop.

We also had our histories with each other: Liz and Ellie, both tall blonds, were old friends, who bickered, as Bee and I did, like a married couple. They had shared all their dramas of coming out while in college. Bee, me, Marianne and Alisa had made a pilgrimage to Graceland during the spring break of our senior year. We slept at campgrounds and smoked pot and chased down adventures in Philly, D.C., Memphis, and Loretta Lynn's Dude Ranch. Bee was filming Marianne feeding one of Loretta's horses with her Super 8 camera when she mumbled to me, "She's so pretty." At one point during that trip, Marianne and I wound up sleeping in a bed together, but Bee squeezed between us, eventually pushing me out. Nothing happened but a little cuddling, as Marianne wasn't so keen for Bee.

Now Bee had a little crush on Liz, but I thought nothing would come of it. We all just went out dancing and drinking and laughing. As I said, it was like college again, a familiar space of living among women, straight, gay and whatever. It was funny to recall what I had thought of Wellesley when I first arrived, what a completely unfamiliar landscape it had been. In the end, I didn't get through it unscathed, but I did learn a lot about women.

———

The Toyota Camry wound its way through the wooded back roads of Dover. My parents were in the front seat, and I was in the back with boxes of my stuff. It was a still, late August morning and we were headed to the Wellesley campus, a half-hour drive from Walpole. *No one's gonna like me at college,* I thought.

The campus was bright green, lush with trees and grass. Cicadas were buzzing at my nerves as Daddy drove slowly so we could find my dorm, Bates Hall. As we approached a brick, institutional building, I spotted attractive, physically fit girls wearing clothes like those I coveted in the Esprit mail-order catalogue. Unloading Mercedes and BMWs were a bevy of distinguished-looking parents, mothers and fathers alike sporting tidy hairdos. Daddy brushed his combover back into place; it had been flying out the window.

As we pulled up to the curb and I felt the urge to vomit, my mother turned around and said, "Now, Nancy, you are probably going to encounter a few lesbians here. I don't want you to turn into one."

She waited for a response.

"Uh, okay?" I didn't want to turn into a lesbian either, but apparently Mumma actually thought it was possible.

Luckily, the shock of the question dispelled my nausea enough for me to unload the car without puking. After we deposited my boxes into a cinder-block-walled room, we took a walk to explore the campus, brick and ivy and designed by Frederick Law Olmsted. Gothic style dorms of towers and turrets were situated among rolling hills and serene meadows. In the quad, a stately bell tower rang its carillon bells and Rodin's *Walking Man* strode towards us. Now, among the trees, I was able to breathe. We were strolling down picturesque stairs which overlooked idyllic Lake Waban when Mumma told me, "You know, Nancy, I wish I could have come to a school like this."

"But you weren't smart enough," Daddy joked.

My mother had attended Rhode Island College of Education to become a schoolteacher. She really didn't have many other options as a young woman in the Fifties, but it had never occurred to me that she had ever wanted anything else, after all her stories about her mother's encouragement to get a profession to support herself. Mumma had just demanded that I not turn into a lesbian; most of the time, she seemed to barely know me, and she didn't seem interested in finding out who I really was: only the end results of my upbringing seemed to matter. So usually my mother's approval of anything I read, wore, or ate sent me over the edge. But now I was touched as she confessed her own wishes to me, her big brown eyes filled with pride and wistfulness.

On the first day of Physics, I was sitting on a lab stool near a strange girl who had placed the hood of her navy sweatshirt over her huge afro. She also had a pubescent boy's moustache over her light brown skin, and big holes in her jeans. It was the hood that got to me, though. She would not take it off. *What a weirdo,* I thought.

When the time came to choose lab partners, I somehow knew Miss Afro Hood would ask me to be hers. *I'm not gonna work with her,* I thought. *No way.*

She sized up all the girls with their neat notebooks before turning to me and asked, "Wanna be lab partners?"

"Okay," I said.

Her name was Samantha. "I've seen you in Bates," she said as I pulled my stool next to hers. "You're a first-year?"

"Yeah. What about you?"

"I'm a first-year, too. I should be a sophomore, but I took my second semester off last year." She spoke in a restrained, cool monotone.

"Why?"

"Girl trouble."

It didn't surprise me that Samantha was a lesbian. She had a tough, messy aura that reminded me of Valerie's friends. I'd spent a weekend at Val's apartment in Jamaica Plain over the summer, after she'd moved out of my parents' house.

"My parents flipped when I told them I was queer," Samantha said.

"The same thing happened to my parents when my sister came out," I told her.

"Your sister is a lesbian?"

I nodded.

"What do you think about that?"

"It was hard at first," I said, "kind of a shock. But then I realized there was nothing wrong with it." It was a relief to say this to someone, finally. I'd never told any of my friends in Walpole about Valerie.

But I wasn't going to become Samantha's friend, even though I was badly in need of one. In the Bates dining hall later that week, Samantha, wearing her jeans with the big holes, the most scandalous of which was strategically ripped near the crack of her panty-less bum, paraded past wide-eyed first-years. Dinner-long blabbing sessions on her bizarre behavior then ensued. Dubbed "Skateboard Sammy" because she darted all over campus on one, Samantha was just one of a notorious cadre of upperclasswomen who were the subjects of first-year gossip. The most notable included Meg Natick, the "big dyke on campus" who resembled a portly Steve McQueen, and Frick and Frack, a deviant duo who destroyed any preconceived notions of the Seven Sisters ivory tower, running around the campus wearing Dungeons & Dragons capes, licking the communal ice cream scoop in the cafeteria before dropping it into the tub of rocky road, leaving soiled tampons on the bathroom floor. I thought it best not to take my acquaintance with Skateboard Sammy further so that I could steer clear of any association with the outcast squad.

One day I was sitting in the common room while two other first-years were having a conversation:

"You know this is the lesbian dorm, don't you?"

"No it's not!"

"Well doesn't it seem like there's an inordinate amount of lesbians living here?"

"I never really thought about it … But now that you mention it—"

"It just doesn't make sense to me how they have sex," the first girl said. She curled her hands into two Os and then banged them together.

I was surprised to encounter lesbians being disparaged at a women's college, but then I realized not everyone's sister was one. It occurred to me that perhaps there were an excessive number of first-years in Bates because few straight upperclasswomen wanted to live in "the lesbian dorm," leaving entire floors available for the lowest class to inhabit.

Just about the time when the lesbian lightbulb went on above my head, the dorm leadership held a special sexuality workshop in the living room. "I would never choose this for myself," Meg Natick admitted, her shoulders hunched forward. "It was always something I felt inside from as far back as

I can remember, before I even knew there was a word for it."

A pale girl wearing braids and a bandanna tied over her head spoke next. She was sitting on a couch next to her boyfriend, a bear of a man with a wild beard. I'd seen both of them in the dining hall before. The pale girl explained she was bisexual. "I feel equally attracted to men and women," she said, her head tilted to one side. "It's the person that I'm drawn to, not their gender." That sounded reasonable.

"How does your boyfriend feel about that?" someone asked.

"I don't have a problem with it," he answered.

"In fact," the pale girl giggled, "I was feeling attracted to his ex-wife, and he didn't mind at all. Now all three of us get together."

Silence.

"What do you mean, 'get together'?" someone ventured.

"The three of us make love," the girl answered.

An audible gasp came out of the crowd and chaos ensued. Ms. Bisexual and her Pervert Lover sat on the couch, stoically observing the resulting me-lee. The Head of House tried to salvage the discussion so that we wouldn't be left with the tone of a *Sally Jessy Raphael* show freak-fest, but it was too late.

In the elevator, on my way up to my room, I talked to a first-year who lived down the hall from me, a blond with wide blue eyes and a girly voice. "You know, except for the weird bisexual girl, I found the discussion help-ful. But I have to say," she paused, bit her lip and furrowed her eyebrows, "I can understand it for them, but I still don't think it's right."

"I know what you mean," I replied. I said it to avoid conflict, but also because I meant it. I really didn't think it was right to be a lesbian, otherwise I would be one.

"Hi Bee," I called out. "Hi Boobie. Hi Bitsy." Pushing a metal cart down the length of the cafeteria into the noisy hall to deliver clean cut-lery and dishes, I was continually greeted by an abundance of first-years. It turned out my self-deprecating personality and monotone elocution came off as deadpan hilarity to the Wellesley girls. All I needed to come out of my shell was a boost of confidence, the kind that often came to me through the process of making one friend. Louise was the one.

I had befriended Louise after I joined the production crew of *A Doll's House*. As Louise gave orders as stage manager, I discovered she was extremely witty. Whenever she opened her mouth, she said something brilliant, in a quick, jaw-oriented manner, using SAT words I'd never heard in conversation before, like supercilious, spurious, and sanctimonious. Her intelligence could be intimidating, but she assured me I was "smart as a tack." Louise had graduated from a prep school in Connecticut and was not impressed with many of the other prep school girls, whom she condemned for being supercilious, spurious, and sanctimonious.

I was putting the utensils in their bins when Louise called out my name. "I want you to meet my mother." Seated next to her at the table was a woman in her fifties with a salt-and-pepper bob, a sophisticated silk scarf swathed around her neck. Louise had told me that her divorced mother had moved with her to Wellesley and lived in an apartment near campus.

"Hi Mrs. Woods," I said, wiping my hand on my apron.

She took my hand gently, setting brilliant light blue eyes on my face. "Hi there. Louise says you're the only redeeming part of that play you're working on."

I shrugged. Louise despised most everyone on the cast and crew. "Some of the people are a little conceited," I said.

"Well, isn't that how theater people are?" Mrs. Woods said. She said "theater" with mock snobbiness—*theatah.*

"No, Mother, not all of them. Nancy's not."

I was flattered Louise thought of me as a theater person, since all I'd done was move props on the last production.

"Do you like Massachusetts?" I asked Mrs. Woods, changing the subject.

"Sure. What's not to like? Do you like it?"

"Well, I've lived here all my life—" I started to explain.

"Where?"

"In Walpole."

"Why does that sound familiar?"

"Probably because it's the site of the state maximum security prison."

"I've heard it on the news. MCI Walpole?"

"Yes. Massachusetts Correctional Institution. My father is the warden."

"Really?"

"No."

"Ha!" Mrs. Woods laughed.

"What did I tell you?" Louise asked. "Isn't she a laugh riot?"

"Oh, she comes off as meek and mild, but she's a hot ticket."

"Now the town wants to change the name of the prison to MCI-Cedar Junction," I continued. "My father says it sounds like a retirement home."

"I like your father. Is your mother funny too?" Mrs. Woods asked.

As Mumma poured olive oil onto the salad, Daddy protested, "You're not using enough!" his head over her shoulder.

"Stop being so nosy," my mother said. Normally, when he interfered in the kitchen, she called him a *djudjuveneh* (which was some kind of Armeno-Turkish slang word that roughly translated to "man without a penis"), but she muted her response in front of Mrs. Woods, who was standing on the step between porch and kitchen, a glass of red wine in her hand.

"I divorced someone who did that to me," Mrs. Woods said. Mumma laughed at that with a snort.

While we ate shish-kebab dinner on the back porch, Mrs. Woods spoke of her pregnancies. She had several children with another husband before she met Louise's father, from whom Louise was estranged. "Oh fuck, the pain!" Mrs. Woods said.

"I was always knocked out," Mumma interjected. "I fell asleep and when I woke up they handed me a baby," she said in her polite school-teacher voice. I recoiled, wishing my mother could be more real and gritty like Mrs. Woods, who drank three glasses of wine that evening; Mumma could barely finish one. Mrs. Woods used the words "shit" and "fuck"; my mother's worst curses were "son of a b" and "damn it to hell." Louise once showed me some proof sheets of her mom in the Fifties at Skidmore when she was a cool beatnik in black capri pants and turtleneck, cigarette sophisticatedly wedged between two fingers. In contrast, my mother appeared in our old photo albums smiling sweetly in a matching green suit and hat, sitting so prim behind her desk in her second grade classroom, and glowing innocently in her white fluffy wedding dress.

It soon became clear that Louise and her mother had a very different relationship from me and Mumma. They seemed able to talk about practically anything, from sex to drinking to politics.

Though I admired their intimacy, I wasn't so sure I liked all of the Woods' ideology. When the school canceled all classes and sponsored a day-long symposium on intolerance in response to several swastikas scrawled around the campus, Louise spent the day at the movies with her mom.

"I don't need lessons on how to be intolerant. I'm doing just fine on my own, thank you," Lou teased, raising an eyebrow.

"That's not funny," I said.

"C'mon! You know it sounds ridiculous."

I watched her, my mouth in a judgmental shrug, as she took a long swig from a vodka tonic—we were having drinks in her room at the end of the day.

Lou continued, "I'm sorry, but I didn't draw any swastikas, so why should I have to spend my day listening to some victimized, self-righteous kikes?"

Lou often slurred anti-Semitic. I stopped protesting because she came back at me with endless retorts: she called people names not because she hated them for their race, she just hated them; by taking issue with certain words, I was mindlessly buying into the facile logic of the politically correct.

Lou also coined terms to express her dislike for certain people. "Larvaed dyke" she used to describe a lesbian who hadn't come out of her cocoon yet. It was troubling to me that she made no pretense about hating lesbians just for being lesbians, but I reasoned that the ones in Bates were different from my sister. Valerie didn't lick ice cream scoops or wear jeans with holes ripped over her butt. So I laughed when Louise made fun of them; I agreed with her when she disdained them.

But I felt differently, polishing off a screwdriver, on Intolerance Day. "There's something I never told you," I began. "About myself."

"What, are you Jewish?" she asked.

"No," I paused a long time. "My sister is a lesbian."

She looked at me a moment. "And?"

"That's it."

"God, I thought you were going to tell me that *you're* a lesbian."

I swallowed. "No, I'm not."

"Well, it's not your fault about your sister. Don't worry about it."

Late at night in the studio, I visited my latest composition—a still life of a teapot, glazed a deep sea green, and two lemons sitting next to it. I worked hard to get the reflections on the teapot right, and instead of painting the two lemons as they appeared, I fictionalized them, covering the background of the canvas with a pattern of flat, two-dimensional lemons, each smeared with a stylized highlight of white.

"Hey," I heard a voice call out, echoing off the dark windowpanes of the studio. I looked up to see Bridget, a junior with short bleached-white hair, coming towards me. I had stopped by the art building on my way home from the library, but I wasn't expecting anyone else to come in this late. Bridget was wearing a navy sailor jacket with white buttons. She was cool.

"Hey," I said. I stopped working while she looked at my canvas.

Bridget laughed a sharp "Ha!" and punched me in the arm. "You are such a goofball!" She had a strong jaw and a flat chest.

"What?" I asked, suddenly insecure.

"You're the only one in here who's doing something different." She turned to look at another easel. "Lame," she proclaimed, pointing to a straight-up composition of a vase centered in the middle of a canvas. "Does anyone here have any creativity at all?"

"I know, people at Wellesley are kind of conservative."

"Kind of? It's a tragedy."

"What do you think of Charles?" He was our painting professor.

"I love him," she said. "He's such a fag." She seemed to be a cross between Louise and Skateboard Sammy, with her blunt pronouncements and her disdain for most everyone but me.

Bridget took off her coat and looked at her painting. "Ugh, I wish I knew what to do with this," she said. "Do you have any suggestions?"

"Well," I said, looking over her shoulder. "There's a lot of empty space in this corner. Why don't you make the kite bigger so it offsets the shoe down here?"

"But then I'll have to start all over again," Bridget said, turning to look at me. "With a new canvas."

I shrugged my shoulders at her.

"You're right, Agabian," she said, raising her chin.

I turned towards my painting and felt a spark of attraction. It was reminiscent of when a boy on whom I had a crush would randomly look my way and I lost my breath and my fingers tingled. Then it dawned on me that the spark had been elicited not from a boy, but a girl. On my way back to the dorm, I reasoned that in a place where there were no boys, it made sense that I would feel attracted to someone who was kind of like one.

The sound was turned down on Louise's TV. It was around eight o'clock, and we were in her dorm room after she'd returned from the hospital. I sat on her bed as she was putting on her sweatpants.

"She asked me if you were a reporter," Louise said. "She thought you were doing a story on her life." She sighed. "Poor Mom."

The night before, I had visited Mrs. Woods at the hospital. It was the start of our junior year, and the last time I had seen her was at my going away party, before I had left to study art in London for the summer. Though she had been diagnosed with lung cancer, and Lou had just shaved her head before the chemo and radiation treatments, Mrs. Woods looked fine, beautiful even, sitting on my parents' back porch. But last night, she was hardly more than a skeleton, her bright blue eyes staring out at me; I barely recognized her.

At one point, Louise had asked if she wanted more ice chips, and when Mrs. Woods moaned, Louise had joked, "I'll take that as a yes." Louise had been so brave, a rock, while I had wanted to hide and fall apart in the corner.

"Tonight she dropped her toothbrush on the floor," Lou said, "and the nurse said she would bring her another one. We were waiting for the nurse to come back and all of a sudden Mom just laughed. And she said, 'What does it matter?'"

I didn't know if Louise was telling me this story to indicate her mother had given up hope, or that she, Louise, had given up hope. She turned to me, crying.

"I'm sorry," I said.

"I know." She sat down on the bed and I rubbed her back with the palm of my hand. I didn't know if it was helping, but I didn't know what else to do. This was the scariest thing I had encountered in my sheltered life, and it felt absolutely terrible, impossible. I stared absently at the little people on the silent TV.

"What you got on there?" Louise asked after a while, wiping her eyes.

"Designing Women," I said. It was one of Louise's and her mother's favorite shows. Mrs. Woods also liked the sitcom *Perfect Strangers,* with Balki, the lovable immigrant. She could never remember the name of it so she called it, "Funny Friends."

Delta Burke was sitting on a couch talking. Louise blew her nose and started making up silly dialogue for her. "Yes, Anthony, I would like to lick your balls."

I laughed. Louise laughed too. Then she started crying again. She was laughing and crying at the same time. "I'm going crazy," she said.

I lay down on the bed, exhausted, and Lou took deep breaths and rubbed my temple. She swirled my hair under her fingers. It felt really good, like when I masturbated. I wanted Lou to stop because I didn't want to feel good, to feel sexual. But it seemed to make her feel better, so I let her.

The painting I was working on now was on a four-by-five-foot piece of canvas pinned to the wall. I painted just my features—eyes, eyebrows, nose and mouth—scrunched into an ugly twist and floating aimlessly on the canvas.

One day I walked into class and at my workplace was a note in the old typewriter I had snagged from the closet at the Wellesley Students' Aid Society. Unsigned, it read:

Hi Nancy. Nice face, you freak. Keep up the good work.

Later that week I walked into the studio and found Bridget, wearing an ascot, standing at my typewriter, pecking at the keys. Caught in the act, she giggled.

"You're the one!" I exclaimed.

"You're the two!" she echoed back.

"I think I'm more of a zero," I said dejectedly.

"Agabian," she asked, "why so hard on yourself?"

"My best friend's mother is dying of cancer," I told her. "And I don't know how to help."

"Who's your best friend?" she asked.

"Louise Woods."

"I don't know her. That's too bad about her mom. I'm sure you're doing all you can." Her usually animated features now settled into sympathy. We chatted awhile and then she left to work on her senior thesis project in another studio. I continued painting, losing myself in my work, and periodically thought about our conversation, welling up with a smile every once in a while.

A week or so later, I ran into her in the hallway outside the studio. Then again at Café Hoop in the student center. Then again at the library.

Whenever I wasn't caught up in my cycle of self-loathing—depression from being lonely, which triggered guilt for my inability to help Louise and her mother—I found myself thinking about Bridget and our interactions: what I had been wearing, what she had been wearing, what I had said, what she had said. Our friendship grew in between the daydreams, and one day we went to an art store in Boston together.

10/19/88

> *…I hate writing this down, but I have to tell someone. I really like this girl Bridget. Oh, I'm going to rip this up. My face is turning red. I'm not gay. I know I'm not. It's just this one girl. I find her so fascinating and I think of her all the time… [Today] she pointed at this queer-looking guy who works at Charrette's and said "That's your future husband."*
> *I said "Yuck, no he isn't."*
> *… Then she said, "Well, who is?"*
> *I felt like saying "You." Auuuggh!*

One night in early November, Louise called to tell me she was home from the hospital.

"She's gone," she said.

I walked into her room and found her in her ripped green prep school sweatshirt. She was on the bed, her back slouched against the wall, as if she were being pushed, and she was crying, her face red, her hair in wisps getting caught in the tears. I tried to hug her, but I couldn't slide my arms around her back, slumped against the wall as it was. So I just stayed there, my body leaning onto hers.

The phone rang three times before Bridget answered it. "Hello?" she asked. I hung up. The sound of her voice was incredible to me, the most beautiful thing, the possibility of something else.

Lately I had become even more depressed, taking up smoking, cashing in my meal credits and living on cheese-filled Combos so I wouldn't have to eat in the dining hall alone. Since it was my junior year, most of my friends had taken the semester abroad. I'd gotten a really lousy number in the housing lottery, so I wound up back in Bates Hall. Many nights, I exhausted myself from crying, falling asleep in my clothes with the lights on. I knew I had hit an all-time low when I walked by the common room and overheard a first-year say, "The Sheriff was wailing again last night." Apparently, wearing a toy sheriff's badge on my fake fur coat for fun had qualified me for membership in the outcast squad. I now suspected that all those freaks I had distanced myself from two years before were all once perfectly fine girls, just going through a hard time too.

I didn't know what was I was obsessing over the most: Bridget, the fact that I loved Bridget, or the fact that I couldn't tell anyone, least of all my best friend whose mother had just died. I started to imagine what would happen if Bridget liked me back. *I'm so happy,* I would cry to her. *But I have to come out now.* Then I envisioned the consequences: Louise would hate me, none of my friends would be able to relate to me, and my parents would treat me as they did my sister. Worse, Mumma and Daddy would probably think I became gay just to spite them. After all, they had never given Valerie any warnings to not become a lesbian—but me? My mother had constantly been drumming it into my head and now I had a mad crush on a woman.

Mumma's tolerance of my sister dating women waned once Val had been with a girlfriend for over a year. Miriam was a writer and she was incredibly sweet and kind. But Mumma couldn't stand her, since it was now clear that Valerie's lesbianism was not just a phase. "It's fine for them to be friends," she'd tell me over the phone. "But why do these women have to have *sex* with each other? Your sister is just so gullible, she just goes along, letting them talk her into it. Don't let anyone talk you into it, too, Nancy."

One night I went to a movie on campus, by myself. As I searched for a seat, I heard someone call, "Hi Nancy." It was Marj, my old Resident Advisor from the year before. She was with a pretty, delicate blond. "Come sit with us," Marj said.

About fifteen minutes into *Tootsie,* when Dustin Hoffman goes on the audition as Dorothy, I noticed that Marj was laying her head on her friend's shoulder. I thought, *Wouldn't it be great if girls could love girls and there would be nothing wrong with it?*

I suddenly felt an incredible sense of freedom and I cried there in the dark. I bawled at the end when Dustin Hoffman convinces Jessica Lange that Dorothy isn't gone but still alive inside of him.

It was gradual, but everything pretty much fell apart after I told Bridget that I had a crush on her.

I had been drunk; she was taken aback. Then she postponed a trip we had planned to visit the Museum of Fine Arts the next day. In the weeks that followed, she tried to remain my friend, but it didn't last long because I would not give up the crush. Most of my friends were fine with the news; I told them I thought I was bisexual. Of my family, I only told my sister; I didn't tell my parents. When I told Louise, she said, "I thought that if you were going to fall in love with a woman, it would have been me." Our friendship, as I had expected, became strained.

Mrs. Woods had asked my parents before she died if they would watch out for Louise, and naturally my parents had agreed. So Louise stayed with us in Walpole during the winter break. Before Mrs. Woods was diagnosed with cancer, Mumma had already taken a caring attitude towards her and Louise. She confessed to me, not too long after she had met Mrs. Woods, that she wasn't the type of person she would choose as a friend.

"She has a difficult personality, Nancy," she admitted. "But I just feel for her. It must be hard to be a divorced woman in a new city." Mumma went ahead and invited Mrs. Woods to all kinds of cultural events; she was an expert from her job as a cultural arts coordinator for the Walpole public schools, a position she had created for herself. Mrs. Woods and Louise, my parents and I, had many dinners and dates together.

It hadn't occurred to me at the time that my mother might have been drawn to Mrs. Woods because of her history with single mothers—her own mother had been one. I just knew my mother felt a responsibility to help people in need. I admired her for this, in an idealistic way; I actually thought it had something to do with being Armenian, that as a people we knew what it meant to suffer greatly and to need help. But in reality, I found it very confusing. A couple years before, she had taken on Colleen, one of my high school friends, a promising gymnast who came from a divorced home, split over religion since her mother had become a Jehovah's Witness. After Colleen dropped out of school, started hanging out with juvenile delinquents from the city, and all my friends abandoned her, my mother encouraged me to not break my connection to Colleen in order to help her. To me, at seventeen, this meant I had to be friends with someone with whom I no longer had much in common. Begrudgingly, I invited her to come with us on our museum trips. Mumma didn't guide me through the distinction between a friend and a person that you helped, so I became angry at her for yet again forcing me do something that I didn't want to do, and guilty about my negative feelings towards Colleen.

Later, I was thankful for Mumma's sense of duty when the Woods needed so much support while dealing with the illness. I was glad too, that Louise now had a place to be, among our silly family, at Christmas time. She laughed when Daddy yelled out to my mother, "Stella, where's the clicka?" referring to the remote control in his Boston accent. She finished her incomplete courses and watched *Oprah* with my mother during the day while I interned at an art museum in Boston. She had her own space in the den, but sometimes she slept with me in my old bedroom, and we spent most of our time together when I wasn't working. I tried my best to be understanding and kind and generous. But it was difficult sometimes, in the emotional state that I was in, less because Louise was homophobic, and more because of my guilt that I wanted to take care of myself. Once we were taking a walk around the neighborhood and I was a few paces ahead of her because I needed some space that day.

"What the fuck do you think you're doing?" she yelled.

I turned around. "What?"

"You're avoiding me."

"No, I'm not."

"I'm sorry you're depressed that you're a lesbian and you can't tell your parents, but my mother just died. Pull yourself together."

But coming out wasn't all that made me depressed. There was something else that held me back from Louise, that made me protect myself, but I didn't know what it was yet.

"You don't want to be friends with me anymore?" Louise asked. She was sitting on her bed in her new dorm room as I sat cross-legged on the floor. We were together at Wellesley again, a little over a year after her mother died; I had spent a semester away at an art school, and Louise had spent the next one interning in Washington D.C., perhaps because we had both been shell shocked. Life was going well for both of us: Louise had met a guy she liked in D.C., and they were still dating. In the meantime, I had been seeing a therapist at the counseling center on campus, had been painting, had been making new friends with Alisa, Marianne and Bee. Things seemed normal again, but I had been nervous about Louise's return, that she would somehow take over my life and swallow me whole.

"I still want to be friends," I told her, my heart beating too fast. "I just can't spend as much time with you as I used to." It was a proposal I'd worked out with my therapist.

"I'm sorry, but I don't see how you can quantify friendship. If that's the kind of person you are, then it's over." Shaking, she stood up and opened her door.

When I ran into her on campus after that, she ignored me, and if I said hello, she looked completely unnerved that I would acknowledge her.

A week or so later she called to accuse me of stealing her mother's jewelry, which she had left in storage in my parents' garage. My hall neighbors then reported to me that they had seen Louise sneaking into my room one day when I wasn't there, presumably to look for it. She mentioned the jewelry to my mother, the possibility that I would have stolen it.

"No," Mumma said. "I'm not going to let you accuse Nancy of such a thing."

"Her mother died," I told Mumma on the phone. "Of course she's irrational."

"Her mother's death doesn't give her the right to act that way, Nancy, I'm sorry. My mother died of cancer when I was twenty and I never acted like Louise."

I exhaled for a long moment. It had never occurred to me before that a woman could lose her mother and not go crazy, not be owed everything. To me, it seemed like just about the most painful experience imaginable, the absolute worst thing.

PART III

"I'm going to the pussy doctor now," Rhoda announced one day at noon.

Keeping my head bowed over the drafting table, I lifted my eyes towards Rhoda, my eyebrows high. This must not have been the response she was hoping for, because she continued, "The doctor is going to look at my pussy."

"That's nice," I said, returning to my drawing. It was of a big androgynous head with two giant foam rollers for a mouth. The mouth was big enough for a young child to squeeze through, in between the rollers. For some reason, the art directors, Rhoda and Gil, gave me a lot of responsibility not long after I arrived as an intern at the production company.

"Nice? You think the pussy doctor is nice? Have you even *been* to the pussy doctor, Nancy?" Rhoda's voice was sharp and lilting.

"I was seeing a gynecologist," Gil droned from his table at the back of the bungalow. "I mean, he and I were dating. I don't actually have a vagina."

"I wasn't talking to you, you big fag," Rhoda continued. "Nancy, it's important to go to the pussy doctor regularly, especially if you're a slut like me. Do you have a boyfriend?"

"No."

"Do you have a *girlfriend?*"

"No." I blushed a saturated pink and Rhoda finally got what she was looking for.

"I knew it! You owe me twenty," she said to Gil, poking a pick through her big brown hair and slinging her leopard skin bag over her freckled shoulder. She walked to the open door; the sun lit up her short white dress and her pink toenail polish gleamed.

"So will I see you two *queers* at Prototypes?" she asked us, putting on her sunglasses.

"What time is Prototypes today?" Gil asked.

"It's at two stupid."

"Are you going to make it back in time?"

"Yes, I'll make it back in time. How long do you think it *takes* to look at my pussy?"

"I imagine it would take a while," I said softly, my voice distant, the air in my lungs compressed, "since there are probably a lot of diseases in there.

You big… whore."

Rhoda lifted her sunglasses and looked at me. I raised my eyebrows at her again.

"Hallelujah! I didn't think you'd ever get broken in," she yelled and tromped down the steps to her Jeep.

It occurred to me that maybe I was being sexually harassed at *Let's Get Messy*, but I wasn't sure because Rhoda was a woman and I wasn't getting paid. At orientation, Mira, the intern advisor for The Armenian Philanthropic Organization, had said that we should take our positions seriously and treat them as we would real jobs. "Don't go in late. Don't steal things from the office," she had admonished with an accent. "This is a very good opportunity for you, and these people have donated their time to help you with your career. Treat them with respect." But Mira hadn't mentioned what to do if our employers didn't treat us decently. I certainly hadn't been expecting the art director of a TV game show for children to have such a nasty mouth. But this was my first job experience in the real world; I had just driven across the country, away from my mother in her nightie, and had arrived in L.A. just two weeks before. I figured I simply needed to feel more comfortable with this particular work environment, with Rhoda joking about sex, and then everything would be okay. Calling her a whore was a good start.

At two, Gil and I walked over to Prototypes, which was taking place in an empty stage across the lot. *Let's Get Messy* taped at the Hollywood Center Studios off Santa Monica Blvd., just east of Highland. It was a polarized part of L.A., with greasy hamburger stands next to film editing establishments, shoddy bungalow courts adjacent to parking lots full of shiny BMWs, and shirtless hustlers swaggering around outside the studio gates.

A few nights ago, Mira had driven us down Santa Monica Blvd. further east a few avenues, where I had been shocked to find Armenian grocers and bookshops and doctors' offices and restaurants. Mira explained that Armenians had been living in L.A. since the turn of the century. The first wave came from the East Coast, looking for farm work. Armenian farmers from Fresno later arrived during the Depression. "But over the last twenty years the population has really boomed," Mira said, "with Armenians from Beirut and Iran escaping war. There are one hundred thousand Armenians in L.A. now."

I had felt estranged from the Armenian community since high school, when Mumma had dragged me to a few dances, which seemed like thinly veiled excuses to indoctrinate teenagers to marry Armenian. Not knowing how to dance, I sat at a table while Mumma told me not to wear such a "sad-sack face," so I went to the bathroom and sobbed in a stall. At Wellesley, my ethnicity became an obvious target of jokes since none of my friends had heard of it before. After the earthquake in December of 1988, which decimated several cities and killed fifty thousand Armenians, my friends quipped, *"Now I hear about Armenia constantly."*

But the spring of my senior year, I took a class called "Lesbian and Gay Literature," with a professor named George Stambolian, a gay man my parents' age who translated Jean Genet and edited anthologies of gay male fiction. We read *Zami: A New Spelling of My Name* by Audre Lorde and *Stone Butch Blues* by Leslie Feinberg. I became rapt with tall, willowy, bald and mustachioed George Stambolian as he gesticulated in front of the class, informing us of his days at Stonewall and Fire Island, popping poppers on disco floors.

One day he approached me before class and asked me where my parents were from. "Cranston, Rhode Island and Oxford, Massachusetts," I stated.

He blinked his elegant eyelids. "Where are your grandparents from?"

"Armenia," I said.

"Where in Armenia?" he continued.

"I don't know," I said.

"You should find out," he said. "It's important."

After the class I called my grandmother. "Sepastia," she had said.

It's a nice name, I had thought, as it appeared in my brain: *Sepastia.*

A warm breeze blew over Gil and me as we walked over to Stage 8. I noticed the sky was bright blue, as opposed to the usual smog gray. Looming above us were the classic white Hollywood letters nestled into the hillside.

"Hey, look at that!" I said to Gil. "I didn't know the Hollywood sign was up there."

"You haven't seen it before?" Gil asked.

"No, I guess it's always been covered in smog." This was a little frightening; the sign and the hills weren't that far away. "You mean to tell me," I asked Gil in disbelief, "this neighborhood is Hollywood?" I never would have imagined that Hollywood was filled with slums and hustlers and scores of Armenians. But I'd literally been living in a haze.

The first prototype was a pizza made of foam rubber, about twelve feet in diameter, covered with red, Frisbee-sized disks meant to be pepperoni, mushroom shapes, and red cherry Jell-O, not fully jelled, for the tomato sauce. The designer explained that two kids from opposing teams were to engage on top of the pizza in a crab-like fashion, on hands and feet with stomachs up, their arms tied to each other. The kid from the red team would kick the pepperoni off the pizza, and the mushrooms would be kicked by a member from the gold team. Whoever moved most of their toppings in a minute was the winner. There was a problem though. The casting director sent only one kid over.

Everyone stood around staring at each other. "Rhoda," barked Dick Messing, the founder of Messy Productions. He looked sickly and came to work in a wheelchair.

"Yes, honey," Rhoda answered.

"Put on that suit and get down on that pizza."

Rhoda looked at him blankly.

"Well someone's gotta get down on the pizza," Dick said.

I looked around and saw that I was the youngest and possibly most flexible person in the room. I recalled Mira's orientation pep talk: "You need to go out of your way to make a good impression, to go the distance in your positions," she had pleaded. "Take opportunities when they come. Make yourself visible."

"I'll do it," I said, smiling into Dick's face. His white-yellow hair and moustache were the same color as his pallid skin.

"Nancy, don't be ridiculous," Rhoda said. I ignored her and grabbed the suit, a yellow t-shirt with "Let's Get Messy" in red and a matching pair of yellow shorts, girls size 12.

As I changed in the bathroom, I discovered that the shorts were so short my pubic hair could not be contained by them. Pulling on the shorts legs to cover the unsightly black fuzz, I cursed the summer I shaved past my bikini line. As soon as I straightened up, the shorts rose to reveal the weedy rebellion. *Oh well, there are plenty of other places people can look besides "down there,"* I consoled myself.

I walked out of the bathroom and sat down on the pizza, making myself visible to the *Let's Get Messy* bigshots. The kid, a twelve-year-old boy from Tarzana who was wearing the red outfit, joined me. As we assumed crab positions and our arms were strapped together, it all seemed morally wrong. The stunt would have been fine for two kids. But a young boy tied to a woman with excessive body hair on top of a giant, Jell-O-drenched, foam rubber pizza? I worried that it smacked of kiddie porn.

The buzzer went off and my opponent kicked the soggy, gelatin-loaded pepperonis like a maniac. I could tell he was having trouble being anchored to my heft and I inwardly cringed as he grunted. Slipping and sliding over the Jell-O, I kicked mushrooms the best I could and tried to have a fun, helpful attitude about the whole affair.

But my shorts rode high and I could not pull them down as my hands were tied. When I looked up to see if people were looking "down there," they averted their eyes: Gil conferred with one of the producers and Rhoda covered her mouth with her hand sideways. The only one who was even vaguely smiling was Dick, but his grin looked slightly evil.

Needless to say, the kid won.

The producers decided to use the pizza on the show, so I assumed my overexposure wasn't so obscene that it ruined the stunt. None of the *Let's Get Messy* bigshots, including Rhoda and Gil, seemed to really appreciate my initiative, though.

———

The green plastic bowl in the bathroom, left behind by previous tenants, reminded me of the one Mumma kept under the kitchen sink, used exclusively for puking into whenever one of us got sick. It was 1 A.M., and I had been throwing up since ten o'clock. Tired of trudging to the bathroom and gagging over the toilet, I set up the puke bowl next to my futon on the floor so I could just shift my head to heave into it.

The first time it happened at Wellesley was the day after I had flunked out of an architecture class. I found myself tromping back and forth between my dorm room and the bathroom about twenty times. At first I thought it was just the noodle kugel served in the cafeteria, but after I had chucked it all up, something yellow and bitter and horrifying emerged.

"It's bile," Mumma told me over the phone. "Go to the infirmary."

After puking up a bedpan of acid, the nurse gave me a sedative and I fell asleep. The next morning when the doctor arrived, he took blood and urine samples but no major problems were diagnosed. It happened again before the Teach For America interview and another time after Louise's mother had died. The procedure was the same: puking, bile, sedative, tests, no diagnosis. I started calling them panic attacks, since I had trouble breathing and they always occurred around times of stress. When I was traveling across the U.S. to California, I was struck as I drove through Yellowstone during a snowstorm. In a motel room, one of my traveling companions massaged my stomach and that did the trick.

I was never able to stop puking by myself, though, except for the first night I moved into the apartment in Venice. Bee had been driving across the country and would move in with me a few days later.

This is where the story gets tricky, reader. You might be wondering where I was right now, and where was Bee. It was a couple of years after the internship had ended. Bee was out for the evening, and I was alone, having yet another panic attack. To recapitulate: Bee had visited me while I made jewelry at the beach, we had gone to the science fiction convention together, she had found a job, I had joined the writing workshop, we had become like an old married couple, and we had just made a proto-lesbian-friendship group together.

So far in this book, I have set up a structure of a twenty-three-year-old me, looking back on my childhood. Childhood ended with my graduation from college, and yet, in the period directly after college, Chapter 9 as it were, when I arrived in L.A. during those first few months as an intern, I was in some nether region of adulthood. How can a twenty-three-year-old look back at being a twenty-two-year-old? In reality, I am forty, writing this to you. My early twenties blur together, much the same way my memories of my panic attacks bleed together, as if I had no body, no sense of time. I was free floating during those years, traveling through a landscape so different from the one I grew up in. I felt some kind of urgency to find myself, to find some strength there, for fear that I might stumble and end up back where I started, in Walpole.

Back in time, as I was waiting for Bee to drive across the country, I had tried to relax, lying on my back, staring up at the ceiling. The lamp-post in the alley was shining an eerie, acetylene orange light onto the newly painted eggshell walls. It reminded me of the bucket of cotton candy pink paint I'd spilled inside a clear Lucite tube that served as a slide on *Let's Get Messy.* Then I remembered how I was supposed to pick up a tarp at a place on Orange and I mistakenly went to Citrus. Gil would be stupid to hire me on his next show. *How am I gonna pay rent?*

Turning my head, I threw up again. And again and again, blood rushing to my head, eyes wide, until the bitter taste of bile came up. Where was Bee? She went out with her Chicano friends. I never had Armenian friends. *Something is gonna break soon.*

I collapsed back from the bowl and lay down, able to breathe again. But several minutes later, my stomach was tight again. I writhed around and tried to calm my belly by physically kneading and massaging it, but the only thing that alleviated the pain for even a minute was heaving into the green bowl. The time in between wretches became shorter and shorter until I was throwing up so much the bile became less bitter. I eventually lost track of my thoughts. I didn't feel like a person anymore, but a system, nothing more than stomach pain and the convulsions that relieved them. *Orange and citrus* repeated in my head to delirium, a trance-like state. By some miracle I fell into the silence of sleep.

———

Though moving to L.A. was an attempt to distance myself from my family, it ironically brought me closer to their people, the Armenians. Every night and on the weekends, the internship progam immersed us in Armenian culture, events led by Mira. Mostly, we just visited Armenians who had lovely houses, poolside, striding the mountains of Glendale. One evening, Mira brought us to her parents' place.

When she approached me as I was waiting in line at the buffet table, I told her, "Your parents have such a beautiful home." The place was huge, with exquisite Oriental rugs on every surface and a pool out back; her parents ran an import business of some sort and had donated money to the intern program. "Did you grow up here?" I asked.

"No, sweetie, I grew up in Beirut. We've been in this house about five years."

"You live here too?" Mira was twenty-six and wore sleek dresses, heels and pearls; she worked in PR at one of the studios. I was surprised she still lived with her parents, that she would be subject to an arrangement that belonged to the realm of previous Armenian generations, totally old-fashioned, not to mention soul crushing. Mira seemed at one with herself though, unlike my older brother who still lived at home, four years after graduating from college, in his old tri-cornered hat wallpapered room.

Mumma nagged Leo to take out the garbage and Daddy bossed him around, as an appraisal assistant, in the basement. He didn't date, as far as I could tell, even though he was tall, dark and some might say handsome. Ever since he had temped for a month at a mutual fund company, he fancied himself a yuppie, wearing oxford cloth shirts he spray-starched.

I didn't suspect just how unhappy he was until I ran into him at a Kitaro concert a few months before my college graduation. Alisa's uncle, Kitaro's road manager, got us into his concert at the Wang Center for free. Unfamilar with Kitaro, I was stunned by the popularity of this long-haired Japanese man in a flowing black robe, playing New Age guitar riffs amidst puffs of dry ice smoke. Afterwards, we were invited backstage, and Kitaro appeared wearing large-framed glasses, a pilly white turtleneck tucked into designer jeans, and white aerobic sneakers with Velcro straps. Tiny, humble and smiling effusively, he projected none of the dark New Age mystery he'd possessed onstage.

When we left the building we found Leonard out in front, smoking a cigarette and wearing an earring. For a minute I wasn't sure it was him. *An earring?* A little diamond stud in his left ear. I quickly did the check that a junior high-aged Leo had taught me—*left is right and right is wrong*—to ascertain if he were gay.

He was dumbstruck when I approached. "Wasn't that the most insipid crap you've ever seen?" I asked.

"Oh no, I thought it was a great concert," he said, taking a drag from his cigarette and I noticed it was a Parliament, a brand that he had informed me back in the Tricky Dick O'Reilly days was the faggiest cigarette of all.

I didn't know who my irascible Republican brother thought he was, pretending to be a Kitaro-loving, earring-sporting, Parliament-smoking gay guy, but it was painfully obvious that Leo had kept this alter ego from our family. I imagined him pulling out of the driveway and shoving the stud into his lobe once the coast was clear at the bottom of our road. His survival was contingent on a certain appearance, sort of like Kitaro, who would never make it in the cutthroat New Age music business if he wore that pilly white turtleneck on stage. But unlike Kitaro's fans, our family was never happy with any illusion presented.

"Of course I live with my parents," Mira said. "I wouldn't live anywhere else." She swished away then, long hair flinging behind her.

I prepared a little plate of appetizers and sat alone at a table. The *boereg* and *choreg* were really tasty, but not as good as my grandmother's.

I thought of her as I tasted the savory flavors and overheard two elderly women conversing in Armenian. I found myself enraptured with the sound of the language, hearing patterns of words—*eench guzes, eench genes*—spoken with Grammy's urgency and accent.

Mira greeted the ladies, kissing them on both cheeks, joining the conversation. She noticed me staring. "Do you understand Armenian?" she asked.

"Hardly anything," I replied sheepishly.

"And your family doesn't speak it?"

"My parents do a little. Mostly my grandmother—" Then I blurted out, as it was occurring to me, "I connect to being Armenian mainly through her." I thought this was a marked difference to the way everyone else at the party was Armenian, embodying it firsthand by living in extended families, within a community and speaking the language. I turned to the old women sitting next to Mira, "It's really nice to hear you talk because it reminds me of my grandmother." They looked at me blankly as if to say, "Well, why aren't you with her?"

"Eench bes es," I heard Lewis, a frat boy from Cornell, suddenly announce: it was time for the interns to introduce ourselves to the patrons of the Armenian Philanthropic Organization. Lewis was wearing a navy blue suit and tie, which set him apart from the other guy interns in sloppy sport jackets and Dockers. "I'm Lewis Der Ananian," he said, smiling broadly, "and I'm going to be a famous Armenian-American sportscaster thanks to the great connections I'm making at KABC News. Thanks so much for this opportunity—*shnorhagalutiun.*" He grasped his hands together and shook them twice at the old Armenian fogies, who were beaming.

Sonya, from Georgetown, stood up next. She tossed her head to one side, swung her bleach blonde bob and explained her internship on *The New Lassie* show. At least, that's what I thought she said; she was speaking in Armenian. The crowd stared at her blankly. Perhaps the men were gawking at Sonya's low cut dress and ample boobs, but I sensed disapproval.

I didn't know what they would make of me, with my hairy, feminist legs and geometric-patterned dress. After announcing as graciously as I could that I had just graduated from Wellesley College and was learning so much at *Let's Get Messy,* I felt queasy.

"Did you see that bitch?" Lewis joked with the other guy interns in the car on the way back to our USC student apartments. He was referring to a patron's daughter; she must have been around fifteen. "What a body. That's some tight pussy there, man."

I glared at him in the darkness of the car. He felt my anger and turned to me. "What?" he laughed. "You jealous?"

<hr>

Incidents like those at Mira's parents' house prevented me from pursuing more contact with the Armenian community once the internship ended. I did have a brief relapse later when Mira told me about the AAAA, Armenian American Arts Alliance, which held a contest and exhibition every year. I had submitted some of my naked self-portraits, including a very large one of myself from the waist up, with a small head and enormous breasts—a skewed perspective. My eyes and mouth were closed and covered with straight black lines, a slit appeared in the center of my chest, and faint outlines of California and Massachusetts surfaced on opposite sides of the page, marked with arrows. When Bee and I entered the exhibition, we saw my giant self-portrait ... fall down. It crumpled to the floor just as we walked in. We stood in front of it a moment, then I spun on my heel and walked out, remaining in the car until Bee came to get me. The drawing was back up but the top right corner was torn and it had not been properly hung, scotch taped to the wall.

Bee grabbed a couple of cups of wine and we strolled through the rest of the exhibit to find endless paintings of Mount Ararat, the national symbol, landscapes like Auntie Agnes had painted of ancient church ruins, and tortured, abstracted figures entitled "Genocide."

"Heavy," Bee commented. I had to laugh. She was always here to help me, to witness. Even my panic attacks.

One time, a couple of days after my big reading at Beyond Baroque, I had spent half the night sitting on the bathroom floor, with its tiny hexagonal tiles, right by the toilet so that I wouldn't wake her. When she awoke in the morning, Bee drove me to Santa Monica Hospital, past palm trees and strip malls on Lincoln Boulevard. She helped me fill out forms at the intake desk while I intermittently puked into a plastic bed pan, then she sat in the waiting room while I was admitted.

As soon as I put on a gown and climbed into bed, I stopped throwing up. A nurse took my temperature and blood pressure and hooked me up to a bag of fluid. "You're very dehydrated," she said. An hour or so later, a dour doctor in big aviator glasses, brown hair parted down the middle, came in to see me. For some reason, he was convinced I was pregnant, though this was before I even met Jesse. Though I let the doctor know I was a virgin, he still insisted on giving me a pelvic exam.

"Hey little one, how was it?" Bee asked when I returned to my bed from the examination room. "I've never had one."

The speculum was freezing and the doctor had been rough. I paused, looked directly at Bee and drolled in my best deadpan, "I've been raped."

Bee laughed as the nurse returned, asking, "Is this your sister?"

"No," Bee said. "Just a friend."

"Your friend had quite a night," she said smiling.

"I know," Bee said. "She's worn out."

"Well, the doctor will be in shortly with your exam results," the nurse said.

The doctor never returned, and after I was hydrated and had stopped upchucking for a few hours, the nurse told me I wasn't pregnant and let us go home. She patted Bee on the back on our way out. "You're a good friend," she said.

Now she was out with some friends that she had made on her aunt's campaign—young, politically oriented Chicanos like herself, just out of college. Before I started going to the poetry workshop, I had tagged along with her to rallies and speeches and got to know her Chicano friends, whom I liked very much. But I sometimes felt awkward, dwelling outside the border of their culture and common interests. It was probably because I was jealous that I had no people of my own, but I wasn't about to seek out friends in the Armenian community, not after the internship. I did what I could just to get through the rest of it.

—◆—

The barber at Farmers Market, at the corner of Third and Fairfax, was an older Jewish man with a big round head and thick glasses. I sat in his chair and he tied a smock around my neck. "How short?" he asked with a Yiddish accent.

"Could you cut it to a quarter of an inch?"

The barber held his electric razor to the top of my forehead. It buzzed against my cranium, tickling, and my brain shifted. The barber, I could see in the mirror, was smiling as he worked, trimming my hair to an even, fuzzy coat.

"Looks good," he said and brushed off my neck.

"Oh my God! You look like Sinéad O'Connor!" Lia, one of the other interns, nearly hyperventilated when she saw me afterwards. "Where did you get it done?"

"The barbershop at Farmers Market!" I proudly answered. Like I was so cool to think up such a stunt; my artsy friends at Wellesley would have approved. What I liked most about my story, though, was that my character had connected with the barber, another character. Two characters connecting made a community.

On the interns' next outing, an Armenian man my father's age said, "Nice to meet you, young man," as we were introduced.

"I'm a woman," I informed him.

"Oh, sorry," he said. "I just saw the short hair."

He must have been sight-impaired because I clearly possessed eyelashes and boobs. But then I realized every Armenian woman I'd met in L.A. had long hair. You'd have to be a boy to have a shaved head. You'd have to be a crazy girl to cut off your hair, to look like a worm, as Grammy had said.

A month later, I went back to Farmers Market to get my hair trimmed, but the barber declined, shaking his head. "You're a girl," he told me. "I don't cut girls' hair."

This was unsettling; I was a paying customer and there weren't any others in the place. "I'd like a haircut, please," I repeated.

"Go to the beauty parlor," he said.

"I don't want to go there," I told him. "They won't do what I want."

"Well, I'm not going to do it," he said.

"You did it before."

He shook his head.

"Please," I begged him. It was unlike me to be so insistent. But I couldn't accept the change in the barber. It seemed he had come to suspect since the last haircut that I was a lesbian. But I was still the same character he had connected with a month ago, lesbian or not; I sat in his chair, waiting.

He eventually approached and I smiled with my lips closed as he tied the smock around my neck, but he wouldn't smile back. He set to work slowly buzzing my hair down, as if coerced into a crime. Little pieces of black hair cascaded over my skin and hands. When I looked down I saw dashes—punctuation that marked an interruption—on the surface of my smock. That's when I spotted the tattoo on the inside of his arm.

When he finished, he swung the smock off of me, and I quietly thanked him and handed him a ten. He wouldn't take it from me, but bundled up the smock instead and turned away.

I could have just left, but something wouldn't let me. Keeping back tears, I placed the bill on the counter.

It was years later, and we were half a world away from each other, but I suddenly remembered my big sister, with all her secrets, on my grandmother's porch, bluntly informing me that I was innocent.

The Korean lady placed the wig—long, black and straight with bangs—on top of my head. I'd passed the wig store in Koreatown several times on my errands for *Let's Get Messy*, formulating the purchase in my mind. It would be easy to slip on over my short hair; it could provide an interesting art experience. I didn't want the Korean lady to know I wasn't buying the wig expressly to have beautiful Korean hair, though; she might get offended like the barber. She daintily combed my wig and said, "Very pretty."

The black hair swished around me as I drove up the 5 Freeway to Lia's apartment in Glendale. During the last week of my internship, Rhoda quit *Let's Get Messy* for a better job and Gil hired me as an assistant. Lia had known I would need a place to stay in a matter of days and offered her apartment while she visited relatives in Iran.

I parked on the quiet side street and climbed the stairs to the back of the apartment complex. I took off my wig and set it on its accompanying Styrofoam head on top of Lia's coffee table. Since the show started taping, I hadn't been here much. I worked from 8 A.M. until eleven or twelve at night, painting sets and running errands. It was Friday and this was the first waking moment I'd had to relax, to have time to wonder if making children's TV was what I really wanted to do.

The apartment felt suffocating, so I went for a walk, the only person on the sidewalk as thousands of cars zoomed past. I stopped by a convenience store to pick up some things, and the lady behind the counter, with dark lipliner demarcating the border of her mouth, spoke to me in Armenian. I had been aware that a lot of Armenians lived in Glendale, but I hadn't yet encountered any. "I'm sorry," I uttered. "I don't speak Armenian."

She looked at me bewildered. "No? Why not?"

I felt like saying, *Look, I'm not a recent immigrant from Iran or Lebanon, okay? My people have been here a long time. Don't you know there are other kinds of Armenians?*

"I tried to learn it but couldn't pick it up," I replied instead.

"Your family doesn't speak it?" she asked.

Uggh. Do I have to get into my whole history here at the ampm on Colorado?

"You should really learn it. It's a beautiful language." I turned around to face a gas station attendant with *Vartan* embroidered on his shirt.

"Okay," I assured him. "I will."

When I got back to the apartment, I drew a picture of the wig and tried not to think about how I was ever going to learn Armenian.

When Lia returned from her trip, she drove me in her red VW Cabriolet up the side of a Glendale mountain to the home of her fiancé Shant, a wealthy, self-made businessman, ten years her senior. He had bought her the convertible and paid the rent on her apartment. They had made an arrangement that when she was done with school, they would marry.

Shant's house was big, modern and beige. His tiny old parents roamed around the shiny marble floors in slippers and mismatched patterned clothes, straining homemade yogurt in cheesecloth to make thick *lebne* and spreading fruit mush onto sheets to prepare *bastekh*. I felt like I had walked into the Armenian version of *The Beverly Hillbillies*.

Lia made plates of *yalanchee*, rice, pita and *lebne* for me and Shant to eat while we watched a rerun of *Taxi*, his favorite show. "I love Jim," he said, bouncing his stocking feet up and down and laughing with his mouth full every time Christopher Lloyd delivered one of his stoner lines. Lia quietly drank a bottle of wine and rolled her heavy-lidded eyes, flinging her long, permed, Julia-Roberts-in-*Pretty-Woman* hair over her shoulder.

During the summer, I had watched the sleek way Lia groomed and dressed and maneuvered her way around guys. She was always eating and drinking to excess, and I thought she was depressed. She told me she thought she was overweight and sometimes at night I heard her throw up in the bathroom. Her parents expected her to marry Shant, but I had no idea what Lia wanted to do.

When I was greeting her right after my college graduation ceremony, Grammy had told me, "I wanted to go to school and learn like you."

"Why didn't you?" I asked.

"My brothers made me get married." She was referring to her two much older brothers who'd arranged her engagement to my grandfather in order to get a stake in his farm.

Though Shant and Lia's arrangement was more modern than my grandparents', it still struck me as old-fashioned, adhering to family expectations. By contrast, I had just moved three thousand miles from my family in order to be whatever I wanted. I just didn't know what that was.

The long black Korean wig was missing from the bald Styrofoam head when I came home from work. Lia wasn't home either.

I was still awake in the sofa bed at 2 A.M. when she stumbled in, wearing a tight black dress, black hose and heels, and the wig, slightly messed up.

"I hope you don't mind," she said breathlessly, running her fingers through it.

I had actually never worn the wig in public besides that first ride home, so I was a little jealous. "Where were you?" I asked.

"I went to some clubs," she smiled.

"With Shant?"

"No," she grinned, her lids ever heavy as she handed me the wig and went to bed.

For some reason, I was reminded of Rhoda. During her last days at work, she showed me pictures of the crew from two previous seasons. In one shot, Rhoda was wearing a turtleneck and big glasses, her hair pulled back with barrettes. In other words, a nerd. A female Kitaro.

"Oh my God, you looked so different!" I had told her. She had obviously undergone some sort of transformation while at *Let's Get Messy.*

"I got contacts," she had said. "No big deal."

Shave a head to save yourself, wear a wig and become something else. I knew it didn't seem like a big deal, such a superficial adjustment, a quick fix, a shift in appearance. But there was a story of something bigger, beyond what my brain realized then; I somehow knew that a person becoming herself, becoming oneself, was a really big deal.

Two years later, not much had changed it seemed. My hair had grown out, grown long, but I was still trying to become myself, I was still having panic attacks. Bee finally came home from her night out with the Chicanos to save me.

"It's happening again?" she asked. "Weren't you out with the workshop?"

"Yeah, but then I started feeling sick when I got home. How was Vic?" I asked. He was a guy from the group of friends she'd been out with. She had gotten to know him, had sex with him, then he dumped her. Now she was obsessed with him.

Bee looked upset. "He's okay. He was with another girl."

"I'm sorry Bee," I said through strained breath. I scuffed in my slippers to the bathroom, threw up, and then trudged into her room.

She had taken off her dress and was lounging around in a black slip. My eyes focused on her breasts which were small and pointed outward, unlike mine which were round and full. I always wondered why hers were shaped that way.

"I'm not getting better," I told her.

"Did you call the guy?" In the back of the *LA Weekly* I had found a listing for a man in the Bay Area who was a panic attack specialist. I would call him and he would lead me through several breathing exercises until I stopped puking, and then I would send him a check for whatever I could afford.

"Yeah, but it helped for only a minute."

"That's weird, it helped before."

I thought I knew why the treatment had ceased to work. I had noticed a pattern to my panic attacks: Bee found a job, I found a job, I had a panic attack; Bee found friends, I found friends, I had a panic attack. As Bee moved forward, I worried that I was flailing away. When I found my place, the stress I'd been repressing would erupt from my body.

But more disturbingly, I had started to feel like maybe Bee and I *should* grow old together, as she had suggested recently. It seemed so obvious, with all the time we spent together, and especially since we had just been dumped by guys. The only thing was, I didn't think I was sexually attracted to her. I mean, she really drove me crazy sometimes. So I had been keeping the idea to myself.

I took a deep breath now and said, "I think what helps the most is when I know I'm safe, that I'm taken care of."

"I'll take care of you," Bee said. "Come 'ere."

I curled up against Bee on her futon on the floor, and she rubbed my back the way Mumma did when I used to throw up into the puke bowl. My spine tightened and my breath stopped.

"Bee, there's something I have to tell you," I blurted out. "Maybe if I say it, the panic will go away."

"What is it?"

"I feel very close to you, closer than I've felt to anyone, and I think, I think maybe we should go further in our relationship and become sexually intimate?" I said it in a rush, in an effort to save myself. Bee breathed through her nose and her nostrils flared. "But I don't feel attracted to you, I don't think," I added, "so I'm confused about it."

Bee looked at the floor and said in a tone of voice I recognized as the one she put on to be serious, grown up and caring, "Thank you for telling me. But I have to tell you, I don't feel the same way. It's more like I love you as a sister."

I took a deep breath. "That's fine," I said. "That's actually a big relief."

10. HOLIDAY BY HOLIDAY

"You're a good person," Pat said.

"Really?" I asked.

"Yes, you are a very good person. And you don't have to do anything to be good. Just sitting in that chair, you're good."

Pat was full of shit, but she was all I had at the moment. A few weeks after Bee had rejected me, I went a little crazy. First, I found her and Liz having dinner one night in our apartment and it definitely seemed like a date. Then some friends arrived from New York, twin sisters, one of whom went to Wellesley and the other to Brown. We had a drunken party and Liz and Ellie took the twins up to the mansion of the famous actor Ellie used to work for. They skinny dipped in his pool and made out in his hot tub. Bee and I had watched them all leave together from our window; we both felt left out, and now she appeared to feel jilted by Liz. Why would Bee have such feelings for her and not for me? Everything came to a head, though, when Bee was offhandedly telling me one morning that she wanted to go to grad school. "You can't go to grad school when I'm not ready for that!" I barked. Bee responded by handing me the phone book and told me to look under counseling.

And now here I was with Pat, a grad student racking up client hours for her certification at the Westside Women's Health Clinic. Pat, with her heels and makeup and full pleated skirts, was trying to perform some of the work my parents had neglected. "You mean to tell me," I began, testing her theory, "I'm a good person if I just sit around all day watching *Doogie Howser, M.D.*?"

"Yes," Pat insisted. Without my consent, tears streamed down my face, and goddamn Pat handed me the box of Kleenex. "Your parents only gave you attention when you achieved. Did they ever tell you they loved you for being you? When you brought home a bad grade? When you made a mistake?"

"I don't think so."

"Nancy, a child needs to feel loved in order to love herself."

"Uh huh."

"Your parents bathed you and fed you and provided for you, but they didn't give you enough emotional support. It's not their fault because their parents probably treated them the same way."

"Oh."

"But that doesn't mean it's fair you lost out on getting your developmental needs met."

I sniffed and looked blankly at Pat.

"Aren't you angry?" she asked.

I tried to imagine Pat's utopian vision of parents nurturing kids without asking for anything in return. I thought Mumma and Daddy had made it pretty clear to me that they wouldn't love me unless I earned good grades, wore clothes that didn't embarrass them, and visited art museums all over the greater Boston area. Now that I was learning about good parenting, there was hope that I might be able to reverse the cycle and help my future kid become her own person. But it seemed I was getting the raw end of the deal. *Why do I have to be the generation to get so shafted, to feel all the pain?*

"You never once told me you loved me!" I yelled at my mother as she was wrapping presents in the den, where she'd set up a secretive wrapping area. It was my second day home for the holidays, and my first outburst, so far.

"I thought I did," Mumma said, matter-of-factly.

"Well you didn't. And I grew up with no confidence because of it."

"Oh now you're going to blame me! You must be going to therapy. All those therapists like to do is blame the mother."

I marveled at her extrasensory perception, stammering, "Well, why shouldn't I blame you if you screwed up?!"

"Nancy, I didn't know I was doing anything so bad. I thought you knew I loved you. You mean I had to tell you?!"

"YES!" I screamed.

"You know, we just don't say things like that in our family."

That had me stumped for a minute. "Well... you never just loved me for who I was," I started up. "You always made conditions that I do things for you, and now I've developed into a person *who always has to please everyone!*" I was running out of breath; the last words came out in a crazed screech.

"Who do you have to please?" she asked. "It's not my fault you can't stick up for yourself."

"All my pain comes from *YOU!*" I exploded.

Mumma shook her head stubbornly and tsk-tsked me. It was hard for me to believe that my last point was delivered in such a way that could not be readily understood by someone with even modest hearing, so I brought out the big guns.

"YOU'RE A HORRIBLE MOTHER!" I screamed.

My mother very rarely cried. To see her crumpled in the den like the wrapping paper she had recycled from last year, mumbling that she'd tried the best she could to raise us kids, was slap-in-the-face sobering; I'd gone too far.

My throat raw, I staggered upstairs and ran into Leo, still living at home. "What are you screaming about?" he asked.

"Did Mumma and Daddy ever tell you that they loved you?"

"No."

"So don't you think that's fucked up?"

"That's what you were screaming about?" He brushed past me to the den then returned instantly. "You made Mumma *cry*," he said accusatively.

"She wasn't listening to me," I told him. "At least now she knows what she's done."

"What did she do?" Daddy asked. He'd come upstairs from the basement.

"Why didn't you ever tell me that you loved me when I was growing up?"

Daddy laughed. "That's what you're yelling about?"

I heard the den door creak and Mumma suddenly appeared, climbing up the stairs. We all clammed up and watched her turn on *Oprah*. Daddy decided to put on a show for her. *"Oh Nancy, I love you!"* he shouted in a pinched joking voice, his teeth clenched and his eyes wide, reaching out to grab me.

"Ick! Get away from me!" I cried.

Mumma ignored us and grabbed a tissue from the side table to dab her eyes. After a fight she usually kept her defenses up, but now she was sniffling and meek and mute.

I didn't feel like a very good person now. I felt pretty shitty, actually.

Mumma, Daddy, Valerie, Leonard, Grammy, the aunts and I were standing around the dinner table. Some of us had our hands cupped heavenward as we recited in unison, *Hayr Mer, vor hergeenes yes, Soorp yeghitzee anoon ko…* (Our Father who art in Heaven, hallowed be Thy name…) Then Grammy started to race through the prayer, forcing everyone else to proceed at their own pace, and all the words tumbled together. I mumbled until people crossed themselves, the big finish. Auntie Ruth berated Grammy that God didn't care how fast she could say the words.

"What?" my grandmother asked innocently. "That's how I like to say it."

"It's not a *race*, Ma!" Daddy chimed in, giggling.

"Aaakh. You say too slow," Grammy popped back, dismissing everyone with a hand wave and a frown. *"Hrammetsek!"* she ordered.

Daddy carved the turkey and scooped out the rice, pine nut, parsley and allspice stuffing and we passed around the cheese *boereg, fasoolyah,* mashed potatoes and gravy.

"Everything looks delicious," Mumma said, the tiniest trace of anger beneath a polite veneer. Mumma never broke her personal code of civility at Grammy's house, except for Easter, 1984. At first she had simply asked, "Where are Sherrie and Tony this year?"

The aunties had given the standard excuse—Tony's run-down 1977 Cadillac couldn't make the drive from Long Island.

"I don't see why no one ever demands that they visit, and yet we're expected to come every single holiday," Mumma said.

"Well pardon us if you don't want to spend time with your family," Ruth said.

"You're not my family," said Mumma. "You're my in-laws."

Suddenly the feelings my mother had been keeping from my grandmother and aunts exploded all over their ham and pilaf dinner. Daddy clenched his jaw; he'd been anticipating this showdown for a long time. Valerie burst into tears, Leo retreated to the bathroom, and I felt sick to my stomach. Mumma's truth was never supposed to be exposed. But now that it had, I couldn't help but defend her. "I think Mumma feels like you guys don't like her or something."

Mel turned to me and said, "*We* don't like *her?* How would you feel, Nancy, if your own sister-in-law never once, in twenty-five years, invited you to lunch?"

"She's a spoiled brat," Grammy said.

Mumma was completely appalled. "How dare you say that when I don't even have a mother?" She stormed out and we followed her to the car while Agnes called from the porch, "Have a nice life," as if we'd never see each other again.

Of course we were there the next holiday; we just went later in the day after spending some time together as a nuclear family. But the Aunties and Grammy pressured Daddy to come earlier and earlier and eventually the allotment eroded over the years till my mother was not far from where she had started, spending most of her holiday not with her family, but with her in-laws.

This year, after we had opened presents and eaten dessert, Mumma approached the den where we were all squeezed in together, watching TV. She looked expectantly at my father. When he didn't stand up or make a move, she said, "It's late, we have to get going," and there was an awkward silence, as there always was, which ushered in the period of grabbing coats, taking home leftovers, securing store receipts and kissing everyone on the cheek.

A couple of days later, Mumma and I were headed to the mall to return some of the Aunties' gifts. I hadn't ridden in a car with her since I was a teenager, and it felt oddly familiar and intimate, the both of us in such a compact space, facing forward, moving through all the New England-isms—bald trees and brown marshes and gray-green hazel lawns. For some reason, I started telling her about the women's multicultural poetry work-shop.

"Nancy, I really hope you're not going to be like your sister," my mother responded.

"What's that supposed to mean?"

"I just don't think you should be a lesbian."

When she'd said it in the past, I just clammed up. But now, after the few sessions I'd had with my therapist, I was convinced I was witnessing a blatant case of poor parenting. I sighed. *I may as well get this over with.*

"Look, Ma, I'm bisexual. I might fall in love with a man, I might fall in love with a woman. I'm not going to fall in love with a gender, but with a person."

"Oh Jesus," she said. "I don't like that."

"It's not up to you to like it or not," I said.

"It's just... unnecessary. These women are independent, which is fine, but then they think, 'Now we don't even have to have *sex* with men!' You know, Valerie used to have boyfriends. I think she's just been talked into this by her friends, she's so gullible."

"I *highly* doubt that. No one can talk anyone into being gay. Valerie has a mind of her own, you know. You're just being homophobic."

"I don't like that word. They're just using it for anyone who doesn't approve of what they're doing."

"Exactly! What gives you the right to approve or disapprove of us?"

"I'm a mother, and a mother only wants what's best for her children. A lesbian, or whatever," she stalled to look at me, the unclassifiable queer, "cannot get married and have children—"

"Yes she can," I interrupted.

"No, she cannot have a normal family with a *normal* mother and a *normal* father."

"Well big deal, I didn't have a family with a normal mother and a *normal* father."

"Nancy, you know what I mean. I just don't think it's right. I feel close to my girlfriends, closer sometimes than to your father. But that doesn't mean I'm going to have *sex* with them!"

"Well, maybe you should. Sounds like *you're* gay!"

"*I'm* gay!" she exploded with laughter. "Ha!"

Obviously we weren't going to come to any consensus, any greater understanding with this conversation. But at least I hadn't made her cry again.

"I'm just calling to let you know I got home safely," I told Mumma on the phone, after the Super Shuttle dropped me off in Venice. She had made me promise that I would call her as soon as I got home, even if it was late, Eastern Standard Time.

"Okay, sweetie, I'm glad you called."

"Sorry I wasn't so pleasant to be around," I said, and Mumma laughed. As we were saying goodbye, she came out with it: "I love you."

The Fourth of July, Labor Day, Thanksgiving. I was happy to spend these holidays hanging out with Bee or friends from the poetry workshop. But I always went home for Christmas, and not just because my family expected me to.

Christmas just wasn't Christmas without my father shuttling a tree a foot taller than him into the big bay window of the living room. Without fat lights and skimpy garlands unpacked from an old cardboard bicycle box from the attic. Without my mother insisting that only she hang her mother's heirloom ornaments—a blue peacock, an old tea kettle, a pink star. Without my father's last-minute shopping spree to Radio Shack to buy us cheap electronic gadgets. Without my mother's tissue paper-sheathed presents, the gift receiver's name scratched in pencil in her schoolteacher cursive. Without going to Sts. Sahag and Mesrob on Christmas Eve, my father purposely singing "Silent Night" loudly off-key so we would be mortified. Without the skinny wax candles we held while singing carols from Xeroxed sheets of music, a feeble old person accidentally setting his songs alight. Without Leo and I repressing laughter over the efforts of the parishioners to extinguish the fire. Without lying in bed at the end of the night, the pettiness of the day wiped away from consciousness, feeling a certain special Christmas sensation I didn't think I'd experience if I wasn't in Walpole reliving the morally imperfect Agabian traditions.

The next year, I arrived in Walpole on the 21st and was helping my parents decorate the tree when my friend Alisa from Wellesley called. We had plans that I would visit her in Vermont, where she now lived. Daddy said it was fine for me to borrow his car for a couple of days.

"You just got here!" my mother shrilled. "When are you going to do your Christmas shopping?"

"I can do it when I get back."

"On Christmas Eve?"

"What do you care? I'm twenty-four years old and you're telling me what to do?"

"I wouldn't mind but you just got here. That Alisa calls and you run."

I hated that my mother still thought I did whatever my friends wanted me to do. It just highlighted what my therapist Pat had said: my mother couldn't conceive of me as an individual with ideas and impulses separate from hers. She saw me as her little robot; if I veered from her wishes, someone else must be ordering her robot around, so she tried to reprogram me by claiming I was nothing but a robot with no mind of my own.

The whole concept was so maddening and absurd and... partially true that I threw three pillows across the living room at her, bam bam bam, right in a row.

"Was that necessary?" My mother asked, her hair mussed. "Throwing pillows at your mother?"

"Nancy," my father laughed. "You lost it."

The next morning, I woke up early and brought my duffel bag downstairs to the living room. My mother was already up, wearing her pink bathrobe and her hair in pin curls, watching The Weather Channel, which was forecasting light flurries. "Nancy, it's going to snow, I really don't think you should go."

"Ma, you're making way too big a deal out of this," I said. Daddy was making French toast at the stove as the snow started to appear, tiny dots in the sky.

"You can't go!" Mumma screamed. "You're going to get into an accident and die and ruin Christmas! Is it really worth it? Just to see your friend?" She was hysterical like I'd never seen her before, her face white, her eyes exploding. The yellow light of the kitchen seemed to freeze everything around her. I could only see her face and hear her screaming; I stopped breathing.

"You're going to get into an accident and die and ruin Christmas!" she screamed again, even louder, so much that I was forced to step out of the moment. This was not a typical mental fit, a struggle for control. This was something different, and it had nothing to do with me. I looked at my mother with both fear and concern.

"Nancy," my father said, looking at me knowingly. "Just go. Go!" He threw me his keys.

When I returned a couple days later, Mumma reluctantly gave me a hug, then asked me how my trip was. She wasn't angry or hysterical as we sat in the living room, chatting over the din of the TV. But she didn't seem to like me very much. "I still don't think it was necessary," she said, lidded eyes examining her nails as she filed.

I passed through Grammy's pantry, which smelled faintly of bananas and onions, and into the bright yellow kitchen. Auntie Ruth and Mel were working on the Christmas dinner. Grammy, standing in the kitchen doorway in her navy blue, belted sweater, wasn't involved with the meal preparation, since she'd been so ornery lately. I noticed she was bent over more from last year. "How are you Grammy?" I asked, standing in front of her. We were the same height.

She was frowning. "I'm awful, honey," she said. "Just awful."

I hugged her stooped shoulders. When I pulled away, she kissed me purposefully on the side of my lips, like she hadn't seen me in years.

"How ya doin', Ma?" Dad asked as he placed a bag of food on the table.

"Oxford yertal guzem," she said. I want to go to Oxford. The house in Oxford, where she had raised her family, which she had been renting out to tenants for the past twenty-five years, was now empty.

"You can't live out there alone, Ma," Daddy said. The house was about a three-hour drive away, in central Massachusetts. "You'll get lonely."

"No," she replied. "I wanna be by myself."

Ruth shook her head and Mel stared.

"You'll get out there and you'll want to come back," Dad said.

"No, I won't."

"You're never happy, Ma," he said.

She swore at him in Turkish and walked out. Daddy laughed.

"It's not funny Tip," Mel said. "We have to put up with this twenty-four hours a day. 'I want to go to Oxford, I want to go to Oxford. Why don't you let me go to Oxford?'"

"Well, why don't you?" I asked.

"Don't be foolish, Nancy," Ruth said, her chin jutting out. "She can't take care of herself. She'll be calling us to come out there and then she'll tell us we're bad daughters for making her live alone."

As we set the dinner table, my sister Valerie whispered into my ear, "Grammy said someone from the Board of Health has been visiting her lately."

"What?"

"I guess Aunties were screaming so bad at her one night that the neighbors called the police. And then Grammy told a neighbor that Aunties were beating her up."

I confronted Ruth during after-dinner cleanup. "Did you hit Grammy?"

"Oh, Nancy, I just pushed her a little. You know how she exaggerates. It doesn't compare to the verbal abuse I get from her. She says I'm running off to have an affair with the mailman or the gardener. I don't know how her mind is working. The other day she accused us of poisoning her." Her down-sloping eyes looked at me sadly.

I empathized with Ruth but wasn't consoled by her admission that she had pushed Grammy. Irrational emotional outbursts ran in my family; I had just lobbed three pillows at my mother's head. Worried about every-one and embarrassed that the Commonwealth of Massachusetts was now intervening, I had no idea what to do.

"I offered that maybe I could live in Oxford with her," Valerie said when we were alone in the bathroom, trying on the new clothes the Aunties had given us, just as we had when we were children. "But Aunties said she wouldn't be happy with that either."

"It seems they just can't accept her wanting to live on her own," I said. "She's driving them crazy but they won't let her go."

"How would you feel if your mother said she didn't want to be around *you?*" Valerie asked. It was hard for me to imagine, considering my mother told me a few days before that I would die if I left her.

Grammy was accusing Mel of stealing the birdseed when I made my entrance into the white, shag-carpeted living room, where everyone was opening presents. Mel tried to deflect Grammy's accusation by taking a deep breath, exhaling the anger and focusing on me. "It looks nice, Nansay. Do you like it?" Her eyes looked hopeful behind her big glasses.

The outfit was a simple, formfitting knit sweater and skirt in navy blue, something I would never wear. "I think it's a little small," I ventured.

"Pshaw, too small. It shows off your nice figure. That's what the young ladies are doing now." She touched my hair. "And why are you wearing your hair like this? Don't you want to look pretty?"

"No," I said.

Grammy suddenly appeared by my side. "Here," she said and gently grasped my hand. She led me up the stairs to the second floor and I followed her slowly, one step at a time, to her bedroom. She pulled up her *yoghan* and instructed me to look under the bed. There was a suitcase.

"My bag is packed," she said. "I'm ready to go to Oxford. You take me to Oxford, okay? You can drive. I want to go to Oxford."

I didn't know what to say. I couldn't imagine taking her out there, to cause more trouble.

"Please take me, okay? I want to go to Oxford and they won't let me go. But you can take me. You can drive. I want you to take me. Please take me to Oxford."

She pronounced Oxford as Ahxfudd. She said it again and again and again. She was reminding me of my mother when she screamed that I was going to get into an accident and die and ruin Christmas. Possessed. Years ago, as a child, she had been displaced from her home, and it had all been beyond her control. And now she wanted to go back, but her return was out of her hands too.

I looked into her brown eyes, ringed with grey, and shrugged my shoulders, unable to give her an answer. I rubbed her back, her scratchy sweater, her hard, bumpy spine. She turned to look out the window.

11. THE LAST OF HER

It was February when Bee moved out of our apartment. She claimed that it was because she had always wanted to live on the Eastside. One afternoon, I found her in the kitchen, dumping her Tupperware into a box; she hadn't told me how soon she was moving, and I was upset. We fought, had a heart to heart, and I got her to admit that she was moving to change the dynamics of our relationship. We remained friends but I spent a few years being angry with her before we truly parted ways.

I was alone, between roommates, when the phone rang on a Sunday morning. I heard Mumma say somberly into my ear, "Hello Nancy, this is your mother." This was an unusual salutation; she normally intoned "Hi Nancy!" in a quick, high voice, as if she'd suddenly caught a hummingbird.

"What's wrong?" I asked.

"It's your grandmother." She paused. "She's been taken to the hospital."

"What? Why?"

"She wasn't feeling well so your aunts called an ambulance. Your father just left for the hospital. I don't think he's going to make it in time."

"What are you talking about?"

"One of the major arteries to her heart was enlarged. The doctors found it a few weeks ago and told your aunts that she wouldn't survive an operation and that…she didn't have much time left."

"They didn't tell Grammy?"

"No, your aunts chose not to tell her. They thought she would be too upset."

"Did you know?"

"Yes, your father told me."

"Why didn't anyone tell me?" I asked.

"We were going to, but we didn't think it would happen so soon, Nancy."

"But there's a chance she'll be okay, right?"

"I suppose. I'll call when I have more news."

I stood frozen in the kitchen by the phone on the wall. *Grammy gone?* I had known she was elderly and that she would eventually die, but I hadn't actually prepared myself, especially for such an odd situation. My grandmother was somehow waived the right to know about her own death. It seemed unfair, though I could understand why my aunts thought the news would have damaged the little time she had left.

I was still standing in front of the phone when it rang again. "Nancy, your father called," Mumma said in the same tone as before, but half a pitch softer. "She's passed away."

I stared at the white door of my refrigerator and cried.

"Nancy," my mother tried to console me, "She led a long, healthy life."

"Okay," I said, crying.

"So many people suffer terrible illnesses for years. She was lucky."

I kept crying. "All right."

"Your grandmother was eighty-six or eighty-seven. Think of all the people who die when they're much younger."

Grief invading my chest, tears streaming, about to hyperventilate, I told my mother, "I think I have to go now." I knew she didn't want to hear me so stricken.

I would have gone to sleep right then, I was so exhausted, but I was still in my work clothes. Working part-time in a printmaking studio now, my t-shirt and pants were covered in various colors of printer's ink, and I didn't want to stain the sheets. *What does it matter?*

It would have mattered to Grammy. She kept everything absolutely clean, always. I stepped out of my clothes and instead of leaving them on the floor, threw them into the hamper.

Daddy met me at baggage claim. He was wearing a gray newsboy cap, khaki jacket and brown pants, the muddy colors matching his sallow skin. "Hi Nance," he smiled, giving me an uncharacteristically gentle embrace. He insisted on carrying my suitcase, walking swiftly ahead of me. "How was the flight?" he asked as we got into the car.

"It was fine," I said. "How are you?"

"Oh, I'm okay," he shrugged. It was one of those oppressively overcast days that never brightens up, and we rode in silence through Boston. I wanted to ask Dad why he hadn't informed me before about Grammy's state. But then he said, "I got to the hospital just a few minutes too late, but they let me in to see her anyway. Her eyes were closed, and she was so pale, and…" He was choking up. "Her mouth was open."

Daddy started to cry quietly, the set line of his mouth wavering. Everything about the way he cried was so particular to him, familiar, and yet it was the most unsettling thing I'd ever seen.

"I'm sorry Daddy," I said. I put my hand on his.

"I know honey," he said, squeezing my hand, a new awkward tenderness between us. We stayed like that, hands clasped, during the minute it took us to brush past the Boston skyline and submerge into the darkness of the Central/Artery Tunnel, then let go.

I peered into Grammy's coffin, expecting my breath to be knocked out of my chest. Instead I faced a grandmother with a bad makeover. Pink and purple powders were dabbed onto the face she rarely painted, just a bit of lipstick every now and again, and her gray-white hair was poufed four inches above her head.

I broke down sobbing.

When I sat back down, my mother whispered, "Nancy, you don't need to cry so much," her breath smelling of Tic Tac. "Your grandmother was old. She suffered very little."

I wiped my eyes and looked up to see Auntie Mel by the casket, lovingly stroking Grammy's new hairdo. "You look beautiful, Mother," she said in a soothing, soft voice. I felt sorry for her, that perhaps she regretted all the times she had lost her temper with Grammy. Then I felt angry, that she couldn't be this nice to her when she was alive. And then I felt sick. There was a certain calm to Mel; it seemed she finally had Grammy right where she wanted her, where she could truly be in control of their relationship.

I looked at my mother with a cool stare. Would I do the same to her some day? She set her jaw and downcast her eyes, shifting in her folding chair. Though my mother's relationship with her mother-in-law was strained, to say the least, it was still difficult to figure out her strange lack of sympathy for the rest of us who were mourning Grammy's loss. "I felt badly when my mother died," I remembered her saying. "But my poor grandmother felt even worse. They say that's the greatest pain there is, to lose a child." Perhaps Mumma had felt less entitled than her grandmother to mourn her mother, dying young and painfully from cancer. What would give us the right, then, she probably thought, to grieve my grandmother who lived a long life, who died pain-free? But, of course, Grammy *had* suffered.

The next day, at her funeral, I told one of Grammy's stories. She had told it to me the previous Christmas when I was asking her about her childhood. We were sitting across from each other at the yellow enamel kitchen table, and she told me that because she was a girl, she wasn't allowed to go to school. I asked her if she worked, and she said no, that everyone else in the family did the household chores. I asked her what she did all day.

"Me? I played."

"You played?"

She said, "I played with the birds. The birds came and I fed them from my hand, and I tied yarn to the bird's feet, so when the birds came back, I knew they were mine."

At the funeral, I commented, "Grammy gave love to her children and grandchildren the same way she tied yarn to the birds' legs. We will always come back to her. We will always be marked by her unconditional love." Then I passed out little pieces of the yarn from her knitting bag, to remember her by.

For my grandmother there were always people coming and going, friends and family, just like the birds. Love wasn't enough for them to return unchanged, still hers; she would have to mark them with something unique, an incredibly sad story, or the memory of an outrageous soul deeper than the deepest well on earth.

When it was time for her to leave, she left quickly and painlessly, as she had always wanted. Her daughter Agnes was by her side in the ER: she stroked her hair as Grammy peered out from her oxygen mask. The last words she heard were, "Ma, you're turning into an angel."

After the funeral, Agnes told Valerie and me the rest of the story of Grammy's exit.

"We were having dinner and Ma said, 'I'm feeling uncomfortable, I need to lie down,' and she went to go rest in the den. We checked on her, and she was sitting on the sofa with her skirt unbuttoned, and her face looked so drained. I asked, 'Are you okay Ma?' and she looked down to the floor at this clump. I didn't know what it was, and then I realized—it was her pantyhose."

"Oh," Valerie said, her eyes tearing.

"That's when we called the ambulance."

The aunts knew the end was imminent when Grammy took off her pantyhose. My grandmother possessed decorum over her body that would never allow her to do such a thing, under even the most extreme circumstances.

When I mentioned this to my sister, she told me that Grammy once insisted that Val wear a girdle. "She said that because of men, even she, an old lady, had to wear one all the time."

I was a little confused. "She felt like she had to wear a girdle to look good for men?"

"No, she wore it to protect herself from them."

The day after the funeral, I somehow managed to convince my parents to lend me a car to drive to the New England Aquarium in Boston. A woodworker from Vermont was driving down to meet me. As I waited for him, I watched the seals flop around in their watery chamber, slipping and sliding off fiberglass ice floes. I thought it unseemly to be having romantic adventure while mourning my grandmother—a woman who, in an effort to ward off wayward penises, wore girdles, or at least control top pantyhose, till the death.

Glenn was a friend of Alisa's boyfriend; when I had visited Vermont a few months before, we spent an evening as a foursome, having dinner and making a bonfire in the snow. I had suspected the whole situation was a setup, and I didn't appreciate it; Glenn was bald, wore a black woolen beret and a long brown beard. He was much older than me and rarely smiled during dinner, and then stared at me sullenly through the flames of the bonfire.

For dessert, Alisa and her boyfriend had made these really rich, alcoholic rum balls, which we were slowly savoring. They had also secured some mandarin oranges, which we peeled in one skin, creating little sculptures. The playfulness must have reminded us of childhood. "I like your braids," Glenn said to me. My hair was so long I could wear it in pigtails like I did when I was eight years old, the Wonder Woman stage.

"Thank you," I replied coolly.

"I remember I used to pull Sandy Sherman's braids when we played 'Boys Chase the Girls,'" Glenn said.

"I played that game too." I recalled.

At the end of the night, after Alisa and William had gone to bed, Glenn and I stayed up to play Gin Rummy. He couldn't stop smiling and I noticed his animated blue eyes and wiggly eyebrows. There was a light coming out of him and I momentarily lost the thread of the game, I was so giddy.

"I'm sorry, I keep screwing up," I said.

"That's okay. I would rather listen to you talk than play cards," he replied, his eyes aglow.

I went upstairs to the guest room and Glenn slept on the couch in the living room. I worried that he was expecting me to get physical with him, to consummate our connection, but I was mortified. Since Bee had left, I had dated a string of guys, mostly poets from the open readings, and the same fear came up with them too, but they were all misfits in some way, depressed or distant, so I hadn't dated anyone long enough for intimacy to be an issue.

The next morning, my door creaked open and I heard someone tiptoe in. Holding my breath, I pretended to be asleep until the footsteps retreated and the door thud shut.

He left a little plate beside my bed. Sections of an orange had been placed into the formation of a flower, and a rum ball was in the center.

Glenn peeked his head in to see if I was up yet.

"Thank you for the flower," I told him.

"I had a nice time last night," he said. He was dressed in his jeans and rumply sweater from the day before, and he lay propped on his elbow by the side of the futon on the floor. We giggled and smiled at one another, my long hair messy, his feet bare and arching nervously, while we ate the flower.

Upon my return to Venice, I found a letter from Glenn. It read, "It was great to meet you," the "great" underlined twice in blue pencil, red dots radiating from the word across the page, like an illuminated manuscript. "If you ever get lonely, give me a call and I'll fly out to L.A., really."

I wrote five drafts of my letter in reply, asking to see some of his artwork. He sent me pictures of bowls he had carved from burls; they were elegant, delicate and in some cases, translucent. I feared what a thirty-nine-year-old guy, who was exceptionally good with his hands, expected of me sexually. At the same time, I hoped he could show me the sex and relationship ropes. And although the three thousand miles between us made getting to know one another difficult, it was also comforting. How dangerous could this get with a whole continent in between our bodies?

Just a week before, I was telling Pat, my therapist, about a poem I'd written on how my Turkish girlfriend Emine and I had not known the definition of the word rape. In the end, my character says, "I wish I would get raped so that I could know what it means."

"A lot of women have fantasies about being raped," Pat said, "because they have confusion about dealing with men and they want to relinquish all control."

"I don't feel that way," I told her. "I'm angry at myself for being sexually inexperienced, and I'm afraid that if I do something wrong with a guy, he'll take his anger out on me."

"Nancy, why don't we talk about your relationship with your father? Was he affectionate when you were growing up?"

"Oh yeah, he was very affectionate."

"How so?"

"Well, sometimes he would get overcome with love and just reach out and grab you and hug you."

"He grabbed you?"

"Yeah, I mean, he wasn't rough or anything."

"But being grabbed doesn't sound very warm or tender. It sounds like an assault!" Pat said, her eyes wide.

"No, it wasn't an assault," I said. "He was never violent." I had just read *Bastard Out of Carolina* by Dorothy Allison, and I had heard stories from women in the poetry workshop suffering abuse far worse than the way Daddy screamed his head off from time to time, than the way he hit Leo with the broom handle.

These memories were streaming through my mind while I waited for Glenn, until his yellow truck interrupted them, as I now watched it pull into the parking structure. I caught sight of his formidable beard; it looked really unattractive and backwater. *Big mistake,* I thought.

My breath left my body as Glenn walked across the plaza. First he was a little man, then he got bigger and bigger and I could see he was wearing his black beret, a black leather jacket and jeans. His hands were in his pockets, his shoulders up to his ears, which were sticking out from the beret.

"Hi," he said, his soft voice belying his grizzly-man exterior. I looked into his blue eyes and recalled the rum ball, mandarin orange flower.

"Michael J. Fox owns the ostrich farm up there," Glenn said, pointing out his truck window at the hill next to his house. This was quite a coincidence because lately I had been having a lot of dreams about Michael J. Fox, who at that time, pre-Parkinson's disease, occupied a place in the public consciousness as an excitable little guy who tried to act like everything was normal when it wasn't.

Glenn shyly took me on a tour of his home, through the living room, sparsely furnished with an old couch and a few of his burl bowls, and up the staircase that led to the second floor. On the landing I noticed a rifle leaning against the wall.

"You have a gun?" I asked him.

"Yeah," he said.

"That's weird. I didn't expect that from you. I thought you were peace-loving."

"I am."

"Then why do you have a gun?"

"It's just…I don't ˌknow. It's just something I have in case of an emergency."

As we walked down the long hallway to his bedroom, I tried to suppress thoughts that Glenn was going to shoot me in the middle of the night.

I lay down on his bed. "I want to rest," I told him, and he lay down next to me and stroked my hair. We started to kiss, then took off our clothes. When he'd visited me in L.A. a couple of months before, we had experimented quite a bit—hand jobs, oral sex—but never intercourse. Now we mutually masturbated, and then Glenn got on top of me to insert himself, but something felt wrong, a sharp, impossible pain. I moved away from him and crossed my arms. *No thanks, Mister. No pummeling today.*

"What's wrong?" he asked.

"I can't do it."

"Don't worry about it. It's not a problem."

"It's not?"

"Well, it's kind of a fun problem. It's nice. It's *real* nice, because, well, you know how good it feels when you hold my penis in your hand? Well, imagine how great it'll feel in your vagina. It's just like kissing." His tone shifted between pleading and reassuring.

"Really?"

"Yes, only it's more intense. And we can practice so that we can even come at the same time."

What in the hell are you talking about? I felt like asking. Glenn was making sex sound like a voodoo ritual. Still, he had more experience than me, so I allowed that there must be some truth to his claim.

The next day when we were in bed, we tried again. I was breathing and relaxing and trying to open myself up instead of tightening myself up. I figured the tightening was causing the pain and I wanted to feel good and open so I was opening and opening and opening, just trying to be open and then he stopped. Everything just stopped.

"What happened?" I asked.

"You squeezed me out," he said.

I looked up. He was kneeling at my opening, flaccid, a disturbed look on his face.

When I got back to L.A., I questioned whether I should be with a guy. Wasn't it pretty obvious I was a big lesbian in denial if I was going around repelling penises from my vagina? It was like I was wearing some kind of an invisible girdle, an iron chastity belt inherited from my grandmother.

"Lots of women have the same problem," Pat assured me.

"Really?"

"Yes, some women have to trust a man on a number of levels—emotional, spiritual, intellectual, psychological—before opening themselves up to men. Our bodies give us messages for a reason."

Why hasn't anyone told me this *before?*

A few weeks later, Glenn and I broke up. It's a sordid story, involving me cheating on him with one of my co-workers at the printmaking studio. There was something very safe and familiar about Gary, since I worked with him every day, told him all my stories and heard all of his. He was my first friend who was a guy, and I'd never really felt like I was friends with Glenn; with his age and advice, he was more avuncular, parental, an authority of sorts.

"So, what, you wanna be with him now?" Glenn asked gruffly over the phone.

"Well, I don't know. He has a girlfriend."

"Nancy," Glenn said, his voice suddenly shifting to his soft, pleading tone, "there's a Taoist theory that when people fall in love, a string connects their souls—they're tied to each other. And other people may get twisted and caught in the string, which can confuse who you're attached to. But you can't just cut the string. The love will always be there."

I imagined all these people tied to each other, floating through the universe, getting snarled in a mass of string. And then I saw them in miniature, bobbing around inside of a mayonnaise jar with holes in the lid. I tried to see Glenn and I tied together, and Gary and his girlfriend tied together, and all our strings caught. But instead I saw Grammy, tying yarn to the birds' legs so she would know them when they came back.

Gary eventually cut his ties with me and returned to his girlfriend, and I reunited with Glenn when we met at Alisa's wedding in Vermont. It was prompted when I gave him a hand job in the cow field right after the ceremony. Later, he invited me to his motel cabin, which was surrounded by pine trees and reeked of Lysol. I drank two glasses of white wine very fast and could feel myself slipping deeper into the freedom of drunkenness.

Before I knew it, we started kissing, and suddenly I found myself naked on the sofa.

I'm going to do it this time, I thought, *no matter what.* I got on top of Glenn and slid his dick back and forth over my crotch and then I slipped it inside me.

No big deal. It felt pretty good.

I looked down. His dick was like a little pole connecting our bodies, and his thighs' circumference looked really small, compared to my fat thighs flopping all over the place.

I tried to bop up and down but it hurt. Glenn put his legs together and that was less painful for some reason. He put his hands gently around my back and said, "Here," and edged me off the sofa while he was still inside me. We landed on the floor with him on top. He thrust inside me in that classic way for a while, and it felt pretty nice, and then he fell out. And that was it. I was glad; finally God, I'd done it.

We went to the bedroom and I caught myself in the dresser mirror: my long hair was snarled, a huge black mess of a nest, and my skin, my breasts, were white and round, my lips flushed. I looked really feminine, and it was disturbing. Ever since I had parted ways with Emine, my Turkish girlfriend, for embracing her femininity—and her sexuality—at the age of fourteen, I had been shunning mine. My insides just never felt feminine; they felt neutral, without gender. My body lived in the real world, and I lived in my head; my feminine appearance dwelled outside the realm of my mind's control, and it could lead to something dangerous, like a scary man wandering around, just waiting to strike. This guy had been with me almost as long as I could remember, lurking at the edge of my consciousness. He shook Grammy and haunted her from the walls, crept around the woods with shoe polish on his head, and erupted out of my father with rage. He beat me up when I made fun of him. He pumped at me as if I weren't there. He kept a rifle on the landing in the stairwell. He was in every horror movie I'd ever seen and loomed in the culture at large. He was not just a regular guy to whom you gave over your tender insides, but a monster to protect yourself from for dear life.

Glenn, wearing a thermal shirt but no pants, walked towards the kitchenette to get a drink of water. I noticed his butt was round and white, his dick swinging as he returned. He told me that some girl had been flirting with him in the "laundrymat."

"Did you ask her out?" I asked.

"No."

"Why not?"

"Too shy."

I was a little jealous, though I had no right to be. "Do you like the Eagles?" I asked. Something about the way he said "laundrymat" reminded me of their folksy yet druggy tunes.

"What songs do they sing?"

"'Take it easy, take it easy, don't let the sound of your own wheels, drive you crazy.'"

"'There's a girl, good Lord, in a flatbed Ford slowin' down to take a look at me,'" Glenn said like he was recalling a poem. He laughed.

There was something about that line that seemed quintessentially Glenn, and it made me queasy. His ideal: a pretty girl flirting with him as appurtenance to a kind of life that only a thermal-shirt-wearing guy who hitchhikes through Winslow, Arizona could have.

Suddenly I felt famished, so I went to the fridge and gobbled down some French bread and cucumbers and tahini left over from the reception. And then in the middle of the night I felt sick and I threw everything up into the toilet, trying to avoid my feminine appearance in the mirror. Glenn was concerned but there wasn't anything he could do: I puked bile until morning when it was time to drive back down to Walpole. It was 5 A.M. on Sunday and there was no one on the road. My window was open and the country was green and still. I heaved into a plastic bag as I drove, the sound of my own retching filling up the space in my ears.

Auntie Ruth moved slowly up the stairs, and I followed her to Grammy's room. The aunts had wallpapered it with a flower pattern, but besides this difference, it was practically the same as before she died. Ruth had recently moved in, out of her old blue room at the end of the hallway.

She opened Grammy's top dresser drawer. "Here, Nancy, do you need some slippers? Grammy never wore these. Oh, and here's some material. Do you sew?" She was breathing hard and avoiding my eyes, trying not to cry. Right after Grammy died Ruth had spent a lot of time here, smelling Grammy's clothes.

I opened the second drawer, filled with little jewelry boxes and gifts people had given her that she kept but never wore. I noticed a round photograph, a picture of me and Grammy, mounted on a button you could pin to a jacket. I vaguely recalled making it at a booth at St. James' annual church bazaar.

I must have been around fifteen. Short layered hair. Wearing a ton of eyeliner, spread into the inner rims of my lids. Just found out my sister was a lesbian. Afraid I was one myself. Posing on a button with my grandmother. She's smiling wide, no makeup, her hair not styled. We made a funny pair; above and beyond everything, she was my friend.

Auntie came towards me holding an old lace dress.

"It's beautiful," I said.

"I was going through her closet, Nancy, and I found this black trash bag on the floor way in the back and I threw it at Agnes, thinking it was rags, and she opened it up and lo and behold, it's Ma's wedding dress, crumpled into a ball. Can you imagine?"

No, not exactly—I couldn't imagine what it would have been like to be expected, no, forced to live an adult woman's life at the age of sixteen, after brutally losing so many loved ones; I couldn't begin to picture her a lifetime later, long after she had been widowed, when she, the most conscientiously clean woman, feverishly wringed a hallowed garment in on itself, into nothingness, like a dirty rag—no, not at all. But a part of me, something in me, could understand that sort of rage.

12. WORDS AND MOVEMENT

Wearing a costume of thin white cotton pajamas, I faced a packed house of Armenians in the tiny back room of a cafe in Pasadena; they were close enough to hear my heart beating. Attempting to manufacture an emotional distance, I looked into the back row and announced in a stage voice, "This performance is called *The Crochet Penis.*"

A woman in her late forties, sitting to my right, our knees almost touching, said with an accent, "Ugh, why they have to call it that?" to no one in particular.

A sixteen-inch phallus, which I had crocheted out of red yarn, lay across my lap. It was connected to a red ball of yarn nestled between my breasts and the opening of my pajama top. I held the phallus with both hands at its center and gently stroked outwards. Repeating the motion methodically, I announced, "It has been a year since my grandmother died. All grandmothers die. It is the nature of grandmothers to die, but fuck you, mine was different. Every time I think she is gone I get upset so I start to think about sex instead. Sex with a man and his penis. Because I met a man and his penis right when my grandma died. So I think about the act of intercourse which I have fear about…"

I continued reciting the poem, changing my movements with the content of the poem: stroking the phallus more quickly; pulling on it so that it flapped; stopping; stroking slowly again; then more feverishly until I was whipping it against the floor.

I had started performing *The Crochet Penis* around town a couple of months before. A series of six poems, the performance was memorized so that I could look directly at the audience. But I was having trouble making eye contact at the Museum Café in Pasadena. A lot of people were looking down, showing me the crowns of their heads. Those who were looking up were staring into space, their eyes glassy. I tried not to look at the lady to my right.

I'd been invited to perform for my first Armenian audience by my friend Raffi, who two years previously had read one of my poems in a local journal and tracked me down. Raffi was something of a provocateur; he had written a couple of plays—one about an Armenian man in love with a black woman, another about a Turk and an Armenian discussing the genocide— that had attracted large Armenian crowds, but he'd received a brick through his window for dealing with such controversial topics.

"Wow," I had said. "Didn't that scare you?"

"Not really," Raffi shrugged. "Armenians have to look at themselves. They don't like what they see so they blame me."

As I started my third poem, I placed the crocheted phallus on the chair between my legs so that it dangled off the front edge. Then I grabbed the ball of yarn between my breasts and rolled it around them, underneath my shirt, reciting a poem about one of my sexual fantasies involving a lingerie model. When I dropped the ball of yarn into my pants and rubbed it on my crotch, the lady who had asked "Why they have to call it that?" huffily stood up and pushed her way out of the room.

In effect, I was fucking a ball of yarn, but in the moment, I thought I was simply executing a movement that corresponded to the text. I couldn't imagine why the lady was so offended. I felt a surge of adrenaline—no one had ever walked out on one of my performances—and continued reciting.

For the last poem, I unraveled the crocheted penis and stated, "I have been tending my mother and grandmother's soft member for years and I don't want to anymore. I don't want to be afraid of my body, his body, her body. I want to make this crochet penis a blood line, a family woman blood line that can be strong too."

The Crochet Penis was a personal ritual of memorized words and tightly choreographed movements. I exorcized my feelings about sex to an audience in order to quell my alienation, imagining that this made for a powerful theatrical experience. But now I worried that people saw me as little more than a perv.

Seated in the audience after my act, I noticed an older couple in their early sixties. His combover and her costume jewelry recalled my parents. Their daughter was reading too, and afterwards, I somehow found myself being introduced to them, suddenly wishing I were wearing a bra. Shaking their hands, I wondered if I should apologize for besmirching their sensibilities with my petty sexual problems. But the mom said, "That was a wonderful performance. You said some very important things."

The dad said, "Thank you for expressing yourself so honestly."

Holy Shit, I thought as I stood there, smiling stupidly. "Thank you. That means a lot to me. You remind me of my parents and I can't invite them here … since they live in Boston." *Never mind that I would prefer to stick my crochet hook into my eye and pull out my left frontal lobe.*

As I trolled the crowd for more compliments, I saw the lady who had stormed out earlier. Her dyed blond hair was a honey color that looked mellowed with age, as if it had been coiled into rollers for thirty years. I held my breath as she passed in silence, pointedly ignoring me.

I was thankful I didn't have to deal with a confrontation, but the lady stayed with me as I rolled ink over my palette the next morning at work: red, then black, then red again.

When the tape finished playing, I turned off the TV and faced my students. "Writing and Performing and Telling the Truth" at the 18th Street Arts Complex in Santa Monica consisted of five students, women ranging in age between twenty-five and fifty. I could barely make it to the class without having a nervous breakdown, until I decided that all I had to do was help the class write and perform and tell the truth as best I could. Still, none of them seemed too impressed with me, until now.

"That was amazing. I didn't know you had it in you," one of them said.

"Has your family ever seen your performances?" another asked.

"No," I said. "They live in Boston."

"So you haven't shown them the tapes?" still another prodded.

I should show my family my work, I thought. *That's what any confident teacher-type person would do.*

But there's no way I can do that, I thought in response.

"I didn't write this performance for my family," I finally answered, ejecting the tape.

The five students nodded their heads, some empathetically, some with no expression at all, but I was sure they were disappointed.

Valerie sat next to me on the couch as I popped the tape into the VCR. She was visiting for Thanksgiving and watching the performance intently, her dark eyes darting around the screen. Slouching into the low sofa, her eyebrows furrowed during the fifth poem when I bound my legs with yarn and then unwrapped them:

> My grandmother was different. She saw her mother die, she saw her sister die, she saw her brother and father get dragged away to die and after a long death walk through the desert in circles she survived disease, death camps, orphanage and rape. After all that and a family she created to replace the real brothers and sisters she was more like a sibling than a mother to them my grandfather said, and she didn't wanna be touched. My father saw this

and he wed a woman, my mother and she didn't wanna be touched, and I saw this and I didn't wanna be touched. I am different now.

Valerie picked a crumb off the couch, looked at it, and started crying. The tears were suddenly streaming down her face.

"Should I turn it off?" I asked, taken aback.

"No," she said. I ran to the bathroom and grabbed some tissue but she was already wiping her face on her pajama sleeve when I returned.

She watched the rest of the video in silence.

"Why did you cry?" I asked as I ejected the tape from the VCR.

"I don't know," she said quietly.

"Was there something that upset you?" I asked.

"I don't know," she said again.

I was confused. "How can you not know what upset you?"

"I don't know. Didn't other people cry when they saw it?" she asked.

"No," I said. "No one cried."

A few days later, Val and I were driving through Santa Barbara, up the coastal Route 1 to Santa Cruz to visit some of her friends. "Want some more 'stachios, Nance?" Val asked. We were an hour into the trip and halfway through a one-pound bag of pistachios.

"No thanks," I said. "Can you put them away? I'm addicted."

"Yeah," Val said. "They're very addictive."

"Hey," I said, as casually as I could, "Did you use to smoke a lot of pot?" I figured while I had her captive in the car I may as well ask her things I couldn't when I was a kid.

"Yeah, I smoked a lot of pot in high school and college and when I lived at 1126."

"When did you stop?"

"Well, when I started going out with Miriam, she pointed out that I was getting stoned a lot. I don't think it's addictive, but I think it takes away your motivation."

We were silent for a while as I tried to figure out how to ask my next question.

"Um, so, did you have sex a lot with guys when you were in high school?"

"No, I didn't have sex until I was with Chuck," she said. "Why do you want to know?"

"When I was in the sixth grade Jennifer Rohner told me that you did."

"Rohner? Oh yeah. I knew her brother. Well, I did fool around with guys, but I didn't lose my virginity until I was with Chuck."

Valerie met Chuck when she was twenty. I was twenty-three when I had sex for the first time, just two or three years behind my sister's estimated virginity-losing age. *Maybe I'm not such a loser after all,* I thought.

When we got to Big Sur, we had our pick of campsites at the State Park, empty in late November. It was dusk as we wandered about, ending up in a circle of five redwoods. They towered above us, the ground concave beneath, like a drooping trampoline. I flung myself against a redwood and closed my eyes and vibrated, the bark rough against my hands and cheek. My acupuncturist told me that hugging trees would be beneficial for releasing the chi of my liver—the source, as she saw it, of my panic attacks.

I peeled myself from the tree and yelled "Let's put the tent here!" to Valerie at the car.

"Okay," she said. She lumbered towards me, a wide-eyed look on her face. When she was close enough to give me the tent, she whispered, "I don't think I can sleep in this spot."

"Why not?" I asked.

"It's too intense."

I looked up at the mammoth prehistoric trees. They possessed a certain sacred togetherness, I thought, like a family. But I didn't mention this to Val—she seemed to have her own primal feelings about it.

"Okay," I whispered to her.

We rustled back to the car and set up the tent nearby. "BBRRRRR!" Valerie said.

"I told you it was going to be cold."

"I guess I didn't think it got cold in California."

Once inside our sleeping bags, trying to get warm, Val asked, "Nance, did you hear that noise?"

"It's the trees. They're so big that they creak when they shift. I read about it at the visitor center."

"Oh, okay," she said nervously.

I put my head down on my sweatshirt, a makeshift pillow. I could hear rustling outside, so I tucked my mouth inside my sleeping bag so that the only sound I heard was my own breathing. I told myself to relax; I'd gone camping plenty of times with friends who felt perfectly comfortable sleeping in a tent, who weren't convinced that a crazed woodsman was sneaking through the forest searching for victims to hatchet to death.

"Nance," my sister said.

"What?" I asked.

"I'm scared."

I sighed and propped myself up on my arm. Val's form was a dark lump. "Can you turn on your flashlight?" The beam hit the tent wall and softly bounced onto her face. Her eyes were smaller than mine, like Daddy's, but very dark. "What are you afraid of?" I asked Val.

"I'm afraid someone will come into our tent and attack us," she said.

"Look, I think we're safe," I tried to assure her, also reassuring myself. "There are people living in those cabins by the visitor center and there's probably a ranger still at the entrance. No evildoer is going to be out to-night, anyway. It's too friggin' cold." It was strange for me to be placating her now, since she had always seemed so fearless to me. I must have been looking at her funny, because her face changed abruptly.

"Okay," she said. "You're right." She turned off the light.

Before I could fall asleep I heard her say "Nance" one last time.

The next day, we were standing in the lobby of Sweet Tomatoes in Santa Cruz, waiting for Val's friends Tracy and Laura. Sweet Tomatoes was a corporate cafeteria kind of place, complete with pumped in music. I was asking Val what kind of earthy-crunchy Santa Cruz lesbians would ask us to meet them here when they suddenly appeared.

Tracy, a strawberry blond in little round glasses, a skirt, and clogs with homemade socks, hugged Val. Laura her butch, Jewish counterpart then followed. "This is my little sister Nancy," Val introduced.

We sat down in a booth, peeled off our coats and attacked the buffet. As we ate, we chatted about celebrities. I was always surprised whenever I found myself discussing pop cultural matters with lesbians. For some rea-son, I expected them to talk solely about their cats and the empowerment of women. At the time, Jerry Seinfeld had just broken up with his nineteen-year-old girlfriend. "Did you know that Jerry Seinfeld's girlfriend was a teenager?" Tracy asked.

"We were *all* teenagers dear," Laura joked.

Then Valerie said, "Nancy wasn't a teenager. She went from being a kid to a sixty-year-old woman."

What? "That wasn't very nice," I said.

"Oh, I'm sorry, Nance. I didn't mean it that way."

"What way did you mean?"

Valerie looked at me blankly. Then she looked at her friends and re-peated, "We were *all* teenagers, dear," and laughed.

I couldn't make sense of Val's jab, which came out of nowhere. Para-noid, I took it as an accusation of never having fun, never having sex, never doing drugs, never doing anything.

After dinner, Val and I were silent in the car as we followed Tracy and Laura back to their apartment. One of us would sleep on the couch and the other on the floor.

"I HAD FUN!" I suddenly yelled. "You have no right to make fun of me and call me an old lady!" I screamed at Valerie.

"I'm sorry, Nance," she said.

"I try very hard," I said, crying now. "I think a lot about my life and who I am and why I'm afraid of sex and I'm doing my best."

"I didn't mean anything about sex," Valerie said, perplexed.

"Then why did you cry when I showed you *The Crochet Penis?*"

"It was upsetting."

"Why?"

"I don't know."

"You don't know why you said I was never a teenager and you don't know why you cried?"

"Nance, sometimes I say or do stuff and I don't know where it comes from. All I can say is I'm sorry."

"Well all I can say is I'm getting the couch tonight."

Later, in the darkness, I gazed at the dolphin-shaped candles and rainbow motif mobile in Tracy and Laura's living room while Valerie shifted on the floor.

I hadn't realized how important it was for her to understand *The Crochet Penis*. I could have accepted her crying at the video as validation. But I wanted words. Val was always more intuitive and free-spirited than me; I believed her when she said she didn't know why she blurted out that I was a sixty-year-old woman. It must have been annoying to have your younger sister telling you who she thought you had been and judging who you were now. And it must have been upsetting to have your family history broadcast back to you on a video screen. I was hurt that Val said I was an old lady, but more disappointing was that she and I didn't seem able to speak the same language.

Leo and I were walking to the beach down Grand, an unusually wide street lined with bungalows, yards overflowing with plants, the scent of jasmine filtering through the air.

"I can't believe how beautiful it is here," Leo said. I didn't know if I'd ever heard him engage in pleasant small talk before. Come to think of it, this was the first time we'd spent time alone together as adults. Leo was visiting me for a week; he'd just arrived this morning, a few months after Valerie's visit.

When we got to the boardwalk, he seemed edgy, consumed with finding the perfect place to sit. He walked with a bouncy gait, in his ironed white polo shirt, turning his head in every direction, searching for a bench, but they were all full. "Why don't we just go down to the beach and sit on the sand?" I asked.

"No, I don't want to sit on sand," my brother said. "Here." He grabbed my hand and led me to a low concrete wall and we watched the skateboarders practice, clacking their boards when they landed.

It was an incredible day. The sky was bright blue, a nice breeze. It was getting to be spring and Leo said, "Well, Nancy, it's time you should know I'm queer."

The word "queer" dislodged me and I laughed. For just a second. I looked at my brother, in his sunglasses, a palm tree behind his head.

I swallowed and asked, "When did you figure this out?"

"I've known for a while. Well, all my life. But I just admitted it a few years ago."

"Really? You've known since you were a little kid?"

"I was hoping it wasn't true."

"Did you go out with any girls?"

"No, not really. I mean, there were a couple that I thought I liked. But then I just realized my attraction to guys was too strong."

"Have you told Mumma and Daddy?" I asked.

"No, not yet. You're the first person in the family I've told."

I looked down at my hands, stunned.

"So my plan is to move out of the house and then tell Mumma and Daddy." He was looking out at the ocean.

"That's great Leo," I said. "I'm really happy for you."

"Do you have any more questions?" he asked. It occurred to me then that Leo must have assumed I was straight. I hadn't told him anything about my life because he had always seemed so rigid, living with my parents, working as a temp at a financial services firm and fancying himself a yuppie. But now he was telling me he was open, amenable even.

"Do you have a boyfriend?" I asked.

"No, not yet."

"Are you going to tell Aunties?"

"I don't know. Maybe."

"You know all those times you made fun of the Dicks? What was that all about?"

"Oh God, well I'm sure I was dealing with my own homophobia."

"What did you think when Val came out?"

"I thought it was bizarre that there were two gay people in our family."

"I'm bisexual."

"You are?" His eyebrows raised above his sunglasses and he opened his mouth wide.

I told him the story of Bridget and then the story of Bee. He listened intently, nodding his head. The fog rolled out and there we were, seeing each other. It was like we were friends. Or something.

There really wasn't anything to see at Florence and Normandie. Just some vacant lots and a shut down mini-mart. But it was ground zero of the L.A. riots, where Reginald Denny was dragged out of his truck and beaten. Leo had requested we swing by. I was curious too, but now as we were nearing it, I felt weird; I didn't think we should be treating it like a tourist attraction.

The verdict was a shock; how could anyone let those cops, beating a black man on videotape, get off? Three days of fires and looting and curfews;

the National Guard closed off the boardwalk; a police state. I went out two mornings later with a broom and helped sweep out a looted Sav-On Drugs, but found it more meaningful to write poems with the workshop: *It's taken me 24 years/ to learn I'm embarrassed/to be dark skinned and/it's wrong.*

It was a year later and there was nothing at the intersection of Florence and Normandie. No people, no buildings, nothing.

"This is it?" Leo asked. "It didn't look like this on TV."

I felt jittery, as if something bad were going to happen.

"Turn around," Leo said. "I wanna see it again."

"No, I don't want to," I said.

"Why not?"

"Because, I just don't!" I yelled. It bothered me that Leo seemed fine and I was a wreck, a scared whitey. I changed the subject. "I wanna take you to Watts Towers."

A local man had built the structures from marbles, bottlecaps and broken dishes, bit by bit in his back yard over the years, and now they were the site of a community art center.

"This is what you wanted me to see?" Leo asked. He had a disgusted look on his face; his lips curled around his teeth.

"Yes, this is what I wanted you to see!" I exploded.

"You're a bitch!" he yelled.

"Don't call me that!" I screamed.

"Well I'm sorry, that's what you are. You're being a bitch to me because I told you I'm gay!"

He threw off his seat belt; the metal part hit the window with a crack and he stormed off.

Lying awake in bed, I wondered if Leo was okay. After we'd returned from Watts Towers, he had taken off for Roosterfish, a gay bar on Abbot Kinney Blvd. It was a five-minute walk from my apartment through the streets of old Craftsmen bungalows. It was silly, but I worried about him walking home alone. I stayed awake until two in the morning when the place closed.

Leo stumbled in around 2:15 and fell on top of my old futon on the floor.

I sat up and looked down at him from my bed. "I was worried about you."

"Don't worry 'bout me," he said. His speech was a little slurry.

"I thought you were dead in an alley over there."

"Oh please, you think those queens at Roosterfish could kill somebody? Honey, they couldn't hurt a fly if they tried." It seemed that Paul Lynde had risen from the dead and materialized in my bedroom.

"Can you keep it down, please," I snapped at him. "My roommate might wake up."

"You're *so* uptight," Leo accused, stumbling out of his pants.

"That's a laugh," I scoffed. "None of my friends think I'm uptight."

"Well, they don't know you like I know you."

"Huh? They know me a *lot* better than you."

"They know you better than your own family?"

The question startled me. Leo was implying his family knew him better than anyone, but he had just told one of us, for the first time, that he was gay.

"Yeah. There are a lot of things I haven't told you," I said softly.

"Like what?"

"I'm not telling."

It seemed then that my problem with Leo wasn't so much that he was gay. Somehow, with all that we had become, he was still my big brother, and I was still his little sister.

The next summer, I found myself in the backseat of Ruth's car, riding with all three aunties through Watertown.

"Nancy," Ruth said, "A friend of your cousin Claire saw you in a play recently."

"Oh really?" I asked. Claire was the daughter of my grandfather Jacob's much younger brother, Max. I had never met her. She was around my sister's age, lived in Marina del Rey, and worked as a publicist. At my aunts' prodding, I had called Claire when I first moved to L.A. Her voice had been kind and upbeat on the phone and we made plans to get together, but her mother Ronnie became ill so we postponed indefinitely.

Claire's friend must have seen me perform and asked her if we were related, since our shared last name is pretty unique.[3] The question was, what had the friend seen me in?

"She said it was a lesbian play called *Buns*," Ruth said.

A deadly tense silence overtook the green Ford Torino.

"Bah!" I burst out laughing.

"Is it true Nancy?" Mel asked.

"No! I was never in *Buns!*" I sputtered.

"See, I told Ronnie you wouldn't do something like that," Ruth said.

I felt guilty that I wasn't confessing the truth, but mainly I was awed that the gossip mill of my extended family had transformed *The Crochet Penis* into a Sapphic production about asses. Apparently it wasn't safe for me to be myself, even in L.A. I had a spy, one with my same name, reporting my un-Armenian activities to my family. It seemed I could either continue living in fear that I'd be found out, or I could just come clean.

My parents were visiting me the following Easter, when I informed them, in the middle of an antiquated 1950s dining room at Canter's

---

[3] Its original version—Agababian—is not uncommon, but Max shortnened it to Agabian when he went to the U.S. Naval Academy in Annapolis, MD in the Thirties, and then my grandfather followed suit.

Deli, that I'd just completed a manuscript of my poems. It was entitled *In Between Mouthfuls,* and there were about twenty-five poems in it, *The Crochet Penis* functioning as a turning point. Placing the manuscript on the table, I said, "There are some poems in here that are about you and they might seem angry. But the good news is that I have less resentment towards you because I wrote them."

"Well that *is* good news," Daddy said in a deadpan voice, rolling his eyes at Mumma.

"I just want to let you know that I don't blame you for anything and that I love you very much. Oh and there's some stuff in here about my sexuality too."

"Well, Nancy," Mumma began in her diplomatic tone, "they say that writers do write about what they know, and I think it's perfectly natural that you would write about us, and that you would see things differently from how we as parents see things. In fact," she continued, "I think even *siblings* see things very differently from each other, you know, because each child is born unique, with his or her own personality. Some are shy, some are more outgoing…"

I tuned Mumma out. I knew where she was going. To the nature side of the nature vs. nurture debate. Standing firm on the nurture side, I interrupted her. "Okay, okay, I get the point," I said, handing her the manuscript.

She laughed nervously and put on her reading glasses, the kind found on plastic rotating stands in drugstores. My mother had about fifteen pairs which she kept in the bottom of her pocketbooks, along with her emery boards. The scratched magnified lenses turned her eyes into saucers, and the passé frames were entirely too large for her face. "In between mouthfuls," she read in a smooth voice, proudly peering at me with her big black marbles.

"Ma, can't you get better looking glasses? Those are awful!"

"Yes, tell her Nancy," Daddy joined in. "She looks like Mr. Magoo!"

"They're just my reading glasses; they don't matter," Mumma said in a surly way and directed her big-eyed focus on the manuscript.

Shit, I thought. *Now she's really going to read it.*

Mumma read the first poem on the first page quietly to herself.

She didn't teach me to clean:

The difference between 6 and 13

foot aches and
ear aches from
growing at night so
I yell "fresh
mil-kie in a gla-
ass" and she

brings it up
the stairs slow
and breathing her
hands always
smell pink and have
that mother
temperature "here

honey" her face

smooths out
above me
I take it in that
lying awkward down
sick-served
elbow mode my older

pubie sister is across

the way watching us and
turning over sigh when
I say thank you
and sip it and put it
on the window sill
leave it there

my mother can't deal

with everything and
forgets so I watch it
turn hard and yellow
smelly like the
teen girl cotton
underpits and crotches
stomped with other
stuff on the floor
and the inside of my
four lower front
teeth she didn't teach me
to clean

"Nancy, this makes it sound like it was my fault your room was messy.
I was always after you kids to clean up your room," my mother said.

"It's not *really* about that," I said.

"You're saying that you didn't know how to brush your teeth because
I didn't teach you?" Her mouth was stretched into a confused scowl.

"Well, not exactly," I hedged. "The poem is about how parents change
when their kids go through puberty. That maybe the parents are repelled by
this formerly cute kid who's changing into a sexual being. So in the poem,
the mother is nice to the little sister, but the older sister is angry because

she's no longer getting the same kind of attention. It's like the parents freak out when their kids go through puberty, and the kids can pick up on it."

"You don't freak out," my mother said.

"You don't," I said flatly.

"No, it's very normal for kids to go through puberty," Mumma said, taking off her glasses. "I really don't think the parents change any of the ways they treat their children. It's the kids who are changing. Maybe they *think* the parents are treating them differently, but the parents know it's normal."

"Look," I said, getting angry. "I know what I'm talking about because I lived through it and I know you treated me differently once I went through puberty."

"Is that so?" Mumma asked, biting her lip.

"Yes," I gulped. "Because *you're* afraid of sex, so you wanted to protect me from it."

"You're afraid of sex?" Daddy asked Mumma.

"I'm not afraid of sex, Nancy," Mumma said, shaking her head.

"Yes you are! If you're not afraid of sex, why did you never want me to have a boyfriend when I was a teenager!"

"I never said I didn't want you to have a boyfriend!"

"Yes you did! You said that boyfriends were unimportant and it was better for me to concentrate on my studies."

"Well, that's very different from telling you not to have a boyfriend."

I can't believe this. Suddenly my mother was Dr. Ruth, and everything I'd figured out in therapy, everything I'd written about, was being shattered.

"I know that you're afraid of sex!" I insisted. "You were never supportive of me as a sexual person!" People at other tables turned around and looked at us.

Daddy laughed. "Nancy, calm down."

"I'm going to the ladies' room," Mumma said.

Now I was left with my father. The feeling was reminiscent of a childhood experience of being taken by him to a doctor's appointment because Mumma couldn't. I could tell he liked being able to share in the experience, never having done it before, but it made me nervous to get naked in front of him. He was my *dad* after all.

I watched out of the corner of my eye as he read the poem Mumma had just read, moving his lips. Finally he sighed and said, "Well, your mother is a little repressed, it's true Nancy. You don't think I'm repressed, do you?"

"Yes," I said through gritted teeth. I resented the way he was taking this opportunity to prove he was the better parent.

"Oh, no," he said. "I'm not sexually repressed."

I prayed for my mother to get back from the bathroom.

"I'm what you call freewheelin'."

"Okay, storytime is over," I said and grabbed the manuscript from him.

My mother came back from the ladies room and sat down. Little old ladies teetering over their bowls of matzo ball soup were looking at us intermittently between slurps, waiting for more antics from the sexually conflicted family.

"I'm not very hungry," Mumma said. "I want to go back to the hotel."

I was about to walk out the door of my apartment to present a new performance, *My Gay Family*, at Highways performance art space, when the phone rang. It was Mumma.

"Oh, hi Ma," I said, a little spooked. This was the fourth time that she called me right before I was leaving the house to perform.

"How are you?" she asked.

"I'm fine, Ma, but I'm about to walk out the door," I said, carefully avoiding the fact that I was going to do another performance about the impact of my Armenian-American family on my identity.

"Oh, okay, I won't keep you then. I just wanted to see if you got the package I sent."

"Yes, yes I did. Thank you."

My mother had sent me a pair of ceramic salt and pepper shakers. The salt formed the front half of a chicken, the pepper its rear.

"Do you like them?" She giggled with anticipation.

I hated them. "Uhm, yeah. Look Ma, I'm going to be late if I don't go now."

"Okay, sweetie, have a good time."

Though I was sure she would never understand me, with our arguments and her bad gifts, the timing of my mother's calls, right before my most important moments of showing myself not to her, but to everyone else, served to remind me that she and I were undeniably connected on some unconscious, mysterious, yet wholly loving plane.

I arrived at the auditorium of the Glendale Public Library a half-hour early to perform my new performance *WANT*. A friend of Raffi's had invited me to perform for an Armenian reading series.

As I walked in, I noticed a woman sitting in the empty seats. It was the lady who walked out on me during *The Crochet Penis* at the cafe in Pasadena. She looked at me, stuck out her hand, and said *parev*.

I took her hand shyly and said, "Hi."

"Are you the one who did the *The Crochet Penis?*" she asked.

"Yes," I answered.

She replied in Armenian.

"I don't speak Armenian," I told her.

"Oh, it's a pity," she said. "*The Crochet Penis* was very powerful," she said in earnest. I wondered if I were mistaken about her identity. She looked just like the lady, though—same old moldy honey-colored hair. "Did you bring your yarn?" she asked.

"No, I'm not doing that piece today."

"Why not?" she asked.

"I wrote it about three years ago and it's hard for me to perform now since I feel differently," I answered, still partly on guard.

"You should perform it. It's a very powerful piece. Especially for Armenians to see."

"Thank you," I said, smiling and completely perplexed.

When it was time to perform, I stood on a chair with a king size white sheet over my head and clutched it around my face, like the Virgin. Then I sang the words to *The Mary Tyler Moore Show* theme song extremely slowly, one word at a time, like a church dirge:

"Who... can... turn... the... world... on... with her smile."

When I got to the word "love" ("Love is all around no need to waste it"), I choked. Then I told the audience about two six-year-old girls, conjoined at the hip, who were two people from the waist up and one person from the waist down. After each comment, I blew into a plastic tube poking out from my sheet. A bulge slowly grew on my left side.

I told the audience that the twins had been featured in TIME magazine, which printed a diagram of their shared internal organs, including a rib cage, a large intestine, and a vagina. I focused on what it would mean to share a sex organ not with someone you were attracted to, but whom you loved. I speculated how the twins would masturbate, separately or together? And then I claimed I wanted to be like them:

> I would finally be connected to the earth if another soul could know what it's like to have my clit, my vagina, my wiggly Kegel muscles. When people are in love, they want to join their bodies, they want to get inside of each other. But this privilege of letting someone into my body has been very hard to negotiate. If I let you inside my body, you are going to take a little part of me with you every single time until there is nothing left inside of me but you. The twins don't have this fear. They are the only people on earth who truly know what it means to love each other and to be joined, to negotiate, to share insides, while still maintaining separate identities.

I took off the sheet to reveal an inflatable doll attached to my hip.

The lady was the first to raise her hand during the question and answer session. "Yes, hello. I saw *The Crochet Penis* two years ago, and I want to know if all your work has sexual themes?"

"Not *all* of it. But a lot of it, yes."

"I saw the television program on the twins," she said, "and it is really a tragedy. They have been in a lot of pain. Their parents should have separated them but now they can't, and I don't think it is appropriate for you to make fun of them."

"Well, that's not the way I interpreted it. I read that the twins didn't want to be separated, and the parents honored their wishes." Then I paused. "Basically I wanted people to appreciate their predicament while making fun of my own problems. That's why I said in the piece I didn't mean to exploit them—"

"But you did," she said sharply. She was hugging her pocketbook to her side. She reminded me of my mother when she got angry. She reminded me of the uptight lady who walked out on my performance. *It's her!*

She continued with her attack: "It was not serious poetry, it was more of a low-class comedy act."

"It wasn't presented as poetry," I responded with a red face, "it was presented as performance art." At this point a few audience members reiterated to her my point.

"I am a literature professor!" she yelled. "I know what I am talking about. I could have told you in private, but I wanted everyone to hear my opinion."

Several people shouted, "Who said we wanted to hear it?"

"Oh, go find yourself a penis!" she yelled, walking out on me a second time.

A young woman with long, curly hair raised her hand and said, "I really liked your performance and I hope you don't stop doing it because of her."

Another woman raised her hand and asked, "What is it about Armenians that makes them so uptight about sex?"

"Yeah, why do we have to act like Armenians are the only people on earth who don't have a sexuality?" a boy sitting next to her said.

Another woman stated, "There are so few Armenians in the world, that we treat each other as if we're all family. That's why that woman felt she could act that way with you."

Later, I wondered how it came to be that the intimacy of Armenian families often took the form of attack and condemnation, leading to self-righteous rejection. The lady's reaction was my worst nightmare come true, how I imagined my family would respond if they ever saw me perform.

For the most part I'd been avoiding the Armenian community since I moved to L.A. because I was sure they would treat me like my family, that they wouldn't be able to tolerate my identity. But the lady who walked out on me ironically proved me wrong. A discussion about Armenian sexuality followed her outbreak. The audience wouldn't have revealed itself to me, to each other, if one crazy Armenian hadn't pushed them, inciting them to speak.

I wasn't so sure I wanted to be like that one crazy Armenian anymore. She asked people to say only the words she wanted to hear and abruptly abandoned all conversation if it didn't go her way. I was tired of pushing for words that might never be spoken, wary of rejecting people who loved me, however imperfectly.

PART IV

13. Seeing Istanos

Aunt Agnes left the message on my answering machine. "Nancy, this man Levon Andonyan has found Istanos, your grandmother's village in Sepastia. He's taking a tour there this September. I want to go, but not by myself. Will you come with me?"

In Arizona at the time, I was visiting a boyfriend who had just gone long distance on me. Artis and I had met ten months before in L.A., where he spent a sabbatical from the university. He was a performance artist and a professor, fourteen years my senior, and Latvian American. We had so much in common and he was a very good communicator, more self-aware than most women I knew. His body was big and blond and slightly chubby, which felt soft and luxurious next to my skin. We didn't have sex the first night we spent together, though; we touched and cuddled and talked for hours, unable to sleep. Another morning a few weeks into our courtship, we were in bed kissing and I just wasn't feeling it. I told him, "I have to stop."

"Okay," he said gently.

"I don't think I'm feeling the same things you're feeling right now."

"That's okay," he said.

"I'm just a bit scared."

"That's understandable," he said. "I get scared sometimes too."

I lay on my back and put his hand over my heart, on the hard flat part between my breasts. I just wanted to know he was there with me. That he wasn't going away.

He asked me, "Are you okay?" And I told him, "I'm sad." And he said, "Do you want to cry?"

I started out slowly. And then I let the sound out of my heart, keening the way I did when Grammy died. He held me and looked into my eyes and told me I was okay.

"I don't know why I'm crying so much," I said.

"Is it a childhood thing?" he asked.

I paused, breathing hard. There were many times when I told men that I needed to go slow sexually; they never seemed to understand, shrugging it off, as if there were something wrong with me they simply had to put up with. "If I didn't want to do something my mother wanted me to do," I said, "there would be a fight, there was always a problem. So it was powerful to tell you I felt differently from you and for it to be okay."

"Wow," he said, hugging me.

It had been a good relationship, the best of my life: he was kind, gentle and caring; we were in love, we had good sex, and I was able to trust him. But we would remain a long distance couple and it ultimately wouldn't work out, something that I sensed as soon as he moved back to Arizona.

Besides the relationship, I was still struggling. Couldn't make ends meet, couldn't get anywhere as an artist. And most significantly, several months before, at the age of thirty, my panic attacks had posed a major problem. They had lapsed a bit, but resurged after meeting Artis, who had to take me to the hospital for a particularly nasty case. When the ultrasound technician, a large Russian lady, rubbed the wand over my belly, I moaned in agony. It was my appendix, the doctor told me, and I needed to have it removed immediately. I had always thought my panic attacks were the result of stress, a psychosomatic symptom, an intensity of being Armenian. But my puking and stomach pains were classic symptoms of appendicitis, a case never diagnosed. I would cry in the middle of an attack that I was so fucked up to be doing such a thing to myself, but it turned out the only thing I'd done wrong was spend ten years trying to solve a problem based on a faulty hypothesis.

In this state of existential uncertainty, Auntie Agnes' message was a welcome opportunity. Ever since I had moved to L.A., I felt intrinsically connected to the desert; I hoped going to my grandmother's village, to stand on the dry land whence my blood evolved, would somehow give me a sense of clarity, of completeness.

"Oh great," I said out loud, after wiping myself to find blood on the toilet paper. *Eighteen hours on a plane and I'm going to be bleeding all the way.*

Into my packed suitcase I stuffed tampons, pads and Advil and brought it downstairs to the foyer of my parents' house. When they caught sight of me, they urgently bombarded me with last-minute travel items: "Do you need a sewing kit? How about film? Do you want some binoculars?"

Daddy and I were about to pick up Auntie Agnes and go to Logan Airport, where we would meet up with our tour group of elderly Armenian Americans, also visiting the villages of their parents in Eastern Anatolia, the region that was once historic Armenia, now modern Turkey.

"What do I need binoculars for?"

"To see ruins from far away."

Though I was flustered at the idea of lugging around binoculars, I still registered appreciation that my mother was acknowledging my trip. She hadn't been happy when she had first heard about it. "I don't understand why you would want to go to Turkey, to the middle of nowhere, and contribute to their economy after all that they did," she had said on the phone.

"Because I want to see where my grandmother came from," I replied.

"But you *knew* your grandmother. I don't understand why you need to see where she came from. It'll just be so depressing. There'll be nothing there. Absolutely nothing there to look at but rubble."

"I'm not going there to have a vacation. I've been writing about Grammy, and Auntie Agnes is the only one who really knows the family history."

"My family has a history too; you never ask me about my family's history."

When I'd asked, she had told me that her father was a year old when he came over from the old country, and her mother's parents had fled Constantinople at the turn of the century—why, she hadn't a clue, since they never wanted to talk about it. "That's because you don't know anything," I said.

"You know," Mumma countered, "your aunt wants to go on this trip just because her cousin Tina went." A year before Tina had visited Istanos, from which her parents also originated. "And Tina hasn't spoken to her sisters in thirty years. Is it right that she's going to Turkey and writing letters to Turkish villagers instead of talking to her sisters?" I didn't know Tina very well, having met her just a few times at family functions down in Providence. She was thin as a rail, very stylish, in comparison to her two sisters Lora and Lucy, "pigasauruses" as an adolescent Leo had called them.

"What does this have to do with me?" I asked.

"Yeah," Daddy's voice came out of nowhere. Apparently he had been listening in on the extension. "What does this have to do with Nancy?"

"Oh I hate when he does that! Get off the phone! Get off the phone!" she yelled.

"Look, Mumma, I'm going. Nothing you can say is going to change my mind."

"Well, I hope you'll be happy in the middle of nowhere where there's nothing but rubble and you can kiss the dirt where your grandmother stood!"

Her vitriol propelled her into a weeklong anti-heritage tour offense, going so far as to threaten my aunt that she would never forgive her if something should happen to me and giving me a bogus report from the State Department that it was dangerous for Western tourists to travel to Turkey. I responded by ranting over the phone that she was in desperate need of mental help and that I had no warm feelings left for her, but Mumma didn't acquiesce until I happened to mention that the tour would spend time in Istanbul, which she saw as a cosmopolitan city, her grandparents' Constantinople, and not just "tiny backward villages."

Now she offered, "Do you want a pack of Kleenex? You need a pocketbook. How about a fanny pack?"

I hated everything about fanny packs, including their insipid name, but disoriented from this sudden barrage of travel accessories, not to mention nervous and menstruating, I actually considered taking the black vinyl pouch dangling from my mother's hand like a possum. *It might prove useful for storing and retrieving small necessities.*

"Here are some earphones for the movie," Mumma said, before I could reply.

"These plastic bags will come in handy," Daddy said, thrusting a handful of gangly white grocery store bags in my face.

They wouldn't let up when all I wanted to do was leave. As I picked up the suitcase to take it out to the car, a whiff of mildew suddenly hit me. The bag, which my parents had convinced me to use instead of the smaller one I brought from L.A., had been stored in their garage.

"I can't use this suitcase," I blurted out. "It smells like mold."

Mumma put her nose to the bag and sniffed. "I can't smell it," she claimed.

Sigh. "It reeks; I need another bag!" I rummaged around for another suitcase in the garage, hoping to find one that hadn't been infected by spores.

"What about this one?" Mumma asked, pulling out a duffel bag I had made in seventh grade sewing class. It was festooned with rainbow-colored straps that resembled Mork from Ork's suspenders.

Okay, don't lose it, Nancy, you're almost out the door, pull it together. I took a deep breath. "No, Ma, I don't think so."

"Nancy, you can just put a plastic bag around your clothes. Or a paper bag. Just put a paper bag in your suitcase and then put your clothes inside of it."

That had to have been the stupidest thing I had ever heard. *Traveling around Turkey for ten days with my clothes in a paper bag?*

"Yes, Nancy," she kept insisting, "you can just put a paper bag in your suitcase and put your clothes inside of it—"

"I'MNOTPUTTINGAPAPERBAGINMYSUITCASE!" I erupted.

The explosion came with such force that my mother had to laugh. Now that I was departing, it turned out that I was the one who couldn't emotionally cope.

As we pulled up, Agnes, in a smart denim outfit, was standing in the driveway next to her luggage. Ruth's dark face and halo of gray hair appeared in the den window and Mel, her hair white and her clothes pink, watched us from the living room window.

Ruth yelled through the screen, "Agnes, you left the front door open!"

Agnes handed Daddy her bags.

"Agnes, you're letting the flies in!" Ruth continued.

Completely nonplused, Agnes asked Daddy to take a photo of us by the car.

"Hurry up!" Mel yelled. "You people need to eat lunch!"

"But we already ate—"

"Just get into the kitchen!" Ruth barked.

We all sat at the yellow enamel table in the breakfast nook as Ruth set the table with paper plates, *lahmejun* and an iceberg and tomato salad coated in olive oil.

"Are you excited Auntie?" I asked Agnes as we ate.

"I'm excited about going to Ma's village and finding the family bible."

"Why do you talk such foolishness Agnes?" Mel spat. "You have to be a nut to think that still exists."

"Ma said her mother left it with a neighbor for safekeeping before they went on the march. It might still exist."

"Yeah, and you might *not* exist if you go around that village asking for it," Ruth said.

"It's been over eighty years, Aghavni," Daddy said. "Are you telling me that in all that time you don't think one Turk decided to burn it?"

"I believe in the good of man, Tip," Agnes said, raising her chin. "And I don't see the harm in looking. All the Koshgarian family history is recorded inside of that bible, all the dates of births and deaths and marriages going way back to when the Seljuks pushed us from Van in the eleventh century. Why not look for it? Isn't it better to try than to not look at all?"

"Yeah!" I chimed in. Even though I knew the bible's existence was far-fetched and that Agnes's quest for it seemed partly due to her propensity for drama, I couldn't help fantasizing about snatching our history back. Given half a chance, I wanted to claim our ancestors' lives from beyond the destruction, to see our existence, our ancientness, instead of feeling like a lost band of orphan-victims.

"You crazy kid," Ruth said to me. "You're not a kid anymore, but you're still crazy."

Daddy smiled at me with what I thought was prideful amusement. Then he said, in his joking little kid voice, "Nancy told me I have B.O." I had complained about it in the car on the way over. "Do you smell it, Razmouhi?"

Ruth sniffed near his armpit. "No, you're fine, Skippy," she said. My father looked at me, his bushy eyebrows raised in triumph.

"Your father always used to make me smell him before he went out," Ruth explained. Not much had changed between them since they were kids, it seemed. Daddy reverted to the role of bratty younger brother whenever he visited his sisters, which I found annoying in my seventy-year-old father, but oddly comforting. I too was welcomed into their intimacy of adolescent bickering, into their clannishness and screaming.

Mel threw our paper plates away and told me to wait, she had something for me. She pulled open a drawer and handed me a five-by-three-inch booklet with the words *Trip Diary* embossed in gold on its orange cover. She also gave me a twenty, "for extras." With her wallet open, she handed a twenty to her sister. "Here Agnes," she said.

"I don't need that," Agnes replied.

Mel kept her arm out with the twenty dangling at the end of it. "Just take it," she gruffly ordered, older sister to younger.

"I don't want it Mel, I have money," Agnes insisted, pushing Mel's hand away.

"JUSTTAKETHETWENTYDOLLARBILLAGNES!" Mel finally bellowed. Her head was shaking and her upside-downish, Dustin-Hoffman-as-Tootsie glasses somehow came askew.

As we hugged goodbye, Mel, still twitching from her fit, warmly told me, "Nancy, this won't be a fancy vacation. You'll get to meet the people of the villages."

I took her to mean that I would visit people like my grandmother's family. Like us.

Later, during the quiet void of the flight, I reflected on how difficult it was for my family to separate for such a controversial trip. I suspected that Armenians became crazy and controlling when they left each other or when they defied expectations because of an ingrained, possibly genetic, survival mechanism: if we didn't cling together as a group, we would get clobbered individually until extinction. It would explain why I still needed my mother's approval to embark on anything risky and why she was so fearful I would die whenever I took a trip. It would also explain the tendency I sensed in the Armenian community towards conformity; since it seemed there were so few of us, any divergence from the traditions of family and church (such as marrying a non-Armenian or being gay) was seen as disunity threatening the survival of the entire culture.

One reason why these dynamics stayed with us: the lack of recognition for the event that had started the trauma. Neither the current Turkish government nor their predecessors have ever acknowledged the truth of the matter, that Armenians were massacred intentionally, over a million lives raped, maimed, beaten, destroyed. Shame and guilt were installed and instilled in anyone who survived, and when it came time to continue their lives, they tried not to think about it. It didn't help that no one else wanted to think about it either. And yet it was impossible for feelings not to erupt; the safest place to have them was with family. Fear and mistrust, enacted over and over again on sons, daughters, loved ones, with no resolution nor apology. You screamed your head off and then you moved on.

I tried to fit together the pieces of the Armenian family puzzle into this historic framework, as the plane moved closer and closer, across the ocean, to Turkey.

Half of Parchanj (pronounced "perchance") was out in the street. After a short plane trip from Istanbul, we were in the village of the father of Harry Najarian, a retired chemistry professor from New Hampshire, our tour mate and in the region of Kharpert, now Elazig. Kamal, our Kurdish driver who resembled Ringo Starr and wore a Shetland sweater vest, dropped us off in front of a small tile fountain where a pipe emptied water into a basin. A few kids filled jugs with water and carried them away, watching us. The girls were wearing skirts over pants and sandals. Covered in dust and dirt, their hair was a shambles, but they were all very beautiful, with bright eyes.

The mayor and a dozen menfolk surrounded Levon, our guide, who was displaying an old map of Armenian homes and orchards, found in a book called *The Village of Parchanj: General History 1600-1937*. A retired architect with silver hair, moustache, and regal visage resembling Prince Rainier, Levon had started visiting the formerly Armenian provinces of Turkey seven years previously, simply out of curiosity. He then lectured on his travels, showing videos at Armenian-American churches and cultural events, which sparked interest in his trips. An Armenian who spoke Turkish, he was an indispensable guide and had been leading one or two tours a year ever since.

The villagers brought us to a grand old house once belonging to Armenians. The current owner, a young man, smiled and welcomed us into his backyard. His wife, a young woman wearing a floral-patterned headscarf, brought us watermelon. As we slurped and spit out the seeds, I recalled Grammy serving us watermelon on a TV tray in her wood-paneled den whenever we visited in the summertime. The neighborhood kids animatedly spoke to us in Turkish, pointing out a large garden like the kind Daddy had recently planted in the backyard of tomato and cucumber plants. Bulghur was drying on plastic tarps on the ground, and I tasted the cracked wheat pilaf my mother had cooked throughout my childhood. Propped around the trunks of trees were large carved stone arches—they looked like the former pediments of an Armenian church. Our hosts gestured for us to sit on them, like benches.

Auntie had to pee so the woman in the headscarf led her inside to use the facilities. "You should have seen the beautiful woodwork on the ceiling," Auntie said as she emerged. "I'm sure it was from the days of the Armenians." I was curious, but I didn't want to see. Though the people were kind and excited, proudly showing us our common culture, it was all so sad to me. What remained of the Armenians we sat on or stared up at.

A group of villagers followed as we returned to the van. As I stood in the doorway of the bus, I passed out ballpoint pens to a group of overjoyed girls. A few old men with grizzled beards and wrinkled eyes approached the van and held out their hands, but I didn't want to give them a thing. For some reason, they seemed culpable for their ancestors' wrongs, even though I did not know who their ancestors were. I was offended that they wanted something from me, and I felt an uncharitable urge to ignore or deny them.

I was about to turn around, but Kamal stopped me. He put his hand on one man's shoulder and said haltingly, "Miss, these are big children." So I gave them the pens.

On the bus, Levon spoke about the mayor of Parchanj. "The mayor's family arrived seven generations ago, when the only inhabitants were four Armenian families. When I asked him about 1915, his eyes glazed over. He said Turks and Armenians had lived side by side in peace before that time. It was the government that forced the Armenians out and gave away their homes to Bulgarian, Hungarian and Romanian Turks. And then twenty years later, the new owners sold the homes to locals."

Some part of me was expecting the mayor to give words of regret, or even apology, but according to Levon's account, they did not come. I wondered why his eyes had glazed over if he knew the truth. Perhaps he too was one of Kamal's "big children": blameless, powerless over the past, and ultimately unable to apologize.

We found a verdant spot, on our way to the next village, to stop and have lunch; there was a spring to drink clear water, and we ate more watermelon and sandwiches. Kamal separated himself for a moment, before we boarded the van, to kneel down to the ground, face Mecca and pray.

"He's very devout," Levon explained.

I thought about Kamal for a moment, a Muslim, but not a Turk, who was helping Armenians. I had read in my guidebook that Kurds in Turkey were treated as second-class citizens, forbidden to teach or publish or broadcast in their language, similar to the status of Armenians circa 1915. About ten million Kurds lived in poverty-stricken southeastern Turkey, a region which overlapped historic Armenian land. Since 1984, Turkish Kurds had been waging a war against the government to gain more rights and establish an independent or autonomous Kurdish state.

"What do you know about the Kurds?" I asked Agnes.

"Your grammy said she would rather play with the Kurdish girls in her village than with Noyemzar. She would have them over for tea parties and feed them cream from the top of the milk can. When her mother asked her what happened to the cream, she said, 'A cat came and ate it.'" Agnes laughed.

Noyemzar was cousin Tina's mother. I frequently saw her at church in Providence when I was growing up. My mother would happily speak in

Armenian with her, holding her hands by the front door of the church as the cold air rushed in. She was an old woman, tiny and bright, with impish eyes and a full head of tight, kinky brown hair.

"How was Noyemzar related to us?" I asked Auntie.

"Noyemzar was married to my father's first cousin. She was also a distant cousin to your grandmother."

"Were Grammy and Noyemzar both from Istanos?"

"Yes, but Grammy didn't really like her. When her mother told her to play with her, she would say, 'I don't want to play with that brush-head!'"

Grammy's feelings about Noyemzar must have changed over the years, by the time they were the last two people left from their circle of family, because when Noyemzar died, my grandmother was very distraught.

"Why didn't you go to church today?" I had asked her, calling the day after the funeral. It wasn't like her to be home on a Sunday morning.

Grammy replied in Armenian and Ruth, on an extension, translated. "She said she didn't bury a turnip yesterday."

"Oh, is it customary to bury a turnip after someone dies or else you can't go to church the following Sunday?"

"What?" Ruth asked. "No, you misunderstand, Nancy. She's not feeling up to going to church because *Noyemzar* was buried yesterday. She buried a *friend*, not a turnip."

"You tink Noyemzar was a turnip?" Grammy replied. She was pretty offended.

I asked Agnes if relations between Kurds and Armenians in Istanos had been friendly.

"Yes, they were friends, I guess, but then the Kurds turned. During the genocide, the Turks promised the Kurds a homeland if they would help kill the Armenians."

We were back in the van now, sitting behind Levon and Kamal. I watched them laughing and speaking in Turkish as Kamal navigated the narrow dirt roads of the difficult Anatolian countryside.

As we drove along a single lane road through pale green hills towards Sepastia, our ancestral province, I noticed the telephone wire drooping between poles with the weight of a single bird. One after the other after the other, the sky a clear light blue. We passed a lone horse in a field, and a man lying on a sack next to a watermelon truck.

"I can't wait to hear some good Turkish music," Harry said.

A Muzak version of "Strangers in the Night" emitted from Kamal's radio speakers, followed by the theme from *Rocky*. Over its triumphant strains Agnes announced, "I think that most of the old Turkish music was written by Armenians."

"Yes, I wholeheartedly agree!" Harry said. "That's why they don't play it!"

"That's how intimidated the Turks are by the Armenians," Harry's wife Arpi said.

I nodded my head. We had already seen an Armenian church with a sign in Turkish acknowledging the year it was built, but no mention that it was actually a classic example of Armenian architecture. This older generation of Armenians knew how exclusionary a dominant culture could be, the same way my queer, multiculti artist friends did at home. It was heartwarmingly bizarre that I now felt aligned with them as I heard them speaking a language I knew so well, that of the silenced minority.

The green hills made way to yellow meadows, then miles and miles of torched, fallow fields. I was half dozing in the hot van when I heard one of the senior citizens explaining that *jingeneh,* the Armenian word for cheap, is derived from the word for gypsy. I opened my eyes and saw a series of round carpet tents, presumably those of the Roma, camped along the side of the road. A discussion on the word *odar* then ensued.

"My mother said that I married an *odar,*" Harry joked, "because Arpi's family wasn't from Kharpert."

"One year at St. Gregory's Church there was a big Malatya extravaganza, but only Malatyatsis and their spouses were invited!" Arpi claimed. "Aren't Armenians funny, how they only wanted to associate with people from their own province?"

I hadn't known that Armenians had so much regional attachment for the Eastern Anatolian provinces. "Did your family only associate with Sepastatsis?" I asked Agnes.

"Well, they owned the farm with Sepastatsis. The Sarkissians and the Agababians owned the farm in Whitinsville. They were also from Istanos."

Auntie told me that the two families were also somehow related; Marta, the mother of my grandfather Jacob, was a sibling to one of the Sarkissians, so she had nephews in their family. Noyemzar's husband was a nephew to Marta, but he was also, incidentally, related to one of Grammy's sisters-in-law, plus he was an uncle to my father's godfather, and Noyemzar was related to Grammy's mother. My head was spinning with names and relations, the chart of a family tree in my mind's eye scrambled like a malfunctioning Etch A Sketch.

I was struck now with how incestuous the Armenians from those little villages were and wondered if their insularity made them especially suspicious of outsiders and their unfamiliar ways. I thought that Armenians in the U.S. had divided themselves into Malatyatsis, Kharpertsis, Sepastatsis and Whatevertsis, associating with one another if they were from the same area not just out of familiarity, but because they were probably the only survivors from their neighborhood left. They took whatever family they could get.

But my theory on Armenians finding family didn't quite explain why

Tina wasn't speaking to her sisters. I wondered if the conformist mania of the Armenian family—"be like us or risk death"—was to blame. I asked Auntie for an explanation.

"Well, Tina was always in her mother's favor because she had married an Armenian, and her sisters married and divorced *odars,* but they also took care of Noyemzar later in her life. When she died, she left more money to Tina who didn't need it. So Lora and Lucy resent her and say mean things to her."

"It's not Tina's fault Noyemzar acted the way she did. I don't blame her for not talking to Lora and Lucy. I mean, why would anyone want to talk to two sisters who are always saying mean things?"

"That's the sixty-four thousand dollar question," Agnes said.

The land was steadily becoming more barren as Agnes told me about our family history in Istanos. I learned that Grammy had two much older brothers, Soukias and Zakar, and an older sister, Aghavni. Grammy also had a brother named Touros, the one who rescued Grammy from the orphanage and brought her to America, but he was actually a cousin. "He was born at the same time as Zakar to another Koshgarian family, but his mother died during childbirth so Grammy's mother nursed him. Zakar *Kery* always used to say, 'we shared mother's milk.'" She laughed.

I asked Auntie if Grammy's father hadn't seen the genocide coming.

"Oh no. Grammy's father once said, after he planted, that he didn't know if they'd even be around to see the seeds grow. He wanted to sell everything in 1910 and leave, but her mother said 'Look at all we have. Why should we give it up?' So he said, 'Okay, well I at least want some of us to get out.'"

So he sent Zakar and Soukias to America in 1913. They were both married but their wives, Enneh and Araxie, were left behind. "Araxie had two little children too, Avedis and Mary. All those little children perished during the massacres."

This was confusing. I had an uncle and aunt, who were brother and sister, also named Avedis and Mary. Avedis died young, before I was born, of a heart attack, but I knew his widow and children, my aunt and cousins, because we spent January 6, Armenian Christmas, at their home in nearby Plainville. It was always a slightly sad affair; hung on their cathedral ceiling was a portrait Agnes had painted of Avedis, looking down at us with soulful Donny Osmond eyes.

Aunt Mary, a tiny yet exuberant lady, lived in Washington D.C. with her husband Jack, a big crew-cut man with a Southern accent, and their three sons. We saw her every few years when they visited New England.

"If Avedis and Mary died, why do I have an uncle and an aunt with the same names?"

"They're the second Avedis and Mary."

"What?"

"Araxie and Soukias had two more children."

My brain had to catch up. "Araxie survived the genocide, was reunited with her husband in America, had a son and daughter, and named them after the ones who had died?"

"That's right," Agnes said.

I turned to scribble in my diary. I'd been diligently recording all the names Agnes had been telling me. Knowing names helped to make the past seem more real; it was one reason why, I thought, that we kept referring to places by the names the Armenians used. Kharpert instead of Elazig, Sepastia instead of Sivas.

Now I was struck by the way Armenians held onto the names of loved ones who had perished. Grammy's mother's name was Razmouhi, which she gave to Ruth, and her sister's name was Aghavni, bestowed to Agnes.

From one angle, the renaming seemed creepy and burdensome, attaching death and loss to an innocent baby. From another view, it seemed like a defiant message to the enemy: "You can kill our children but you can't kill their memory." And from yet another perspective, it seemed incredibly bittersweet, as if in naming their children after family who had died, my great aunt, uncle and grandmother were communicating to their living children their importance in love. The family relationships, sister mother daughter aunt, were smudged into one sense of family love, like a mother nursing a child related to her husband's cousin.

Kamal pulled off the highway and let Auntie and I take our picture in front of the sign. After I developed the film, I would see how nervous we were, arms around each other, shoulders hunched. *Çimenyenice,* the Turkish name for Istanos, was stenciled in black on the white arrow behind us.

We slowly motored down a dirt road, through a pastoral setting. I could see goats, geese and the Alis River, a calmly flowing stream. A man in a field pitched hay with a fork. We passed down the road a bit, to another cluster of homes, and Kamal parked the van next to a dried up field. This was it: Istanos, on September 8, 1998, 9:30 A.M.

My heart pumped as we stepped out of the van and walked by a pair of crumbling mud brick houses. "Armenians probably once lived in these ruins," Levon said. The walls were covered with circles of dung drying in the sun, to be used as fuel in the winter. I smelled an open sewer and spotted a satellite dish atop a roof. Someone was screeching "Whoop! Whoop! Whoop!" and then a mentally retarded man with an impossibly large nose appeared, twirling a string: the source of the hoopla. "That's the village *ghent,*" Levon informed us. "The result of inbreeding."

As we made our way through the village, a few shabby kids watched us, but they were not filled with wonder. Our hard candy made no impression—they wouldn't touch it. The sturdiness fell out of my stomach and I wandered about, hoping for a sign that we were in the right place. High walls surrounded us; there were very few windows and doors. Some men emerged to greet Levon, including a large, stern man with a distinguished beard who appeared to be the mayor. He and his posse looked at us sideways, surly and suspicious.

We made our way up a hill, towards the houses that Levon believed belonged to the Koshgarians, as the villagers tentatively followed. We walked as far as we could, to a ledge overlooking miles of fields below. Levon pointed directly below to roofless ruins of tiny rooms, like monks' monastery cells. "Those were the Koshgarian homes," Levon said.

"No, that can't be," Agnes said, her voice high. "My mother said our house was the largest in the village, and that the people had their marriages in the courtyard. And the doors were so tall and wide a man on a horse could ride through them." I smiled at my grandmother's grandiose description. "So this can't be it," Agnes continued, gesturing to the ruins. "The house was on top of a hill, across the street from a church."

We happened to be standing next to a big house, on top of a hill, across the street from a mosque. "What about this?" Agnes asked, looking up.

The house possessed wing doors, though not big enough for a man on a horse to pass through. As I took a picture of them, a smiling girl stepped into the frame of my lens. She was bright and lively, about ten years old, wearing an orange outfit and a headband over her shiny black hair. I looked out from behind my camera to smile at her and then snapped the picture. Many kids we'd encountered had been wearing clothes emblazoned with English words: "Baseball Legends" and "Tweety Bird." The front of this girl's sweatshirt was divided into four sections, each with a cartoon character labeled "LC Waikiki."

Auntie asked the girl her name—it was Ana. She lived in the big, wing-doored house with her family. There was a car parked in front, a rarity in far-off villages, reminding me of Grammy's claim that her family was the most prominent in the village. I looked carefully at the house, trying to determine if this had been her home, and found a date carved into a cornerstone: 1954.

After lengthy negotiations, Levon convinced Ana's father, a handsome man in his mid-thirties, to let us inside the home. We walked around to the other side of the building and entered a storage room; from what I could tell, the 1954 cornerstone was part of its outer wall. The room was connected to the main house, and it was about the size of a one-car garage, with piles of wheat on the ground and old farm implements hanging on the walls. There was a diamond-shaped hole in the ceiling, framed with large timbers. "Look at that," Auntie said, pointing. "This must be a very old building since this land has been deforested." Auntie had told me that, incredibly, the arid plains we had crossed today were once covered by oak forest. There was even a legend that a Persian king had to chop the trees down in order to battle the Armenians.

"That hole was built to let the smoke out, from when people lived in here," Levon said. He pointed to a huge fireplace, about ten feet wide and six feet tall, taking up most of the western wall. "Oh my goodness!" Auntie said. "That must be the *tonir!*" she exclaimed. "My mother said she fell into the *tonir* when she was a baby!" I had read that a *tonir* was actually an oven dug into the ground, which would explain how a child could accidentally fall into one. Nevertheless, I said nothing as Levon took a picture of me and Auntie standing inside the oven while Kamal, our traveling companions, the bearded mayor, Ana's family and a half dozen village kids looked on.

"I could see a wedding party inside this room," Agnes mused. The light was soft from the hole in the ceiling, from the small windows high up in the wall. There was an old TV in one corner, and underneath it, a wooden trunk with elaborately carved designs on the side, just the sort that would hold an ancient family bible. In order to get a closer look, Auntie pretended to wipe off the dust with a Kleenex. "It's an antique," she said.

Agnes produced a chart of the Armenian alphabet and told the mayor if anyone found a book with such writing, to let her know. "I pay you big money," she said, playfully touching the underside of a boy's chin. The mayor, via Levon, said it was unlikely, since the generation before had found those kinds of things. Ana's father said he had been thinking about tearing the room down. "If you come here in a year this might not be here," he said. Still, ever the optimist, Agnes gave him her phone number in Watertown.

We emptied outside. Levon made Auntie and me re-enact entering the house for the first time, so he could videotape us, while the villagers watched. I'd really hoped to avoid the kind of testimonial Levon had been taping of our traveling companions as part keepsake, part documentation, part advertisement. Dramatizing an event that just happened was slightly less odious than exclaiming how wonderful it was to visit a village cleansed of our ethnicity, so I obliged.

"I really think that was the house," Agnes said as we walked away. I didn't have the heart to tell her about the 1954 inscription, that the room was probably built long after Grammy's family had been banished. Because even if the building wasn't her house, this place was her home. I could imagine her stealing the cream off the milk to give to the Kurdish girls, playing with birds outside, and looking out over the plains below. Perhaps my logic was being clouded by the need to find my heritage, but I didn't care. Given the options of dignified sentimentality and healthy cynicism, I chose the former. I didn't think that Grammy would have minded what my attitude was in Istanos, just as long as I didn't forget her. I remembered her wrinkled hands and her dark eyes ringed with gray, her short white hair and her scratchy voice, always insisting that people treat her with respect. Did it really matter that I sat in a fort, built with a hole to let smoke out? That I was drawn to the woods to conjure fear and ghosts, that the sun pounding my black hair in the high desert felt like home?

I turned around to get one last look of the site and waved to Ana. Later, when I saw the photo of her in front of the wing doors, I noticed on her American sweatshirt, appearing in the quadrant over her heart, the word MEMORY.

As we passed through the dung covered ruins where we had entered earlier, a Çimenyenice family invited us for tea. We were ushered into a small room with an upper ledge where men sat leaning against the walls and a lower level a step down for the women. There were rugs covering the seating surfaces and family pictures on the walls. Neighbors streamed in and out of the house during our visit.

Levon turned on his camera and asked my Aunt if she'd ever imagined this.

"I don't imagine anything. Who am I visiting?" she snapped.

"This man's name is Sarkut. His grandfather was a Sarkissian who converted to Islam. He's a distant relative of yours."

"A second cousin of Boghos Sarkissian, I think. He looks a little like him," Agnes said with awe. The man got out his photo ID, which read Neset Sarkut. It didn't give the date of his birth, but he looked to be around Auntie's age, perhaps younger.

"And these are two of his daughters. He has five."

Sarkut's teen and twenty-year-old daughters served us tea. They were wearing colorful, mismatching sweaters and skirts. Their headscarves were cotton and covered the buns on top of their crowns and at the napes of their necks, lending their heads the shape of gourds. I wondered what they made of me, in my fat pants and long uncovered hair pulled back. One of them, whose name was Cameh, had light hair, a soft voice and a very sweet smile. Her darker sister Esgu was flustered with excitement, kissing us nervously on the cheeks in greeting.

I was feeling shaky. I didn't know what to say or do, and I felt I should, I should know what to say or do, I should have Levon translate something for me, some questions, but I didn't know where to begin. If one of my ancestors had converted his faith, I wouldn't exist, and part of my spirit, I imagined, would be living here with them. Was it living here now? Had it ever?

After tea we posed with Sarkut and his daughters, our arms around each other, for a picture. Simultaneously wanting to scream and cry, I quietly quaked and refrained from breathing. "Agnes," Levon said, "you're getting the royal treatment here. The father threw Tina out of the house after a few minutes." So these were the Turkish villagers to whom my cousin

Tina had been writing letters. Standing between Cameh and Esgu, I found myself too shy to look into their faces, but their warmth rose up in me.

The family walked us to our van and some of their neighbors followed, and then there was another round of arm-in-arm pictures. Auntie disentangled herself from the crowd and kissed everyone on both cheeks, and I followed, smiling at people as my face approached the skin of their cheeks. But then I winced when Auntie gave a travel size bottle of Keri moisturizer to a big village crone with hands like leather. She looked at the foreign object completely baffled as we boarded the van.

While Levon was panning his camera over the countryside one last time, I ran into a field to gather some dirt into a tiny film container. When I returned, he commanded me to do it again so he could get it on videotape.

"No, that's okay," I said.

"Yes, do it again," he ordered. "Dump out that container and refill it."

I considered telling Levon that I wouldn't be a part of his ridiculous fake documentation that cheapened my experience in the home of my ancestry. But I couldn't. I knew if I said one thing, it would betray all the rage in my heart, and I didn't want to admit I had rage in my heart right then and there. Levon didn't make himself readily available to translate, so I didn't communicate at all with these distant relatives who were friendly, who kissed both my cheeks and posed for portraits with me. So I couldn't know if I was having a real experience with them or not.

But the dirt was real. The dirt was what I had envisioned, what I had imagined would be so powerful to stand on, that back in America my mother had spitefully told me to kiss. All I wanted was to have my moment with the dirt, to feel its properties, to be joined with my heritage through its minerals, and here was Levon, exploiting my moment. I seethed while scooping up the soil my ancestors were composed of, so that Levon could get his shot of an Armenian girl returning to her homeland, an advertisement for young people to take his trips, just as he wished.

When I was done with my faux filmwork, I turned around to find Cameh holding a plastic bag and a twist tie. She kneeled down to the ground and helped me fill it with dirt.

Now it became clear why Tina would write letters to these people while she was estranged from her sisters. She was finding family where she could. Who wouldn't be inexplicably drawn to distantly related strangers who couldn't speak, i.e. criticize you, who weren't acting out the particular mania of Armenian-American families?

Unable to communicate to Cameh beyond a smile, I turned to watch Levon, who was still in the field where I had left him, videotaping. (Later, as I watched the tape with a friend who translated the Turkish, I learned that he and Kamal were constantly grilling Sarkut on the possibility of the family bible, urging him to remember names of Armenian families, of any place of where it could exist. Unbeknownst to me as I stood in the field, he had been my advocate.) Cameh turned and looked at him too before we retreated to the van. As I walked with her, I felt her gentle jitteriness, the flipside of the explosive feelings I'd experienced leaving my family back in Boston. I sensed that she knew the significance of this moment: we were inexplicably brought together for an hour on an ordinary fall day, decades after world events had torn everything apart. I'd come here to stand on the land, but found that living, breathing people were more important.

Later when I watched the video, Cameh and I appear to be very tiny, just a couple of characters in an old country tableau of villagers and tourists, trees and chickens and a wooden barn door. But she and I turn our searching faces—two blank, bright, featureless ovals reflecting the sun—at the exact same time.

14. HEARING HER STORY

"K-A-*sha* ..." Grammy spells her maiden name tentatively, using the wrong English vowel and adding *sha,* an Armenian consonant. She bluffs a couple more letters and prematurely sums up, "Koshgarian."

"Half Armenian, half English!" Auntie Agnes half laughed, half coughed. She was sitting on the couch in the den at Oliver Street, her large bosom settled just under her chin, her ears activated to my grandmother's voice.

The smooth-voiced interviewer announces herself: "Hera Hagopian, interviewing Mrs. Zanik Koshgarian at her home in Watertown, Massachusetts on January 9, 1979. She was born in the village of Istanos in 1905." The tape had been made as part of an oral history project conducted by the Armenian Assembly of America, an advocacy group. I had secured a copy of Grammy's tapes from ALMA, the Armenian Library and Museum of America, located in an old bank building in Watertown Square, where we used to walk to Woolworth's, holding hands. Though I couldn't understand Armenian, Grammy's voice on the tape was so distinctive, childlike and scratchy, that the sound activated my memory of her smell and appearance and aura. It was like she was alive somewhere, talking to me.

She was probably upset that I had finally moved back East. "Why didn't you come back when I was alive?" she might have been asking in Armenian. In a sense, I *was* here to make her live again. I had moved to New York to go to graduate school, to write more about her. I needed to figure out what exactly she had given to me, to understand who she really was, to know all of what she had left behind.

Agnes was helping me to understand Grammy's spoken words. Auntie was fine this morning when I spoke to her on the phone, but I arrived five hours later to discover she had developed a bad cold. This was the best time to do the translations, though, since both my parents and the other two aunts were away and wouldn't be able to meddle.

"What are your earliest recollections?" Agnes translated Hera's first question.

"The war," Grammy said. "First they came and took all the guns."

I turned off the tape to write Grammy's words in my notebook. I envisioned the Turkish gendarmes seizing the weaponry.

"Then they came and took the boys. Her brother Haroutioun was taken. He was twelve years old; he was too young," Agnes coughed. "Too young to ship to America."

I turned off the tape again. "Why was Haroutioun taken?"

"They said they were taking boys for the military. But who knows what happened to those boys. Ma never saw him again."

"So he was lost, basically?"

"Yes."

It was a bit confusing why Grammy said so little about her lost brother. I had never heard of him, till now, and it seemed my aunt was also not aware of his existence. There was too big a gap of history, which I didn't understand. I had a hunch that my aunt wasn't translating every word. "I think I'm going to play shorter segments so we don't miss anything," I told her.

After the gendarmes collected the guns, horses and the boys, they came back a week later and surrounded the town. The villagers received word that each Armenian family would be relocated and that they could pack just one oxcart with belongings. Then the Armenian priest, the schoolteacher, and Grammy's father, who was a village leader, were chained together and brought to the courthouse at Hochasar, the county seat, and tried for treason. Grammy's mother brought money to her husband, but he told her that the money wouldn't help this time, that she should use it to save the children because he had been convicted and would be killed the next day. "He cried. There was nothing he could do."

"Remember when we went? It was quite a ways from Istanos." Agnes interrupted. "I wonder how Grandma got to Hochasar to see him?"

After we said goodbye to the Sarkut family in Istanos, Levon and Kamal had taken us to Hochasar, where we peered into the locked doors of the former courthouse. I took a photograph through the window of a room with a map of Turkey on the wall and rows of folding chairs. Levon videotaped Agnes telling her grandfather's story until some men who'd been loitering on benches approached and said it was unlawful to photograph military buildings. So we took off. Later, we were exploring another little Sepastatsi village, with an Armenian church in ruins being used as a barn, when we were detained by seemingly friendly villagers, the men in their newsboy caps and knitted vests, who brought us *tahn* to drink. Kamal was led away and interrogated; when he returned twenty minutes later he was sweating, hand on his hip, other hand rubbing his brow. "Not good," was all he would say. Then a squad of young soldiers with machine guns showed up in a   truck and escorted our van back to Hochasar. The ten-minute drive seemed endless, until we saw we were back at the courthouse.

The soldiers eventually let us go, after taking our passports and making a series of calls to Ankara to make sure that I, Kamal with his bad back, and the senior citizens weren't terrorists. Levon thought that one of the villagers simply decided to be a big shot by blowing the whistle on a group of Armenian Americans and a Kurd. Still, Agnes and I couldn't help feeling that the whole harrowing experience had somehow been our fault.

"Yes it was quite a ways," I told Agnes. I took a deep breath and pushed PLAY again.

"*Cah-leh, cah-leh, cah-leh, cah-leh,*" Grammy says.

"We walked and walked and walked and walked," Agnes says.

"She says you have to walk, there was no other way to go—"

"She says they never told them where they were going. They just made them walk—"

"She says there was no water, nothing to eat, just walk—"

The gendarmes led the caravan through several villages, Kotni, Janjin and Yarasar. When they arrived at Sourouj, they were massed together with other villagers into one big group, and then corralled through a narrow mountain pass. The wagons started to fall apart. "*Jampa ya chee gah,*" Grammy says.

"There's no road," Agnes says. "Purposely they made you go through these narrow passages so you fall down and drop."

"*Ghagh oh dereh,*" Grammy says on the tape.

"They went by this place called 'Murder Mountain,'" Agnes says. "*Ghagh oh dereh.*" It's difficult for her to say the *ghs* with her cold.

"Murder Mountain," Grammy says quietly in English.

"Because it was very difficult to pass," Agnes explains.

"Because!" Grammy yells in English.

"Why is Grammy so angry?" I asked.

"Because Hera's asking foolish questions," Auntie answered curtly. "She told me later this was her first interview and that she didn't know what she was doing."

"What did she ask?"

"'Why did they call it Bloody Mountain?'—Because that's where everybody dies!"

"Well, she wants to know for sure," I said.

"For sure, for sure it was!" Agnes said, her eyes wide. "She told her before it was a very narrow passage. I wasn't there, Nancy," she said, as if she were a modified version of Grammy losing patience and I was Hera asking too many questions, "but I'm just visualizing it because I've been in that neck of the woods."

Sigh. The translation process continued on like this, an irritable Grammy leading a novice Hera leading a sickly Agnes leading a completely baffled Nancy through unbelievable, otherworldly material. Grammy sounded like she was here in the room talking to me, but her story was still out of my reach, garbled and impossible.

As I was looking for information on the Armenian Genocide in the stacks of the library, I found myself staring at the spine of a book: *Survivors: An Oral History of the Armenian Genocide.*

Survivors was written by a husband and wife team, Donald E. Miller and Lorna Touryan Miller, and published in 1993. I glanced through the introduction. It seemed the Millers' oral history project started after Lorna's father, a survivor, suddenly became ill; it seemed necessary to record his stories before he wouldn't be able to tell them any longer. The Millers then felt compelled to record others like him, and soon began to understand the importance of what they were doing in terms of genocide denial:

> Denial is motivated in part by our own fear of suffering and death, but beyond that, genocide is a moral embarrassment that the perpetrator, as well as the observing world community, often seeks to repress. It is only the victims who struggle with the problem of forgetting.

My face twisted into tears. That last line called up a truth that I had inherently known but had never read before. On a daily basis, my grandmother embodied the "struggle with the problem of forgetting," with her impetuous insistence that people listen to her. Here her troubles were clearly distilled, eloquently stated in the printed pages of a scholarly book.

I checked it out of the library and brought it back to my room, discovering similarities between Lorna's father and my grandmother. Varham Touryan was seven or eight in 1915; he lived in Eastern Turkey, and his father was a village leader who was unjustly accused of treason and killed. His family was told that they were being relocated, but instead they were sent on a death march.

A gendarme became entranced with Varham's older sister, and he placed her atop a horse to take her away. The girl insisted that Varham and another younger brother ride with her. But when it was time for the gendarme to part ways with the caravan, he took the younger brother off the horse. Varham and his sister were led away, "while their mother and the remaining children went down the opposite fork in the road, presumably to their deaths, for they were never seen again."

I was struck by the matter-of-fact way such a heartrending moment was told, with no explanation for the gendarme's decision, nor the emotions that followed the moment of separation. It reminded me of Grammy's spare words: "My brother Haroutioun was twelve years old. He was taken away."

Most of the people the Millers interviewed were around eleven or twelve years old during the Genocide, so events were told through the eyes of children, from a distance of over sixty years. The Millers found it necessary to look at accounts that were written as the catastrophe was taking place. One was written by Consul J.B. Jackson, who was stationed in Aleppo, Syria, and sent to the U.S. Ambassador to Turkey, Henry Morgenthau. It was dated March 4, 1918 and described the caravans from Sepastia, like the one Grammy had traveled with:

> One of the most horrible sights ever seen in Aleppo was the arrival early in August, 1915, of some 5,000 terribly emaciated, dirty, ragged and sick women and children, 3,000 on one day and 2,000 the following day. These people were the only survivors of the thrifty and well to do Armenian population of the province of Sivas, carefully estimated to have originally been over 300,000 souls! And what had become of the balance? From the most intelligent of those that miraculously reached Aleppo it was learned that in early Spring the men and boys over 14 years old had been called to the police stations in the province on different mornings stretched over a period of several weeks, and had been sent off in groups of from 1,000 to 2,000 each, tied together with ropes, and that nothing had ever been heard of them thereafter.

It confirmed what I'd heard on the tape about Grammy's brother and father, but I also noted condescension ("from the most intelligent it was learned...").

> Then I read a survivor's testimony incorporated into Jackson's account: On the 52nd day they arrived at another village, here the Kurds took from them everything that they had, even their shirts and drawers and for five days the caravan walked *all naked* under the scorching sun. For another five days they did not have a morsel of bread, neither a drop of water. They were scorched to death by thirst. Hundreds over hundreds fell dead on the way, their tongues were turned to charcoal [...] At another place, where there were some wells, some women threw themselves into it, as there was no rope and no pail to draw water but these were drowned and in spite of that the rest of the people drank from that well, the dead bodies still staying and stinking in it.

Charcoal tongues? The part about the wells was more comprehensible, but it was difficult to read of the degradation forced on the victims, the madness to drink or die.

If I had trouble taking in these accounts, I could imagine that it would have been next to impossible for survivors to tell them; to translate an other-worldly experience into a normal life would involve horrible, unendurable feelings. It's no coincidence that not one survivor volunteered to speak with the Millers; all the oral histories were solicited, and many of those who were invited to participate declined to tell their stories.

Grammy might have spoken of losing her brother in such simple terms for the very same reason, to avoid remembering in too great a detail. It was an obvious point, but I had somehow missed it as I was searching for her precise words, the answers to all my questions.

On the first day of "Armenians and the Middle East, 15th-18th C.," the professor explained that the course would examine the dark ages of Armenian history. "Most people want to hear about the Armenian kingdoms, the last of which fell in 1375. But Armenia has always dealt with overwhelming powers on all sides." There were only a few periods when the historical homeland of Armenia wasn't lodged between or ruled under warring powers, he explained. I hurriedly tried to get down all of Armenia's imposing neighbors throughout history in my notebook. "Assyria; Persia (before Alexander); Rome and Parthia; the Sasanians, Rome and Byzantium; the Arabs; the Khazars; the Seljuk Turks; the Mongols; the Ottoman Turks…"

I felt myself shrinking, like Armenia in the "Land of Pride" filmstrip from Sts. Sahag and Mesrob's Armenian School in Providence.

"… the Safavid Persians; Russia and Persia; Russia and Turkey; NATO and the Soviet Union." I looked around at the other students, mostly Armenian-American undergrads; none of them seemed too bothered by this litany of oppressors. When the professor asked us in the midst of class where we were from, in order to prove the effects of a nation long under siege, I discovered my classmates were from Lebanon, Iran, Egypt, Turkey, Canada, even Ethiopia.

Over the course of the coming weeks, the professor outlined the geopolitical forces that contributed to Armenia's subservient place in history. A high, mountainous region between the Black Sea, the Caucasus Mountains and the Syrian desert, Armenia's location was desired strategically by warring empires because it was easier to order troops down a plateau than up it. Armenian leaders, scattered throughout the rugged terrain, had little contact with each other, so opposing forces found Armenia easy to conquer. But the difficult landscape also ensured that Armenian culture, along with the idea of a homeland, could survive in remote locations, no matter who was ruling.

When the dominant cultures were friendly, Armenians adapted their foreign traditions: worshiping Greek gods, adopting Greek and Persian words, marrying Parthian royalty. They also converted to Christianity to counter the Zoroastrian Persians and to align themselves with Rome. But when the Byzantines put on pressure to adopt their theology, Armenians broke away and started their own Apostolic church, which turned out to be a pretty shrewd move, considering the church helped maintain a cultural identity during all the years Armenians lacked a homeland.

Armenians were dispersed from the region starting in the eleventh century, after the Seljuk Turks arrived, and even more Armenians vacated the plateau during the sixteenth century, when the Ottoman Empire and Persia battled over the land. When Shah Abbas deported the Ottoman Armenian population to Iran, hundreds of thousands perished, but he also created the city of New Julfa just for Armenian merchants, who soon established trade routes with Moscow. In the years that ensued, many of these deported Armenians relocated to Russia, and by 1828, after two Russo-Persian wars, Armenia was split between the Russian Empire and the Ottoman Empire, a.k.a. Eastern Armenia and Western Armenia. By the nineteenth century, with communities scattered between the Occident and Orient, Armenians had become worldly, learning concepts of enlightenment and self-determination.

Learning this history challenged my previous notions of Armenians as an insular, conformist people. Armenians did cling to their language and religion, as I had learned in Armenian school, but they also have been composed of many communities that adapted the best aspects of various cultures. When one Armenian community was suppressed, another one thriving elsewhere picked up the slack, maneuvering for greater freedom, maintaining the culture and identity. What allowed Armenians to survive, then, was their diversity.

After class, some of the students stuck around to socialize, but I took off. Though history was teaching me that a progressive might actually have a place in Armenian consciousness, I was pretty sure that the historians had never received Diggin Arlene's scorn for being an Armenian dunce. It was only a matter of time, I was convinced, before I would get shamed by the Armenian students for not speaking the language, so I couldn't even make small talk, never mind ask for help in translating my grandmother's broken story.

Outside of class, I started to do my own reading about the Ottoman Armenians, my forebears. It seemed to me that they were like any other oppressed minority within a larger culture; whenever they demanded more rights, they faced incredible backlash.

For example, I learned about the *millet*—a subsystem of government for religious minorities, which offered protection for Jews, Greek Orthodox Christians, Armenian Apostolics and Coptic Assyrians. But it also segregated these groups from the Muslim population at large. Armenians lived in their own quarters and were not allowed to bear arms or serve in the armed forces, for which they paid high taxes.

The majority of Ottoman Armenians were peasant farmers who lived in tiny villages, like my grandparents' families. In addition to the Sultan's tax on their Christianity, Armenian citizens were often forced to pay high tariffs to local Muslim leaders. Their farms were often looted by Turks and Kurds, who were rarely punished. During the Russo-Turkish War of 1877, Armenian villagers cheered advancing Russian soldiers, hoping they would be victorious and thus protect them against increasing Kurdish and Turkish oppression. Now perceived as traitorous, Armenians saw their conditions worsen. The Sultan armed bands of Kurds, called the *Hamidiye*, to terrorize their villages.

In response, Armenians formed their own defense groups, *fedayees*, which later morphed into the first Armenian political party, the Armenakan, in 1885. Several political parties sprouted up until most of them organized under one umbrella organization, the Tashnagsoutioun, or Armenian Revolutionary Federation. As the Armenian political parties began demonstrating, rumors spread in the mosques of imminent Armenian assaults, with calls to punish the infidel Armenians. What resulted was a huge wave of violence, hundreds of attacks on Armenian villages. Between 1894 and 1896, approximately one hundred thousand Armenians were massacred in pogroms in Constantinople and Anatolia. These were the years that my mother's grandparents had left the region, never to speak of it again.

Ottoman Turkish liberals, including the Sultan's nephew, were disillusioned by the massacres. They organized a party called the Young Turks and joined with the Armenian political parties to fight for reform; in 1908 the Young Turks staged a coup and deposed the Sultan. Together, Armenians and Turks celebrated in the streets. But the unity didn't last long. In 1909, the Sultan's supporters waged a counterrevolution in Constantinople, prompting a backlash at the Armenian population in the region of Cilicia,[4] particularly in the city of Adana. About two thousand Armenians were killed during ten days of massacres. Young Turks eventually sent troops, many of whom, instead of halting the massacres, joined in the spree to kill twenty-five thousand Armenians.

Concurrent with this increasing culture of violence towards Armenians, Turkey grew fearful for its future in a changing world, moving away from Empire states and towards nationalized identities. After losing the Balkans in 1912, the Young Turks thus turned ultranationalist under the CUP, the Committee of Union and Progress, which sought to unite the nation through a Turkish ethnicity. But the world (or, the West) was watching and demanded reform; by 1914, both the Triple Entente (Russia, France and

---

[4] An area also known as "Lesser Armenia" located further west than the Anatolian provinces.

Britain) and the opposing Central Powers (Germany, Austria-Hungary and Italy) agreed that the Armenian provinces should be divided in two and overseen by European governors.

The Turks were sure that this reform was a step towards complete Armenian sovereignty, similar to the recent Balkan independence. If Armenians were able to secede and take their land, rich in agriculture and part of the Turkish homeland since Seljuks arrived in the eleventh century, it would spell the end of the Empire. And then who knew what the Russians or the Europeans would do?

In November 1914, Turkey entered World War I on the side of Germany. Over one hundred thousand Ottoman-Armenian men fought in the Turkish army, although some Tashnags fled across the Russian border to join four voluntary units led by Armenian generals, including the famous Antranig. The Turks lost important battles in Anatolia in the winter of 1914-1915, some due to the efforts of these Armenian volunteers.

In a misguided response to this loss, the CUP disarmed Armenian soldiers in the Turkish army and put them in brutal work battalions, which exhausted the men to their deaths. Then, on April 24, 1915, about two hundred Armenian intellectuals, including writers, poets, artists, teachers, lawyers and other community leaders, were rounded up in Constantinople, deported to the interior, and killed.

The rest of the Armenian population was then subject to an extermination plan: Armenians were disarmed,[5] and mounds of guns, many culled in dubious ways, were photographed to prove their treasonous aims. Able-bodied men were taken away and shot. Local leaders, like my great-grandfather Stephan Koshgarian, were charged with treason and killed. The women and children and elderly, like Grammy, her mother, her sister, her sisters-in-law and their children, were given short notice to pack their belongings and told they were to be relocated. During the deportation, women and young girls were abducted and raped and taken into Muslim homes as slaves or servants. Shell-shocked caravans were denied food and water. The Armenians encountered dead bodies of other Armenians along the road. Their clothes fell apart, their shoes fell off. They searched for water. They walked and walked and walked.

As I read *Survivors,* my grandmother's experience became less singular and I suddenly realized the immensity of the Genocide. Few Armenians, helped by kind Turks or Kurds, were spared. I had heard the number estimated dead—one and a half million—countless times. The Millers stated in *Survivors* that this could be a high estimate, with the lowest possible figure at eight hundred thousand:

> An accurate generalization, however, is that approximately half of the Armenian population of Turkey died as a direct result of the Genocide.

---

[5] Aremenians in the Ottoman Empire were allowed to bear arms from 1909.

Worldwide, one third of the total population of Armenians died. Surviving Armenians included the several hundred thousand who were living in Constantinople and Smyrna who were not deported, children who were adopted into Kurdish and Turkish homes, perhaps three hundred thousand Armenians who escaped across the Russian border, and the pathetic remnant that survived months of deportation.

The killing of the Armenians stemmed from a racist mistrust, the first seeds planted with the *millet* system, growing evermore rapidly as the Ottoman Empire was crumbling, as regular Turkish citizens came to direct their fear and anger at anyone who was different, especially the Armenians who demanded more freedom. Their hatred was a cancer, long validated by law; there was nothing Armenians could do to stop it. It was miraculous that anyone survived, never mind a young child, like my grandmother.

I thought of how most Armenians in America were descendants of "the pathetic remnant." Suddenly the volunteers at Armenian school, Diggin Arlene and Diggin Carol, in their efforts to maintain Armenian identity, seemed like valiant souls. What right did I have to make fun of them? What right did I have to be embarrassed of my heritage, of my grandmother unable to spell her name on her oral history tape?

When I arrived at the hall, I lingered by the refreshment table, away from the other students of my Armenian history class. I wasn't a caffeine drinker but I grabbed a paper cup and filled it with coffee from a stainless steel cistern to occupy myself. I sipped and stared at trays of cookies covered in plastic wrap as my classmates took their seats and waited to hear the esteemed genocide scholar Vahakn Dadrian give a lecture. The event had also been advertised to the larger Armenian community.

"I say we take that cellophane off," an older man suggested to me, nudging my elbow.

"I don't know," I said. "I think they're for later."

"You're drinking coffee," he said accusingly.

"I know," I answered, as if he were my uncle. "But it wasn't wrapped in cellophane."

"It wouldn't hurt you to be a bit *moogovchee*," he said. I hadn't heard that word in a while. My mother used it for my Uncle Joseph when he came to our house and put *choregs* in his pockets, storing them for later.

The man lifted a corner of the film, grabbed a peanut butter cookie, and sat down. It was a matter of seconds before everyone was pilfering the refreshment table, including the students from my class.

One woman, an Armenian Studies Ph.D. candidate named Lori, approached and said hello to me; she told me she was studying literature about the Armenian genocide, and we chatted about survivor novels we had read. In the midst of our conversation, her face shifted to a more personal, almost pained expression, and she said, "Did you know the art historian Sophie der Nersessian?"

"No," I told her.

"That's too bad. She was a wonderful woman. She died last year. You remind me of her. Your face." I smiled at Lori. Here was a note of acknowledgment; even if I didn't feel Armenian, I appeared to be one.

From my seat in the second row, I had trouble hearing Vahakn Dadrian as he began his talk. A serious, stoic man in his seventies, wearing a brown, three-piece suit, he spoke in dry academic language with a French accent, outlining the forces that made the Genocide possible.

About halfway through the talk, strange ambient music from another part of the building encroached on his lecture. It was pretty loud, but Dadrian kept going. What else could he do? The circumstances were appropriate considering Dadrian was stressing the passivity of Armenians. He claimed that the inability for Ottoman Armenians to defend themselves took its toll on their psyche, even after they were able to bear arms; they became experts at compliance. When they found themselves in situations where chances of winning were slim, they submitted rather than fighting to the death. He gave an example of an elderly Armenian man from Constantinople who had been given a gun by a British officer during the 1894-96 massacres. When the man was physically assaulted by a Turkish authority, he failed to use the gun to protect himself and was beaten to death.

Just as long as Armenians had been victims, Dadrian stated, Turks had been invested in a dynamic of inequality, casting themselves in the position of power, due to their version of Islam. The Turks believed their religion to be superior, just as other ardent believers of monotheistic religions have the same tendency. Though the Koran preached tolerance, it also stated that there could be no equality between Muslims and non-Muslims. Hence the reason the *millet* would degrade into a program of oppression. The Turks also possessed a long history of solving problems militarily; they were expert soldiers and masters of war.

I had read in the *Survivors* book that genocide often occurs during periods of political instability. The perpetrators make the victims into scapegoats and identify them with the enemy; because some Armenians had allied themselves with Russians, Turks saw the presence of all Armenians as a grave threat that had to be dealt with. Additionally, genocide often takes on an ideological justification for the loss of human life. In the Armenian case, Turks believed they had to protect their empire from collapse at the hands of Armenian betrayal—it's this very same justification that modern Turkey uses today to explain the Armenian deaths. Although they defend the killings in the name of national security, the perpetrators are ashamed of their actions, so genocide is often committed during times of war, when there is little outside intervention, when it can be covered up.

The Millers purported that denial is actually the final stage of genocide. Since representatives of the Turkish government have consistently denied the Armenian Genocide since 1915 to this day, they are still occupying the final stage, still perpetrating genocide on the children and grandchildren of survivors.

This last thought clung to me as I made my way back to my apartment, alone.

Sitting at my desk, trying to write a passage that combined my newly acquired understanding of the Genocide with my limited knowledge of Grammy's story, I conjured the situation in my imagination as if my relatives where characters in a novel. It was going well until I imagined Grammy's mother, Razmouhi, seeing Stephan, Grammy's father, in Hochasar:

> She brought all the money she had in an effort to bribe her husband out of jail. She went up to his cell and showed him the pouch of gold coins and asked him what she should do. He told her through the bars that he didn't need the money, that she should use it to care for the children. There had been a trial, and he had been found guilty. He told her, "They're going to kill me tomorrow." And there was nothing he could do. There was nothing anyone could do. So he cried.

> I see my great-grandfather, looking like some version of my father, a stocky man with dark skin, a large nose, and a graying beard. He breaks down with his head in his hands. Crying. I see my great-grandmother crumple over with grief and horror, the air choking her.

> And then I don't see anything. Do they try to hold each other through the bars? How do they say goodbye? I can't see because I am crying. I can't see for the feelings, which I have never experienced before. I am crying strongly, it takes me over, the way I cried when my grandmother died, in mourning.

> I cry for a man I never knew, who knew he was going to die, who was forced to not care for his family anymore.

> For my grandmother who loved her father, who lost her father.

> For my father who never said in words that his grandparents had been murdered.

> For all that hasn't been said, and the simple words that have been.

> And all that I don't know how to imagine, but everything that I have known, somehow, through blood.

The next day I fell ill with the flu, and I couldn't complete the story.

"Catastrophe is the translation of *Aghed* and the name that the Armenians gave the event," Marc Nichanian said with a French accent. The director of Armenian Studies and a Sorbonne intellectual with Albert

Einstein hair, Marc was teaching a class, my following year in grad school, called "Literature and Catastrophe." He was explaining why he preferred to use "Catastrophe" to refer to the massacres of 1915, a controversial practice to most Armenians since any word other than genocide seemed to signify denial.

"Genocide" was coined in the 1940s by Raphael Lemkin, a Holocaust survivor, and adopted by the UN to label "the systematic, planned annihilation of a racial, political, cultural or religious group" an international crime. Marc agreed that what happened to Armenians fit the UN's bill. But the word genocide was imprecise since it was anachronistic and did not evolve from the event nor the language of its people. In addition, Marc purported that what marked the genocidal will of the Catastrophe was "the interdiction of mourning" it incurred; both the lack of proper burials during the event and denial afterwards took away the humanity of the victims. By demanding the use of the word genocide as a code word of justice, Armenians today were still trying to prove that the event took place, preventing the mourning process.

In the class we studied texts by and about genocide survivors and witnesses. We read first person accounts by Holocaust survivors Primo Levi, Jean Améry and others, but there was no equivalent literary account of the Armenian holocaust for us to read, written by someone who went through it at the time.

Zabel Essayan came close though. An Armenian writer living between Paris and Constantinople when the 1909 massacres in Cilicia took place, Essayan went to Adana immediately afterwards to help the victims, particularly the orphans; she wrote about it in her book, *In the Ruins*.

In one passage, Essayan travels to a village where victims of a massacre live in tents swarming with infection. She encounters a dazed, childless mother who smothered her infant so as not to give their hiding place away to Turks. Essayan constantly wonders about the trauma contained within each body she meets, about the unimaginable events in their horrified eyes. At an orphanage, she is confronted at night by a slip of a girl with wide eyes, which makes her cry. The orphans hear her sobbing and they are slung back into their moments of grief and then they cry too, a chain reaction.

Essayan survived the round up of intellectuals on April 24, 1915 in Constantinople by disguising herself and escaping to Paris, but she did not write a word about the Catastrophe. Her only effort as a writer to inform the world about it was to record, very faithfully, the oral history of a survivor. She did not interpret his words, or add any of her own experience. The only thing she did add was an introduction, in which she stated:

> Painfully imbued by the task that has fallen to my share, I considered
> that it would have been a sacrilege to transform into a literary subject the
> sufferings in which a whole people agonized, the unutterable story of the

profaned girls and the wrecks of a civilized nation that has been reduced to the level of animality by pain and misery, of crowds that were dying of thirst while they looked at the water on the banks of rivers, of ghosts that still lived in heaps of corpses, of young women and ladies transformed into commodities as devaluated objects, of women wounded to death in their maternal feelings. Consequently I approached this work with utmost simplicity and respect.

According to psychologist Dori Laub, a survivor won't speak unless there is a witness who listens and who respects her silences. Though I couldn't physically sit with my grandmother and I possessed only her recording, I was still a witness. And I hadn't done a very good job of it: I had trouble listening, I was bothered by the silences, and I became embarrassed, so I questioned her, asking (via Agnes) to prove herself as an authority. After reading Zabel Essayan, it seemed the critical component I needed in hearing Grammy's story—in honoring her silences, in separating myself from my own shame, in mourning some of our pain—was the right amount of distance. I couldn't identify so much that I felt personally victimized, nor could I step aside to ignore, resist, or condemn her. She had told me her story when I was an innocent child, before I could become resentful like all the other adults in the family, and before I was responsible enough to know what to do. Now it was time for me to mourn, like Essayan weeping with the orphans, in lineage and empathy.

A few weeks later I asked Lori to translate Grammy's oral history tape.

15. THESE WORDS ARE BEING WOVEN

The river was full and fast. It was May when Zanik marched with her family, first along the banks of the Alis River through several towns to the outskirts of the city of Sepastia, and then, after the men had been separated from the caravan and shot, by the wider Murad, the eastern branch of the Euphrates. The women and children climbed a path by the river, which led to the bridge. The water echoed loudly, "shagul, shagul," and the path narrowed. Everyone slowed down to navigate the treacherous point, but the gendarmes pushed them. Zanik slipped and nearly fell into the river, to be washed away by angry mud, but her sister Aghavni, who was pregnant, caught Zanik by the arm and pulled the child with all her strength onto the bridge.

Zanik's mother picked her up to carry her, though she was exhausted and covered with dust, having walked most of the day and night. Early the previous morning, she had said goodbye to her husband forever, left the family bible with the neighbors, then packed one ox-pulled cart. The women and children had walked out of town, guarded by gendarmes carrying long rifles and wearing woolen uniforms, the color of a muddy river. Zanik looked for her playmates to come out of their homes to say goodbye. There were thirty Turkish families and several Kurdish families in the village, but none of them came out of their homes as the Armenians were leaving, not one.

Later in the afternoon, bands of Kurds rode up on horses. Some of them grabbed girls and carried them away, screaming. Others slashed at the folds of older women's clothes with their knives, plundered carts and stole the oxen. There were little provisions now, no food or water.

A bit past the Murad River bridge, they traversed a narrow path up an incline. "Where are they taking us?" one woman asked.

"We have no idea," said another, answering for everyone.

Zanik says these words later as an old woman; she acts them out. "Where are they taking us?" she asks the young woman sitting by the tape recorder in her kitchen in 1979. "We have no idea," she answers herself.

The hill is tall and the path is long. Zanik holds onto her mother's neck, feeling her strong body rising, up up up. Gravity pulls down. They walk all day and most of the next night. Her mother grows tired. Zanik can feel the muscles waning from her bones, step by step. "*Mairig*, let's sit down and rest," she says. Her mother says nothing. The gendarmes beat up those who lag behind or walk on the edges. Those who fall behind are snatched by the men on horses. Everyone smears themselves with mud to appear as repulsive as possible so that no one will want to touch or take them. "After all, they're virgins," Zanik says. "Sisters and sisters. What happens to them?"

The passage up the mountain becomes rocky and barely discernible, "hardly as wide as the palm of your hand," Zanik says. It is so easy to fall, to drop to one's death. "Murder Mountain," it is called in Kurdish, "Hill of Blood," in Armenian. If you look down you'll get dizzy and see death. Souls decomposing down there. Zanik watches people weak from dehydration trip and tumble down. "'Let them perish in that pit,'" she says, as if quoting the cruelty of the gendarmes.

Back on the flat of the plateau, the caravan is far from any river or spring. The search for water becomes everything. The deportees suck condensation from the morning leaves, their only source of water until someone spots a pool ahead. "A little bit of water," Zanik says. "Let me drink a little bit of water." As they approach, a stench hits them. At the water's edge they see. It is a pit and there are dead bodies in it. "They shot and shot them there, corpse upon corpse. Half dead, half alive. Oh Lord, *aman*."

Then there is a well. Someone manages to draw a pailful but people are crazed with thirst; they collapse upon each other straining for a few drops. The crowd grabs the bucket and dumps it; Zanik cups her hands under the deluge but someone snatches the water from her palms. She pushes her way out of the mob to lick the remaining moisture but she is too late, her hands are dry.

Cah-leh cah-leh cah-leh. They reach a place where Kurds are selling grapes. Razmouhi, Zanik's mother, buys a bunch with a gold coin. The family lives for two weeks eating the grapes one by one, one a day. Razmouhi parcels them out to her daughters, her sons' wives, and her little grandchildren. By the time they are done, the grapes are desiccated raisins, little more than dust.

Cah-leh cah-leh cah leh. Once more they are thirsty. They come to a place where Turks are wrangling with the dried skins of goats, filling them with water and selling them. But the family doesn't have any money left to buy. Razmouhi had swallowed the last of the gold coins as safekeeping from Kurdish and Turkish marauders, but when Araxie, her eldest daughter-in-law, poked through her shit with a twig, she never found them. "We don't have a container to drink from. The Kurds have stolen everything," Zanik says. "My sister had a pail to carry water and they beat her up and took it away."

"We don't eat unless the Kurds sell us food. Otherwise we walk. Walk walk walk. Two, three months we walk until our shoes are rotten and we are barefoot. They are taking us through the woods where there is no road. My feet are swollen, filled with thorns."

Caravans of the near-dead arrived daily to Aleppo, Syria. "The entire place was refugees when we arrived. The Red Cross brought us food. They gave a loaf of bread to every single person. But there's nowhere to sleep. It's just a field." The Syrian governor defied the orders of the Young Turks to kill the Armenians and instead tried to help them. "There is food but I don't even know who's giving it. The Arabs? The Red Cross has abandoned us."

An influenza epidemic hit the camps, so the refugees were loaded onto open trains. "Dirty trains. They brought us to Hama, the Arab land. It's a mountainous area. On either side of the train you can see many homes. But they don't take us there. They'll put us on camels and take us into the Arabian villages." The refugees would be caravanned further into the desert from Hama, to the rocky canyon of Der-el-Zor where thousands would die, a final stop.

But Razmouhi said, "Oh no, there will be no more moving. If we die, we'll die here."

Araxie saw a place she thought would be safe, where they wouldn't be moved again. "She pointed to an opening in a cave. We went into the cave. My mother said, 'We won't leave here. Whatever happens, stay here.'"

The women were skeletons, shrouded in rags. They were in the cave just a few days when Aghavni suddenly felt birthing pains.

"How could she have survived the deportation *pregnant?*" Lori asked as she held her tape recorder, rewinding and replaying the segment, her thumb pushing buttons. We were in her office overlooking a busy Manhattan avenue. "How could she sustain a baby on one grape a day?"

Every Saturday we met for an hour for nearly six months. Lori listened and transcribed Grammy's story into her notebook, and I sat by her side. She told me how hard it was to hear the story, to listen and write down each word. She asked me questions and if I didn't know the answers, I consulted Auntie Agnes' translation, made calls to my family, and read history books on the Genocide and on village life before 1915. But I didn't know how to answer Lori's question about Aghavni surviving a three-month march of 250 miles through the desert while pregnant. Like many other stories of women who live beyond themselves, there is no answer, no logical explanation.

A refugee woman in the cave knew to cut the umbilical cord. But there was no clean cloth in which to hold the baby. "My mother ripped off half her apron so she could swaddle the child."

A family of Greeks came looking for children to adopt. Aghavni didn't want to give up the baby, but she had nothing to feed, her breasts bone dry. Her other children had already died and so had Avedis and Mary, Araxie's children. "They come in the mornings with carts and collect the dead and take them to the top of the hill where there is a pit and they will pile them up there, and they took that child. Those Greeks took it."

Enneh, Zanik's other sister-in-law, had enough strength to leave the cave during the day to find food. She saw the refugee tents, where one could get tea and bread with tahini and sugar. "Come on!" she said.

"But we were so weak and tired, it was just a mile or so to the tents but it took us from morning till dusk to reach it. When we got there, everyone had influenza.

"'I am cold, I am cold,' my sister said and she took me in her arms to keep her warm, she was holding me tight. I went to sleep like that in the tents. I am a child, I fall asleep. In the morning, I wake up, I am lifting her up, lifting her up, she won't stay up.

"I am screaming, I am screaming 'She won't get up! My sister won't get up!'"

The night was never the same; Zanik hadn't slept much before; now she lay terrified. Day and night were the same when she noticed full families arriving at the tents, with men and boys who hadn't been separated and killed. At first she was afraid, but a sister-in-law told her that these were the caravans from Aintab and Marash, southernmost cities of the Anatolian provinces.

Soon after Aghavni died, an Armenian man told Razmouhi that he would take Zanik into his family. Razmouhi replied to the man, "I have only this one child left. Let her stay next to me until my eyes close." Then to Zanik she said, "Don't forget, you have brothers in America."

Her mother is not like how she remembers her from home, a sturdy woman wearing skirts, glints of pretty jewelry on her wrists and ankles. Hands ruddy with work. Thick hair she brushes into her kerchief. She is dirty and sick and barely clothed, bones stretching her skin.

"Zanik," Razmouhi mumbles in a grainy haze, her eyes black towards her, the strongest part of her body, "I am sorry."

In the morning she is stiff. They brush the dust from her face; they comb her hair with fingers and say a prayer. The cart comes and takes the corpse away to be thrown on the pile.

Zanik didn't speak for days. She cried and cried though it wasn't long before her body wouldn't allow tears to flow from her eyes, but still she wept. She eventually broke her silence to ask her sisters-in-law, "What's going to happen to me?" She was near death, her thorny feet swollen like watermelon, lice in her snarled nest of hair; an undernourished calf, limbs like sticks and a bloated belly.

Araxie answered. She was in charge now that Razmouhi had died. "The Arabs come and take the children away. You can go too, you know. The next time they come to collect the children, you go with them."

One day, two Arab women enrobed in black, covered from head to toe with only their eyes showing, stood above Zanik. "Then my sister-in-law came over and said that these two wanted me. She said, 'Get up and go with them. At least you'll have a chance to stay alive. You'll die here for sure.'" Zanik saw the women pass something, maybe some coins, to Araxie. "I don't know what they gave to that sister-in-law of mine."

Then the black figures took Zanik by the hand. "I am going. Crying, crying crying. I am going. I don't know where I'm going. I don't know who they are. I can't even see their faces. My legs are trembling. What if they want to kill me?"

The two Arab women took Zanik to a large house of white stone. They wouldn't let her come inside. "They made me sit in the courtyard. Then they came and took off all my clothes. They cut my hair. They gave me some of their clothes to wear. They brought me food but I couldn't eat." When night fell, they instructed her to sleep on an old straw mat. She fell asleep crying.

The next morning the two women took her away from the house.

She asked in Armenian and Turkish where they were taking her and they answered in Arabic. She feared that they were taking her to be killed. "It turned out it was a bath. But I'm still afraid that they'll kill me." They rubbed a rough stone over her skin; she thought they would rub her skin right off. They poured cupfuls of water over her head, one after the other, without stopping. *Why won't they just drown me in the water?* she thought.

A razor was brought to her head and she screamed. "I wouldn't mind if they cut my hair, but they *shaved* it." Then they shaved her body. "They are kneading my crotch, kneading it, they are going to kill me. They did it, they did it, they did it," she repeats of those who sought to purify her, cleansing her of those who had touched or taken her: "They rubbed me till there was nothing left."

They brought her back home and led her to a small room and she fell straight to sleep, then woke up crying. Bread was left by her side but she was unable to eat. "I am sick, I am going to die. 'Oh God, why can't I just die and be free?' I am telling myself. 'Who are these people I've been left with?' I thought about running away, but I was too weak to leave."

In the morning the two women, without their black clothing, examined her crusted eyes and her feet, still swollen. One of the women made the sign of the cross, and Zanik discovered she was Greek. She was also the lady of the house, the master's wife. "He must have snatched her from somewhere," Zanik thought. "This is why she saved me." The hanum[6] called a doctor to care for Zanik's feet three times that week. He also cured her pinkeye, trachoma, so her eyes could open in the morning.

When she recovered, Zanik cleaned and cooked for the Mohani adi Alli family. They fed her and housed her and once a year they paid her a thin gold bracelet. She learned their language and told their folk stories and the hanum often claimed that she would marry Zanik off to a relative. She was thankful to be alive, but with resentment she remembered how her own family had given food to the poor people who came to their door. "Now they looked down on me as if I were a beggar."

One day her hanum told her to make bread, and Zanik obliged, until the hanum demanded Zanik make more than the dough in the bowl. "I'm from a good family!" she yelled. "I was raised on butter and oil. You are taking advantage of me!" She threw balls of dough to further make her point. Later, in her memory, she saw the soft flesh hit her hanum's face, stupid and alive and clean, unlike her own hands, dough beneath her fingernails.

Zanik didn't leave the house. She was able to perform all her duties indoors, and she felt more safe inside. "I had been there about two years and I had not seen anyone. One day my hanum decided to send me to the

---

[6] A Turkish word, a servant's name for the female head of the house.

market. She put a basket in my hand and told me to bring back this and that. My hair had grown long by now and I had healed, I had put on weight."

One day in the marketplace, she saw a woman with a mole on her right cheek—she looked familiar. "My memories flooded and my brain turned. That woman had held me as a baby, had strolled with me through the village." Her name was Shushan Neh-neh, a neighbor from Istanos. Zanik struggled with how to approach her, to introduce herself. What if she were wrong, or what if Shushan Neh-neh wouldn't remember her? "I went to stand behind her so that when she turned around to leave she would face me." Shushan Neh-neh's eyes met Zanik's. "*Vay yavroum,* my Zanik!" she cried, her voice falling and rising with glee and sadness.

Zanik brought Shushan Neh-neh to the house. They told each other who was still alive, who had died. Shushan Neh-neh didn't know about Araxie and Enneh. "Now if you see my sisters-in-law you can tell them where I am," Zanik told her quietly in the kitchen while Shushan Neh-neh gobbled down bread and *madzoon.*

Six months later, a knock came on the door. "My hanum said, 'Zanik, go see who is at the door.' I was walking towards it when I heard a voice."

"Zan-eeek, Zan-eeeeek," the voice cried, knocking the breath from her chest. It was exactly like her mother's. "She's back to life? Oh God, my legs are shaking." She stood in her tracks, holding onto the wall until the cries were just outside the door. "I opened it to see that it was my brother's wife." Araxie.

They cried and cried and cried. "She was out of breath from crying. 'Akh *yavroum,* what are you doing? *Yavroum,* you are alive! They've kept you so well, your hair's lovely, you're here, my Zanik!'"

Araxie and Enneh had survived the intervening years by living on the street. When they couldn't get into one of the refugee camps, the Red Cross or Near East Relief, they begged for food, they begged for money, they prostituted themselves, most likely, to survive.

Now they asked Zanik to go back to Istanos with them. At this time, around 1917-1918, the surviving Armenian refugees in Hama were planning to return to their villages since Turkey and Germany were losing the war.

"I told them, 'You couldn't even get a piece of bread with tahini for me and now you want me to go with you?'"

Araxie said, "No, no, no. We'll take good care of you. There are two volunteer soldiers who are willing to take us back to the country." An Armenian Legion of volunteers had formed at the outbreak of the war made up of Armenian men from Russia, Europe and America, fighting on the side of the Allied Powers.

Zanik didn't care if the *gamavors* would help them. "I do not want to be left out on the streets again. I will not go."

So they left without her.

"But then something happened. I became emotional. I cried over why I didn't leave with them." Suddenly, she was alone with the hanum again, a stranger's girl in a stranger's home. The next morning, Zanik packed food and water into a blanket, bundled it up and tied it to her hip. "Now I'm just a young girl," twelve or thirteen, "where I am headed, I have no idea." Zanik saw an uncovered woman in the market who she thought might be Armenian.

"Do you know where the Armenians are gathering to go back to their country?" Zanik asked the woman.

She turned to look down at her, and Zanik was surprised by her bright blue eyes. "Oh, you poor, poor girl. You believed there was such a thing as going back? Only a fool would go back and get slaughtered a second time. Stay where you are. At least you have bread to eat." She turned away.

"I won't go back," Zanik said to herself. "What kind of dignity will I have?" Even if her hanum had rescued her from death, she was still a servant, some might even say a slave—she had no freedom to leave, nowhere to go.

"My sister sent you?" she was asked as she entered the home of her hanum's friend.

"I ran away," Zanik said.

Her masters were sent for and arrived shortly. The hanum said, "Do you have any idea how upset we were?" They had been looking all over, asking everyone on the street if they'd seen her. "We were looking after you like our own child," the hanum claimed. When they got home, she asked Zanik to do her chores: bake the bread and fill the oil canisters.

The letter was written on thin tissue paper, in an even Armenian script, so her hanum could not read it to Zanik. Supposedly, it was from Zanik's brothers to a nearby orphanage, announcing that they were looking for Zanik. Her hanum looked at it suspiciously, at the unfamiliar characters. It had been brought to the house by Mairam Chavoush, an Armenian refugee who took it upon herself to rescue the Armenian girls in Arab homes so that they wouldn't become lost forever. Shushan Neh-neh had told her about Zanik working in the Mohani adi Alli home, that she was losing her tongue, and that Zanik had brothers in America.

The hanum harrumphed and sent her away, but a few weeks later, Mairam Chavoush stopped by the house again and insisted that Zanik come with her to sign for another letter that contained money for her passage. The hanum was enraged. "That letter is a fake. There is no salvation for the Armenians, they're dispersed all around. If you leave here again, it will be the end of you."

At the time, you had to be a bit crazy to believe that an Armenian could live anywhere, after seeing so many of them practically dead or soulless. But Zanik knew her hanum wanted Zanik to stay and serve her. But Zanik remembered the words of her mother to not forget her brothers in America.

It turned out the hanum was right, the letter had been a fake; there was no money from her brothers. And the orphanage was a barn. It was filthy and everyone was covered in fleas. The orphans, miserable and sick, wailed into the night and wet themselves. Their condition was not much better than during the death marches. There were no beds so they slept on chairs pushed together.

But she would not go back. The Armenian orphanage sent her name to the agencies in the diaspora, who printed it in the Armenian weeklies. If her brothers saw her name, they would send for her.

"Your brother is here. He's been looking for you." Zanik stared at the woman delivering the news. She was the *Mairig* of the Red Cross orphanage in Aleppo, where all the orphans had been transferred, a safer location and a better facility, with a school where Zanik was re-learning her language. The orphans dressed in white and slept two to a bed and the *Mairig* watched over them. Now Zanik wasn't sure if she had heard her right. "Well," the *Mairig* said, "go to him!" She pointed out the window at a group of people near the main gate.

"But I don't know what he looks like," Zanik said. She approached a young man wearing a Russian Army uniform.

"Zanik, is that you?" he cried.

"Touros?" she asked. She had always heard about him when she was growing up, a mythical figure who had shared her brother's mother's milk; she was only four when he had been drafted into the Turkish Army. Touros had survived the forced labor battalions until he was captured by the Russian Army and sent to Siberia for three years. After the Red Army released all the prisoners of war at the start of the Bolshevik Revolution, he joined General Antranig in 1917. A year later, after Armenia became independent, Touros set out to find his relatives.

After the orphanage, he left for Hama to find Araxie and Enneh. Two months later, he returned with them, and they all went to Smyrna, now Izmir. Their money soon ran out, so they lived in the yard of the Armenian church for a month until Touros could find the money for their passage to America on the Panama, a Greek ship.

Araxie and Enneh were sick for days, but Zanik had the time of her life. She watched a couple of girls who were holding some strange yellow fruit with a rubbery skin. She'd never seen anything like it. They broke off the tip and peeled away the skin in sections and then bit into the long fruit. Zanik couldn't help laughing. The girls noticed and offered her one. She laughed and laughed while she tentatively chewed it, the yellow pulp brightening her mouth.

In Providence, she lived with her brothers and sisters-in-law on the top floor of a triple decker until there was a strike at the foundry where her brothers worked and they were left jobless. "Now all of a sudden there is a story circulating. Whenever I enter a room my brothers quiet down. One day I said, 'There's something you're keeping secret from me. What is it?'"

"Zanik," Soukias said. "This is the situation. We have no jobs and no income. You've arrived, and Jacob Agababian has a very large farm in Oxford. If you marry him, we can become partners with him."

"I saw that man and I won't have him. If you want to be partners in the farm, buy it from him."

"Our money is not enough," Soukias said.

"Let me go to school, please, don't make me marry him." But her brothers wouldn't listen. Though she was precious, the only one of their family left besides them—father, mother, brother, sister, all gone—she was still a girl. She was going to grow up and get married anyway, so why not marry now while they needed an income to survive? "We had just arrived and we were hungry." It was 1920.

"How old were you then?" Hera asks Grammy. She has asked it about nine times during the course of the interview. When the soldiers were collecting the guns and the horses, Grammy answers, "I was about four years old, but things are so branded in my mind, what child can remember age?" When Hera prods, Grammy replies, "Who knows about age when it comes to war? Does age stay on one's mind? I was little."

Hera asks for her age after Touros collects Araxie and Enneh to bring them all to America. Grammy loses her top. "Who knows how old I was? Who asks about age?"

"It wasn't necessary," Hera complies.

"Here they ask; they want to know about age," Grammy laments. "One day seems like a thousand years for me."

"Why can't she just tell her age?" I asked Lori.

"It's typical of Armenian women of that generation to be vain about how old they are. My grandmother and aunts were exactly the same way," Lori said.

But as I thought more about the situation, I realized that Grammy wasn't even sure what year she was born since her birth records were destroyed. Her predicament was such that she couldn't control much of what happened to her life, even the fact of her age.

But she could control the telling of her story. At the time of her engagement, Grammy estimates, "I must have been ten to fifteen."

"Fifteen," Hera confirms at the older end of the spectrum.

"*Barely* fifteen," Grammy bargains. "These words are being woven."

Jacob was a cousin of Zanik's sister-in-law Enneh, on his mother's side. "But my parents never would have arranged that marriage if we were in the old country. His family wasn't good enough." Jacob was ten years older than Zanik and she thought he was dark and ugly. She didn't know English and couldn't speak to the neighbors. Girls came to visit her, "But I don't know a word to say to them… There was nobody. Not an Armenian girl for me to say a word. No one to listen to your problems and empathize."

Six months later, the farm was faltering and there were job openings in Providence. Her brothers told her she could leave Jacob.

"No way," she said. "You got us engaged, you praised him to heaven saying what a nice fellow he is and now suddenly, six months later, he's not so good? I wanted to go to school and you wouldn't let me and now you'll just take me and give me over to somebody else. I won't have you making decisions for me anymore. I won't go." Besides, she felt sorry for Jacob, at least that's what she told her daughters later.

Zanik didn't talk to her in-laws unless they spoke to her, according to custom. "I did not speak and could not look in anyone's face: I was nonexistent." Her mother-in-law asked her to cook meals whenever relatives came to visit. Zanik had to do everything her mother-in-law said.

It was just like the old country again. The family under one roof, the chores, the animals, the food, the *dahn deegeen* in charge of everything. Among the Irish Catholics and French Canadians of Oxford, a little piece of Istanos. Armenians in a safe part of the world had preserved the culture, and Zanik was plopped into it.

After her mother died, friends turned to enemies and then to friends again: Araxie, her hanum, now her brothers. She was still being bought and sold, still being forced to go from one undesirable place to the next, forced to ally herself to those who had more power. Her life seemed to parallel Armenian history then: during the darkest periods she struggled for dignity, she couldn't help the drive for self-determination.

Near the end of her life, I had thought she wanted to return to Oxford because it was her home. Now I realized that she also wanted independence and recognition of the self. She constantly expressed this wish, telling whoever would listen her hopes, her complaints, her regrets, her story. She spit it into her dough, she screamed it at her daughters when she demanded that they take her home, she scrubbed it into her granddaughter's skin, rubbing me till only my birthmark could stay her memories.

16. SECRETS OF THE *UNDANEEK*

Zanik was alone with her youngest daughter Ruth who was sick with a cold, feeding her *panjar abour,* when a man came to the door.

"What?" she asked, staring at his suit and hat.

"Lady, you owe me two dollars for the silverware set." Zanik listened to his speech, tilting her head closer in his direction, her eyes squinting. Her English was getting better, but the sounds Americans made with their tongues were so unfamiliar; she thought she knew the words, but had trouble understanding intentions. She looked for clues in the man's pink face and the placement of his body, his barrel chest and thick arms.

"I know you remember me," he said. "There," he pointed to the soup spoons on the kitchen table, "the silverware, you owe me."

"I don't have money," Zanik said quickly, understanding completely. "I give to you next month." She moved towards the door.

"You owe me two dollars now," the man said, more insistently, "and if you don't pay up, I'll call the police."

Ruth was sitting on the side of her mother's sewing machine, a makeshift highchair, and she started to cry at the sound of the word "police."

"I don't have it!" Zanik yelled, disturbed that her child was now upset. She pushed the man out the door and slammed it shut. She took a deep breath, told Ruth to stop crying, and fed her some more soup. "I never should have married him," she said under her breath.

By 1928, eight years after her wedding day, Zanik had birthed five children, losing one. The dairy farm continued to falter, so Jacob decided to sell the farmhouse and 250 acres, keeping only three and a half acres on which to build a new two-family house on Main Street in Oxford. He planned that the upstairs would house his mother and younger siblings, and a downstairs for his four little girls and young wife.

Zanik had thought he was crazy, that he could have instead bought two or even three wire mill workers' homes with the same amount of money. But Jacob insisted those shacks were lice traps and that it was far better to build a safe secure clean house. He even decided to quit his job to oversee the carpenters, to be sure they weren't using one nail when they should be using two.

"Don't leave your job," Zanik had told Jacob. "If they don't give it back, what will we do?"

"They'll give me my job back," Jacob said. "What could happen?"

The Depression hit and Jacob and Zanik owned a house but not enough money to pay the taxes on it. They would have lost it to the bank, if it weren't for the cash they managed to raise last minute from relatives. But now Zanik barely had enough money to buy food for her family, never mind silverware.

They lived off the vegetable garden that Jacob planted on their three acres. In the summer they ate green beans with pilaf, green beans with to-matoes, green beans with green beans. Hazelnuts and blueberries grew in the woods surrounding their neighborhood and the kids collected them in baskets. Zanik made pies from the blueberries, cookies with the nuts. Every month she made huge batches of *choereg* and *paghach* that lasted weeks. She sewed the childrens' clothes, and Jacob fixed the holes in their shoes and carved wooden *tavloo* boards and toys. The neighbors came to Jacob to fix their broken-down cars and beat-up sewing machines, but he never asked for anything in return. There was a welfare service but Zanik and Jacob were too proud to apply.

Relatives visited from Providence and Zanik made huge meals for fifteen to twenty people on two burners, all by herself, and asked none of the children for help. When the girls grew older, they helped bake bread and sew sheets to the *yoghans* every week; they cleaned the house and washed down the walls and changed the curtains every spring. They assisted with the canning and pickling.

In the winter, the house was frigid because they couldn't afford heat; only the kitchen was warm, so everyone would rush into it from their beds in the morning. The girls readied themselves for school, competing for one mirror, applying lipstick, fixing hair, adjusting dresses; when they started to push and shove each other, their father would throw a towel over the look-ing glass to hurry them up. There were two double beds in the room the girls shared. Mel and Ruth in one, Sherrie and Agnes in the other. The girls made jokes at night while the flowered wallpaper on the walls made faces at them, and the whippoorwills would coo and soothe them to sleep.

Jacob had wanted all the girls to be boys; each and every time Zanik was pregnant he prayed for a boy. He had become so desperate that when he found out at the hospital that Ruth was a girl, he said nothing and went home without even taking a look at his daughter.

Zanik taught the children to be neat and polite and to work hard in school. She always stressed the importance of education, encouraging all of her children to go to school, to study as much as they could. The Oxford schoolteachers gave her children American names, which bothered her, but what could she do? There were but two Armenian families in town; most everyone in Oxford was of French-Canadian descent. When they asked the Agababians what they were, and the Agababians answered, "Armenian," the French Canadians would answer, "Oh yes, Indian."

One day Zanik caught two boys stealing the tires off her husband's truck, so she brought out her husband's shotgun. "Get lost or I'll call the cops!" she screamed from the front door, gun pointed directly at them. The boys brazenly ignored her so she went inside and made the call. The Oxford police stopped the boys, returned the tires, and brought them in, but then let them off with just a warning. It didn't surprise Zanik.

She told her children what the Turks did to the Armenians. She described the march, she told her children how she lost her parents and brother and sister, sparing them the gory details. Her story was still difficult to listen to. "Oh, Ma," Ruth used to say when her mother would mention something particularly tragic, "I don't want to hear it right now."

So Zanik would tell other stories. She recreated the folk tales that she had learned from her Arab family in Hama. She gossiped about the Oxford villagers and made fun of her neighbors and the police chief who spoke with a nasal voice. She had all the kids laughing so much at the table they physically couldn't eat their supper.

When I asked Mel, Agnes, Sherrie, Ruth and my father for specifics, though, to tell her stories to me, they couldn't remember.

"Did people in your generation feel pressured to get married?" I asked Auntie Agnes.

I conducted interviews with my aunts, partially to construct their family's early life, but also in an effort to get at the stories of those wedged between Armenia and America. As I spoke with each aunt, trying to ask open-ended questions which I hoped would produce long historically important answers, I was thinking about all the stories I had always wanted to know but was afraid to ask.

"No, because there was nobody to marry," Agnes said bluntly. "All the boys in my time went into the service [to serve in WWII]. And they all came home and they started out with entry-level jobs and we already had good jobs. You know, you're not gonna take a step backwards to go forwards. I don't know, the timing wasn't right." Then she added as an afterthought, "And besides all of which, my father always used to say, 'We're lost in this country. Let's help the ones in Beirut, let's help the ones in Armenia, but we're lost in this country, we'll never amount to anything.'… I don't know, he always talked as though we were gonna assimilate and be nothing."

Aunt Sherrie told me her engagement to Uncle Tony lasted five years because of their difference of religion. Mumma had told me that Sherrie was asked to sign papers stipulating her kids would be raised Catholic and Grammy threatened to disown her if she did. "Were your parents concerned about you marrying someone who was of a different religion?" I asked, sitting in her living room in Long Island, like I was the Agabian Mike Wallace.

"Of course. We heard this all our lives. To marry an Armenian boy, find a nice Armenian boy and get married. That was one of the things you were brought up with. And we traveled in the Armenian circles. I certainly gave it enough time. We went to all the conventions and all the dances… But nothing worked out. What can I say?"

Since she was the only aunt who moved away from the family, I was curious how Sherrie had managed to break from her parents, if they were worried about her when she left home to live in New York. "Oh yes, they were concerned, but they also weren't the type to tell you not to do something. They told you to try it and if it didn't work out they would be there to help."

Agnes said something similar when I asked if Grammy got nervous about her travels abroad. "No, not really. She wasn't the type to worry like that."

This wasn't the Grammy that I knew. It seemed the aunts were reluctant to say anything negative about their parents. They all spoke of how much they admired their parents for raising them during the hardship of the Depression, for all that they sacrificed. But I was longing to hear stories about the difficulties of being their children; I wanted to hear resentment, to find the source of all their screaming.

I wasn't nervy enough to ask Aunt Mel about the marriage proposal of her paraplegic boyfriend, but she spoke extensively of her work on the spinal cord unit of the V.A. hospital, detailing how emotional it was and how much she admired her patients. "If there is any sacrifice, bodily injury… amputation and anything else, there's means of getting around, there's still a lot that you can do. But if you have a spinal cord injury—that is rough, Nancy. And they're wonderful people… To this day I'm amazed that they can have enough spirit in themselves that they handle it as good as they do. You know, it's really something." I imagined that for my aunt, watching a man physically embody triumph over unimaginable loss must have been incredibly touching; I couldn't expect her to tell me a complex, intimate story of losing such a person.

But Ruth revealed herself, briefly, when she told me her father's reaction to her birth. "Who wants the fourth daughter?" she said, annoyed at her lot in life.

Later, as an adult, Ruth was deserted by her siblings, who all left home within a six-month period. In 1952, Mel went to nursing school, Agnes to the art institute, Sherrie left for New York to find an airline job, and Tip was drafted into the Army to fight the Korean War. So Ruth was the only child left with their parents at the house on Main Street.

During those years, Zanik and Jacob fought over everything, screaming and yelling. "Maybe mother was discontent, that she realized her life wasn't all she wanted it to be," Sherrie said. Zanik was often suspicious of Jacob and accused him of looking at other women. "She didn't treat Pa very nicely, and he put up with it, because of what she had gone through," Agnes said.

When I asked my father how his parents got along, he replied, "Uh, my parents got along very well at times and very poorly at other times. Like any relationship, it would go sour from time to time... [My mother] would get bent outta shape and uptight about various things she didn't think were right, and so their relationship would get contentious, and it was never kept from us children; we experienced all of those difficulties that they had through the years."

I asked what his parents' arguments were like.

"Well, there would be some yelling, but then it would subside and then there would be not too much conversation between the two and you knew they were not on the best of terms. They wouldn't talk and sometimes you'd have to relay messages from one to the other."

"Were you ever afraid they would split up?" I asked.

"I suppose there was some of that fear, but they would always get together eventually. When you were a young child you were concerned it might happen, but as I said, they would always patch up their differences after a while and so you would go on to the next episode." This sounded familiar.

That kind of constancy made me think of Auntie Ruth. She had never lived apart from her mother, and she was the one with her father at his death, though he had shunned her at her birth. She described to me how he was driving her to a baby shower in a snowstorm when his heart suddenly seized and he nearly drove into a snowbank. She rode in the ambulance with him and squeezed his hand and he would squeeze back, fainter and fainter until she was afraid he would stop squeezing. By the time they got to the hospital, his hand was limp.

"All in all they were good parents. Believe me," she said, as she cried and blew her nose. "We were very lucky when I think about some of the people who had these weird parents and you know, hardships. Thank God for, you know, our good parents. Really."

"Yeah," I said. "It sounds like they really loved their kids."

"Yes," she said. "Just like your folks."

Ruth was showing the pattern to me: her parents loved their kids, so my parents loved me, Leo and Val; it was clear that relationship difficulties also resurfaced in the later generation. But considering the news came from Ruth, it seemed that love outweighed all of the dysfunctional troubles.

"Why did your parents separate?" I asked my mother. Now I wanted to find out about the legacies from her side of the family. An inexperienced (and sort of sadistic) interviewer, I started with the hard stuff.

Mumma made a face, curling her lips and shaking her head and making the thumbs down sign, as if the tape recorder was a blind stranger in the room she was trying to elude. I watched expressionless and waited for an answer.

"Well," she began, "I really don't know the reason. It may have been money. We moved into my grandparents' house on Crescent Avenue and it was in a very rural area…" She described the trees in the neighborhood and her grandfather's egg business and chicken coops, indicating that she wasn't going to talk about her parents' separation on record, even though she had told me before that they split up because theirs was an arranged marriage and they had known each other hardly at all before they wed.

"What was your mother like?" I asked.

"She was very very loving. And was always keeping the house neat, and took as good care as she could for us, and insisted that I go on to college even though she could have used the money and really didn't have much of anything at all, but insisted that I went."

"And uh, what did she look like?"

"She looked very much like you, Nancy. In fact when I look at you I can see my mother. You even have some of her facial expressions." She had told me this before—once, she saw her mother in one of my charcoal drawing self-portraits. It gave me a funny feeling. I was special for looking like her mother, for whom she had so many feelings, great love and sadness, but it was the same sort of special as nearly dying at Children's Hospital, or realizing a relative had been named after a dead baby from the genocide.

"Did she seem happy?" I asked my mother. I wondered if we looked alike, did we have similar dispositions?

"At times she was happy and at times she was not so happy. It wasn't so easy."

"Did she ever get depressed?"

"At that time I did not use that word," Mumma quickly said, annoyed. "I'm sure and I know she had her bad days. It was not an easy happy life."

Her mother depressed, I noted. "What was your father like?" I proceeded.

"My father was always very friendly and a lot of people seemed to like him. It was just too bad they had difficulties in their earlier life because I think he changed his mannerisms and his outlooks."

"How did he change?" I asked.

"Well," she started reluctantly, "I got the feeling from what my mother said that they seemed to be a little more amiable, maybe because a number of years had gone by."

"And did you see him much when you were growing up?"

She curled her lip and shook her head and made the thumbs down sign again.

"And why are you making those weird facial expressions?" I blurted out.

"No, I did not," Mumma acquiesced. "It was just she and I, so we were very close. We would talk a lot together. And she was always interested in what was happening to me in school. So I would unload on her and she was always very empathetic, and sympathetic."

This last comment bothered me, and I could not hear it, nor imagine the close relationship she described. I could only question why my mother had not been more empathetic and sympathetic towards me. I took a deep breath. "Tell me about when your mother died," I asked.

"Well, when my mother died it was very much of a shock because she really hadn't been ill with any terrible amount of illness, and so it was very sudden, and they discovered she had lung cancer and there wasn't much they could do because in those days there was no chemotherapy. I don't even think there was radiation. They tried to operate but they said they couldn't get through the operation, that she would die, so they brought her back out of the operating room, and it was very very sad because it was a matter of only about four or five months. And it was a very traumatic time for me, because I hadn't expected that she would die this young, and it was very, very, very difficult for my grandmother because my mother was her only child. And so it was extremely difficult for her afterwards, and I had to kind of help her along."

"How old were you when she died?"

"I was just nineteen in my second year of college. And my mother would say to me when I would go to the hospital to visit her, 'Why are you coming to visit me?'" Mumma choked up and her eyes watered. "'You should be in school,'" she said through tears.

"Oh, Mumma, I'm sorry." Turning off the tape recorder, I silently passed her some Kleenex.

I felt my face tighten towards tears, but I refrained from crying. We went over a few last questions, and then I went upstairs to my old bedroom and cried, releasing all the emotions I'd hidden away in the tight muscles of my cheeks and eyes.

My mother and father met at an Armenian dance in Boston. Mumma and her best friend Rose missed the last train to Providence, so my father and one of his friends from Worcester offered them a ride home. It had just started to snow; about halfway to Providence, the sky was white, the roads were covered and traffic slowed. "She was better looking than most of the other Armenian girls. She seemed to have more of a sense of humor and was more interesting to talk to," Dad said. At the next dance in Providence, he asked her out.

My mother was taken aback. Daddy had not made a good first impression on her; she thought he was a jerk with all his jokes. She said to Rose, "Oh can you imagine, he's here and he asked me out on a date. I don't think I want to go." And Rose said, "Oh Stella, just go, it's just a date.

Why not go?"

"And so I accepted, and that was the beginning of the end," Mumma joked.

"And what did you think of him when you went out with him?" I asked.

"Well, he appeared to be a lot different [from the first impression]. And as I got to know him then I liked him even more."

"What was it about him that you liked?"

"Well, I don't know, we just had a good time talking, and we had a lot in common, being Armenian." And then she laughed. "And it was just like a romance was brewing, I don't know how it happened." She was silent a moment. "I did go out with someone else for quite a while, almost a year and it was pretty serious, but he being a little younger than me, and going to Harvard University, it was kind of hard for him to keep up the relationship. And so that romance broke off. He's a professor at Harvard now."

I wondered if she were telling me about this guy to prove my father wasn't her only choice. Or that he was second choice. She was feeling societal pressure to marry and her mother had died; the pull to wed and start a family was strong. She thought my father's family was nice enough. "But if I had known what they were really like, I never would have married him," she always said.

This was an echo of my grandmother's claim that if they had been back in the old country, she never would have married my grandfather.

"One time, and I'll never forget this, I had been engaged to your father for a few months," Mumma said, "when your grandmother asked me, 'Where's your mother? Why don't you have a mother?'"

The question shocked Mumma because she had told Grammy on a previous occasion how her mother had passed away several years before. "I'm just asking," Grammy explained in Armenian, "Because sometimes people have a mother hidden away."

Mumma was flabbergasted, her eyes wide. "What?" she asked.

"If she's sick or you're ashamed of her," Grammy explained.

"Can you imagine?" Mumma asked me. "That's how insensitive she was."

But maybe Grammy was asking because she was the one with the mother hidden away. I had never heard Grammy speak of her *mairig* until the day I listened to her oral history tape.

I watched from my old bedroom window as U.J.'s car pulled into the driveway. He walked up the flagstone steps to the front door and rang the bell a million times, just as he did when I was a child. He would be my final interviewee; I was hoping he could fill in some of the gaps about my mother's family.

My mother's older brother was an upbeat, eccentric character who insisted on driving far below the speed limit and obsessed over bowel functions. The formal term "Uncle Joseph" didn't seem appropriate, so Leo had given him his nickname, circa 1979. He now sat in one of the soft chairs in the living room and looked up at me with his big eyes, which looked even more bulbous than my mother's behind his thick glasses, and he smiled at me with his full lips and white moustache. He was wearing a dingy blue and gray knitted sweater over his big belly; what was left of his white hair was disheveled.

"My paternal grandfather, Harry Messerlian, held court every Sunday for dinner," U.J. said, immediately launching into a story, without my prompting. It was curious to me that he would start with his paternal grandfather, from the side of the family from which he was estranged (due to the separation of his parents), rather than his maternal grandfather with whom he lived and grew up. "Harry would clear his throat and everyone would stop what they were doing. He would have everyone kiss his ring, you know, the way the Priest does it in church." Obviously, U.J. had a propensity for the dramatic gesture; I imagined he had some mythic memories of those estranged relatives of his father.

U.J. went on to tell me that Harry Messerlian owned a grocery store, but he also pooled his money with his brothers and bought and sold buildings in Providence. "There was always wheeling and dealing. They wore big diamond rings and bought Cadillacs and Buicks." Harry had four children, including my grandfather John, with his first wife, who died when my grandfather was twelve. A year later, Harry married his deceased wife's sister, his children's aunt; they had two daughters, Jan and Polly.

"Everyone knew them as the Two Bitches," U.J. said. "You know why they were called the Two Bitches?" he asked.

I shook my head no.

"Because they would fraternize with sailors in Newport. You know what sailors want, don't you? S-E-X," he spelled. "And they didn't use condoms."

"So your father was an older half brother to these—"

"Two Bitches."

A year after my grandfather died, Jan produced an I.O.U. on a restaurant napkin which John had supposedly written; she sued Mumma and U.J. for the inheritance money. There had been a rift between Jan and my mother ever since.

When Harry retired from the grocery store, he bequeathed it to my grandfather, who worked eighty-to-ninety-hour weeks, dutifully giving Harry a large share of the profits, even during the Depression, when he needed to pay the mortgage on his house. When the bank foreclosed, U.J. claimed, John's wife Vivian and two young children, four and six years old, moved into her parents' house.

"Why didn't he move with you?" I asked.

"How could he?" U.J. asked. I took him to mean that John couldn't defy tradition to move in with the parents of his wife, or that Vivian was deeply unhappy and prompted the separation. It must have taken a great resolve for Vivian to defy the wishes of her parents, move back in with them, and to leave a husband within the traditional Armenian community of the 1930s; she struck me as a strong woman.

John rarely saw his estranged wife and family, except to occasionally bring them meat during the war since he had access to the black market. U.J. went into great detail then, about the food he was raised on; his mother and grandmother made Imam Bayaldi, an eggplant dish called "the priest fainted," and chocolate pudding with walnuts. I tried to imagine those times his father stopped by the house to bring meats and rare goods. Did they yell and scream, or did they keep things in? It seemed to me my mother's grandparents were prone to swallow and hide, like their tragic past of which they never spoke in Constantinople. I imagined it was tense, that people would rather ignore the obvious and eat Imam Bayaldi and chocolate pudding.

Of his maternal grandparents, Levon and Mari Biberjian, U.J. told me they had emigrated from Istanbul, fleeing the 1894-1896 massacres, and married after they met in Providence. U.J. remembered that they spoke vaguely of how the Turks had betrayed them, but other than that, they didn't speak of the old country. He knew that his grandmother Mari had lived in an orphanage, where she had learned to become a seamstress. He also recalled a Mekhitarist priest coming to visit her one day, which upset his grandfather; Levon chased him away.

"I think it was her brother, or something," U.J. said. *Yeah, right,* I thought. What man would chase away his orphaned wife's brother? The priest must have been someone from Mari's past. Naturally, I imagined some sordid love story.

I tried to track down records of this Mekhitarist priest, to find what information he might bring about my great-grandmother, but when I emailed their monastery in Venice,[7] I never received a reply and so Mari's priest remained a mystery.

Mumma's cousin Leon would call me in a year or so, in the course of assembling a Messerlian family tree, and would fill in some of the other holes for me. He informed me that Harry's mother—my great, great-grandmother—was quite the matriarch, giving birth to fifteen children in twenty-seven years, only seven of whom survived. According to legend, she was so strong that she was out doing wash in the village the day after one of her stillbirths. A widow in 1899, her eldest son had immigrated to America

---

[7] The Mekhitarists are an order of Armenian Catholic priests who have occupied the island of San Lazzaro in Venice since 1717.

a few years before, during the start of the pogroms, and she brought the rest of her children, plus their families, a group of twenty-six people in all, over from Kharpert to Providence; she didn't know French or Arabic or English but navigated their way to the port of Marseilles and then to Ellis Island. Her youngest was just two years old, only a year older than my grandfather, her grandson. This lady was so remote to me; Leon wasn't even sure of her name, as everyone called her Annah, but this is also a term of endearment for "a great mother" or head of a clan in Arabic, used in Turkey at the time. Though she died in 1943, Mumma had never known her, and had never even mentioned such a legendary character from her father's side of the family.

I was also shocked to find the plentitude of aunts and uncles and cousins my mother had, with names like Crosby and Baxter and Oscar and Zeek, Evelyn and Melina and Pearl and Arlene. I couldn't remember meeting any of my mother's relatives; they had never once come to visit our house. But Mumma knew all about Daddy's family, every relative and their accompanying stories. In some ways she was a *hars,* adopting the family of her husband, but it was by choice, perhaps to make up for the disappointments and silences of her own family.

When I questioned U.J. about his mother, he said, "She was a very loving woman. The sweetest angel. A classy dresser." Mumma once told me that Vivian often patiently helped U.J. with his schoolwork—he was often missing school due to sickness and had to catch up with his class.

"She was always thinking about her darling daughter," U.J. said sarcastically about my mother. I guessed he was jealous of their close connection. Mumma had told me that when they moved into her grandparents' house, her brother had his own small room off the living room, while she and her mother shared a bed. It must have been humbling for Vivian to move back in with her parents; perhaps that close connection Mumma described might have included Vivian confiding or revealing her depression to my mother.

"She was concerned, one night," U.J. continued, "that your mother didn't have a ride home from the movies." Vivian insisted that they drive to the theatre in his 1939 Chevrolet, because Vivian didn't want her daughter to walk home in the rain, but on the way to the movie theater, they were hit by a drunk driver. U.J. was gouged in the face, his mother suffered from a huge blow to her ribs. They cracked and pushed into her lungs.

"That car accident caused her cancer," U.J. said.

"What?"

"She complained to the doctor that she had pain in her side," U.J. continued, "but they insisted it was nothing. That it was from the accident. But it turned out to be lung cancer. She died the week before Christmas."

I stared at my uncle; it was preposterous to think a car accident could cause cancer. U.J. seemed to be implying that my mother was somehow responsible for Vivian's death.

You're going to give her bruises and the bruises will turn into cancer! Mumma would shriek when Leo pounded me. *You're going to get into an accident and die and ruin Christmas!* she screamed when I took the car to Vermont.

I didn't mention what I'd learned from U.J. to my mother. Instead, after his visit, I went upstairs to my old bedroom, to the pink walls, the cold air, and the rocking chair where she used to sit and hold me as an infant, to calm me down. Here, I felt those old pains, and I let myself cry again.

PART V

When I walked into my first meeting of the Armenian Gay and Lesbian Association of New York, I sized up all the members. It seemed they fit into two distinct categories: Young gay men who were dressed up, and middle-aged butch lesbians who weren't.

Normally I would have been attired in comfortable jeans and Doc Martens, like the dykes, but because I was nervous about attending my first meeting, I decided to wear a pair of olive capri pants, a purple short sleeve sweater, and around my neck a yellow pendant enameled with a flower.

I immediately regretted my appearance. Even though the president, a bushy-browed young man, greeted me warmly, I knew shunning would begin posthaste. Prior to the meeting I had imagined being interrogated, ridiculed, dismissed, or at the very least, cast bad vibes. Now the fear became more specific: I was scared the lesbians would disapprove of my bisexuality.

I had first looked up "Armenian" and "gay" on an internet search engine in 1998, but there was nothing listed. Then in the summer of 2000, a friend of a friend told me about the Armenian Gay and Lesbian Association and directed me to their website. The AGLA was founded in May, 1999 with separate chapters in Boston, New York, Washington D.C., London, Paris, and L.A.

It hadn't really occurred to me until now that my bisexuality would be an issue. However, as more people filtered into the room the AGLA rented every month at the New York LGBT (Lesbian, Gay, Bisexual and Trans-gendered) Community Center, I realized it wasn't unusual for me to bridle in a group situation: with my childhood playmates, Wellesley girls, L.A. Armenians, extended family, the human race.

The AGLA president asked me to introduce myself. I took a deep breath and said, "My name is Nancy Agabian. I'm bisexual. I'm a writer and performance artist and a lot of my work has to do with being Armenian and queer." I had often made statements like these before, in connection to my work, but I always felt some hesitancy and a little twinge of shame. Now, as I spoke, I looked at the faces of the people who sat in the circle—active, listening, interested, some smiling, other nodding their heads, all eyes on me. It seemed I had found a group of people for whom it was vital that my two disparate parts existed in one person. I had never felt this way before in my life and joy seeped through my veins.

But I still couldn't help thinking that the butch lesbians were looking at my capri pants with suspicion.

The president then started the meeting, announcing that he had decided not to resign, even though some had voiced discontent over his leadership. The three gay boys expressed their support, and the three butch lesbians said nothing and cast each other discontented glances. Seems I'd walked into the middle of a rift between two factions of the Armenian Gay and Lesbian Association.

As I pondered whether the conformist mania of Armenian families— "be like us or risk death"—had infiltrated the AGLA, a polished, straight-looking woman, wearing a white cardigan and khaki pants, walked into the room. She too didn't fit into either of the opposing AGLA factions, in looks or language. She was speaking a dialect of Armenian that no one could understand. Those who spoke Western Armenian, i.e. those who had learned the dialect spoken by parents or grandparents originally from the Turkish-Armenian provinces, assumed that she was speaking Eastern Armenian, the dialect spoken by Armenians from Iran, Russia and the current Armenian republic. (Both Eastern and Western Armenian developed as standardized Armenian languages in the mid nineteenth century as a way to remove Turkish idioms in the West and Persian and Russian in the East. They were both based on spoken dialects and composed in an effort to unify Armenians from different villages who often had a hard time understanding each other. But the Eastern scholars modernized the language thirty years earlier than the Westerners did, resulting in two different Armenian languages: similar vocabulary, but different grammar and different pronunciation of several consonants, perhaps as close as Spanish and Portuguese.)

But the polished woman was speaking a version of Armenian that was neither Eastern nor Western. One of the gay boys asked her in English, "What are you speaking?" and when she answered *"Hyeren,"* the Armenian word for "Armenian," he insisted, "No you're not." A few members whispered that her dialect sounded like Turkish. Everyone was suspicious. She seemed like a straight spy, a straight Turkish spy who had come to kill the entire AGLA.

Recently, there had been a feature article about the organization in *AIM: Armenian International Magazine* and everyone was a bit jittery with all the publicity. I had actually been interviewed for the article, but my comments were cut because the writer thought it was enough for *AIM*'s audience to contemplate the possibility of gay Armenians, never mind the complicated topic of bisexual ones. Hate mail had shown up on the AGLA website soon after the article appeared: "Gay Armenians don't exist," "You're nothing but a bunch of Turks," and "Death to all Armenian fags, bisexuals and lezzies." They were disturbing to read, though I found myself oddly appreciative of the death threat's inclusiveness of bisexuals.

As the others interrogated the newcomer and tried to decipher her dialect, I sat there totally clueless. Still stumbling over words, I had just begun refreshing my memory of the alphabet at a beginning Western Armenian language class that Lori was teaching at the university. But it wasn't helping me here. I watched this woman trying to communicate, calmly speaking as if she knew she would eventually be understood. She was thin and her shiny hair was cut into an elegant bob an inch below the ear, her fingernails were manicured and her skin was moist with makeup. I wondered if she had to bleach her moustache like me. Her voice was slightly low and mellifluous, and I noticed the width of her neck.

She's a trannie, I thought.

Soon enough, the word, "transsexual," came out of her mouth.

The group was able to discern this much: the polished woman who turned out to be a transgendered woman had read about AGLA in an Armenian newspaper published in Turkish. She was from Istanbul and had just moved to the U.S. and worked in a jewelry store. Her name was Adrineh.

I looked at her in awe. I could only guess at how Adrineh felt like an outsider for being born into a sex that didn't feel right. The meeting was conducted in English, a language she didn't understand, yet I didn't see her quivering with paranoia.

The meeting adjourned and dinner at a nearby Chinese restaurant was to follow, but not everyone, including myself, could make it. I lingered in the lobby and chatted with the lesbians about my gay siblings, my parents' attitude toward us, and gulp, how I was dating a man just then. They didn't seem to mind the last entry.

When it was time to say goodbye, everyone—Harry, Fred, Raffi, Alec, Ara, Natalie, Anahid, Stacey and Adrineh—according to custom, kissed each other on both cheeks.

As my friend Sally and I tromped from the subway down the Greenpoint streets in our heels, I taught her to say *odar*. We were on our way to the annual AGLA Christmas party, held in the Brooklyn loft that the president, Alec, shared with his partner José. I thought if anyone asked Sally if she were Armenian (she was half Latino and could pass), she could reply, "I'm an *odar*," to much ironic delight.

To my surprise, the group of about twenty folks in the candlelit loft wasn't entirely Armenian. I recognized members of the AGLA mingling amongst a mostly…well…*odar* crowd. Raffi asked Sally if she were Armenian, but her rehearsed response didn't induce the chuckle I had anticipated. "Isn't it sad the only Armenian word our friends know is *odar?*" he joked to his friend Houri. I felt a little twinge of guilt. "Here's a better word for you to know. *Miaseragan.*"

"What does that mean?" I asked.

"It's the word for 'gay' in Armenian. *Mee-ah* is the root for only, and *ser* means love. *Mee-ah-ser-a-gahn,*" Houri explained.

Me as her again, I repeated in my head to remember.

I had no idea there was even a word in the Armenian vocabulary for gay. I looked at Houri in awe. She was cute and energetic with curly brown hair. After a few moments of conversation, she indicated she had a boyfriend; I then noticed her kissing a bevy of gay boys on both cheeks and complimenting their outfits.

In order to prevent myself from asking Houri the Armenian word for fag hag, I made my way to the food table and scoped out the crowd for potential dates, but no one looked good—it had been only three months since Artis, my long-distance boyfriend, and I had broken up.

Our relationship had become even more long-distance after I had moved back East. We had both been hoping that he would find a job in New York but nothing ever panned out. Then he got a job in Chicago, and I spent a summer there, but we fought the whole time, mostly over housework.

Making matters worse was the fact that his friends and colleagues, when introduced to me, often mistook me for a former student because of our age difference. I tried to not let it get to me, but I couldn't help feeling slighted. He would always be older than me, he would always be the one with the more important job. I saw my life before me: a professor's wife stuck raising a baby by myself with no friends to confide in, no time for my writing.

When he broke up with me over the phone a couple of months later, he said that while I was in Chicago, he had wanted me to make him the number one priority in my life, to take care of him full-time and not write. He immediately started dating a woman, he made a point of telling me, who was not an artist.

Sally approached the food table as I was reaching for what I thought was *lahmejun,* but turned out to be *mole* inside a tortilla. She was chatting up an AGLA member, a mustachioed and ponytailed man, what I imagined an Armenian freedom fighter would look like. It turned out he was born and raised in Providence.

"I'm from Massachusetts," I said. "But I have a lot of family from Providence. And I grew up in the Sts. Sahag and Mesrob Church."

"I went to the *other* church in Providence, Saint Vartanantz. I can't talk to you," he joked and disappeared to say hello to someone else.

"What, you guys had rival softball teams?" Sally asked.

"No, the Armenian church in America is split because of political differences." The details of those differences, I had no idea. As a kid, I was periodically reminded that there was a group of Armenians, called the Tashnags, with whom we did not associate, but who practiced the same religion we did in churches that looked like ours, singing the same liturgy, led by priests wearing the same vestments.

This always creeped me out. Part of Armenian identity entailed feeling like a rarity, a member of a tiny tribe. Whenever my parents overheard Armenians in far-off locations on our family vacations, they were elated. *Who are you and where are you from?* Every once in a while we would run into some Tashnags, though, and the celebration invariably cooled.

My mother had claimed to me recently that the division didn't matter anymore—both sides wanted to forget their differences. It seemed to me from the freedom fighter's reaction, though, that the hatchet wasn't exactly buried.

My eyes were then drawn to a chocolate cake so round and smooth with cream frosting that it was practically a fetish object. As I sliced into it, I thought about my Tashnag pocket calendar at home. After the earthquake in Armenia in 1988, I had requested info from the Land and Culture Organization, an NGO that transported Armenian Americans to help rebuild the disaster areas. I discovered LCO was affiliated with the Tashnags when a pocket calendar arrived in my name to my parent's house the following January, from the *Prelacy* of the Armenian Apostolic Church of America. (The church that I was raised in, that of the rival political group, the Ramgavars, is a parish of the *Diocese* of the Armenian Apostolic Church of America.) Every year, I would flip through the list of Prelacy churches in the back of the calendar and periodically reflect on our dopplegangers' existence before tossing it. Last year, from an envelope filled with post-Christmas trinkets from my mother, the Tashnag calendar tumbled, apparently slipped in by my father as a joke. On one corner of the cover there was a splotch of dried spaghetti sauce.

"The Tashnags killed the Archbishop! On Christmas Eve! During church services!" exclaimed Fred, an older gentleman in a spiffy red and green sweater. He was explaining the cause of the rift to Sally.

I had forgotten the Archbishop's murder. Agnes had painted the gruesome picture for me when we were in Turkey. The Tashnags somehow struck the Archbishop when no one was looking; His Holiness suddenly appeared with a knife in his belly to everyone's complete and utter horror.

"It happened here! In 1933! At Holy Cross in Washington Heights! They have the vestments he wore on display!" Fred said.

"Really?" I asked.

"Yes, you can see the knife hole!"

On a cold January morning, the youngest priest I had ever seen, about my age, which was thirty-three, opened his door and greeted me at the Holy Cross Church. "Hi Nancy," he chimed in a sing-songy upper register, smiling at the doorstep, "I am Father Khntoun." He was dark with black, close-cropped hair, a stubble of beard, and bright eyes covered by a unibrow.

"Hello Father Khntoun," I said, trying to correctly make the khhh expectorant sound. Lingering too much on the khh would signal me as an amateur Armenian. Not using any back-of-the-throat emphasis, opting to call him Father Kintoun, would make me sound like a complete assimilation case.

"Please come in," he said, ushering me inside. Father Khntoun had explained to me on the phone that he had just moved to the U.S. from Armenia four months before and did not know English well; every statement he made thus sounded like a phrase he was learning in ESL class. "This is my office," he said, standing straight, legs together, gesturing his arms at a dark, bleak room with cracked linoleum, fake wood paneling and scuffed office furniture.

"Oh," I said, trying to come up with an appropriate reaction. "It's nice?"

"Would you like to see the Archbishop's tomb?" he asked.

"Sure," I said, a little baffled. I hadn't known there was a tomb. The day before I had queried the church's answering machine as to whether the Archbishop's vestments were on display. "Yes, it is true, they are here," Father Khntoun said when he called back. I imagined them hanging in a display case, the knife hole in view, next to yellowing typewritten labels: a kitschy vitrine of documentation, the perfect detail in a literary nonfiction quasi-journalistic piece like the kind I was reading in school by Dave Eggers, David Sedaris and David Foster Wallace. I was here to ace an assignment, but I really did want to find out the source of the split of the Armenian church, a public manifestation, as I saw it, of the MPTAF.[8]

Father Khntoun led me up a flight of stairs and through a small passageway into the church. When we neared the altar, Father Khntoun made the sign of the cross before making a quick left, to a chapel, where there was a marble slab on the floor, carved with Armenian letters.

"This is where he is buried," Father Khntoun said solemnly. He read the Archbishop's name, Leon Tourian, and the date of his death, December 24, 1933. "It's very sad," he said.

I feigned a melancholy look for Father Khntoun's sake. "Yes," I said.

"Do you want to see the vestments?" he asked.

"Okay."

Father Khntoun walked into a closet filled with fancy priest robes and pulled out a cardboard box. He placed it on a nearby table and opened it up. It was filled with green and gold brocade covered in large blotches of dried blood, as if it had been soaked. I wasn't prepared to be disturbed by so

---

[8] Mania Particular To Armenian Families.

much blood, nor by the fact that the stains looked new, comparable to the
menstrual blood that spotted my underpants the day before yesterday.

Father Khntoun did not take the vestments completely out of the
box, but he unfolded them to reveal where the knife had torn through the
vestment. "See?" he asked. Then, "Do you want to see more?"

My polite instinct told me to say no, I had seen enough blood, but
my sensationalistic side won out: "Sure," I shrugged. Wrong answer. Father
Khntoun sensed my lack of respect and said, "I think that's enough," and
closed the box.

"Were they ever on display?" I asked.

"Yes."

"Do you know when?"

"Maybe fifteen, twenty years ago?"

"Why have they been put away?"

"Because," Father Khntoun was searching for words. He stood holding
the box in his hands. "It's better to put this in closet. It's better Armenians
forget this."

He returned the box to the closet and led me to a small room by the
front door, walls lined with old pictures of Primates and Vehapars,[9] bearded
holy men, wearing pointy hats draped in black cloth that fell just above
their eyes. Gravely serious in their matching black robes, they each wore
several bejeweled crosses spread across their chests.

Father Khntoun pointed out the picture of Leon Tourian who had a
doughy face, with round eyes, nose and mouth, the only man on the wall
not completely frowning; I could detect a faint trace of a smile across his
lips.

"He looks nice," I told Father Khntoun.

"Yes," he said, looking at the portrait wall lovingly as if he were gazing
at family.

Until now, I hadn't really thought of the Archbishop as a person. He
had just been the victim of a murder that was incredibly dramatic and cartoonishly violent. Over the years, I had seen Armenians act incredibly dramatic and cartoonishly violent, particularly within my own family. So I
treated the murder lightly, expecting to find at the Holy Cross Church in
Washington Heights something I could make fun of. Faced with the visage
of a real person, I sobered up.

Back in his office, Father Khntoun and I sat facing each other. He
crossed his legs. So did I. He wiped the perspiration off his brow with a
hanky. I looked at my notes and shyly asked, "How do you like being the
priest here?"

[9] The name of the leader of the Armenian Apostolic Church, equivalent to the Pope. Also known as Catholicos.

Father Khntoun expressed himself with his eyes before he could respond in English. They widened and looked surprised. "I like very much," he smiled and said in an "of course" kind of way. Then his eyes fell to the floor.

I hoped I wasn't making a faux pas. It suddenly occurred to me that Father Khntoun might not appreciate a woman questioning him, since he had been operating within the Armenian church for some time now, and the culture is still very patriarchal. Women sit on the parish council, but they aren't allowed to become ordained as priests, even though there is a shortage of clergy due to the split.

I thought of the stern, salt-and-pepper-haired priest I had grown up with at Sts. Sahag & Mesrob in Providence, the Der Hayr, Lord Father, Dikran Hovanessian. My only contact with him was during communion when he would tower and glower above me in his glittering brocade robe, monitoring my communion-receiving technique as he pressed a wine-drenched piece of the wafer onto my tongue. I was told in Sunday school to swallow the host whole or else I'd be sinning, but I could never resist sinking my teeth into the gummy sweetness.

In an effort to shut out the memory, I proceeded, "How many people come to church here?"

"We have ninety-five members. Forty are active." During the '30s and '40s, Holy Cross was home to the largest Armenian Apostolic parish in America, but in the late '60s there was a large exodus of the parish to suburbs in New Jersey. Today's church members, Khntoun told me, consisted mainly of recent immigrants who had moved to Washington Heights for the low rent. There was only one elderly parishioner who had been at church on December 24, 1933, but he had been a very young child, too young to remember.

"Do they know about the history of the church? About the Archbishop?"

"Yes, they know. On Christmas Eve we do special service. I give sermon about him."

"What did you say?"

He answered with his eyes again and then shrugged, as if it should be obvious. "I say it is sad moment in our history."

"Do you think some people would rather there be no service about him? To forget the whole thing?"

He shrugged. "I don't know."

"The murder caused the church to split in two. What do you think of that?"

This time Father Khntoun spoke before his eyes did. "I think it is the baddest thing to happen," he said quickly. "The worst thing."

"Why?"

"Because, a body can't have two heads. If there are two heads, the body is sick."

I had been wanting to get a tattoo of a two-headed bird lately, as part of my post-breakup campaign to try new things. I had seen the symbol carved into a ruin in central Turkey on my trip with Agnes, and the two heads seeing both sides, seeing all sides, clicked with me. A quick internet search revealed that a two-headed eagle was a popular symbol adopted by the Hittites, Byzantines, Imperial Russia, Hungary, Serbia, Albania, the Greek Orthodox Church, not to mention the Freemasons. In 1993, Boris Yeltsin re-adopted it as the national emblem of Russia, prompting many to dub it the "Chernobyl Chicken." But it wasn't until I found a two-headed bird engraved on the doors of an Armenian church in Douglaston, New York, as a symbol of "the universal Church reaching east and west" that I decided it wasn't an appropriate image for my right hip.

Father Khntoun reminded me that Armenians splitting in two was nothing new; the Armenian Apostolic Church had possessed two Catholicoi since 1441, one located in Etchmiadzin, Armenia, and the other originally in Cilicia, now in Antelias, Lebanon. Originally, there was just one in Etchmiadzin, built the year after the Armenian nation accepted Christianity in 302 A.D. But because the region was engulfed in turmoil with Persians and Seljuks and whoever periodically ransacking the land, the See[10] would be uprooted to ensure its safety, eventually winding up in Cilicia in 1062 A.D. Things were peaceful till Cilicia came under Turkish rule in 1375, and a culture of corruption proliferated among the priests. When several Catholicoi were assassinated by their successors, some powerful bishops in Anatolia called for the transfer and election of a new Catholicos to occur in the original location of Etchmiadzin. But the Cilician Catholicos did not step down from his post, so the two Sees have thus oddly co-existed since 1441, with the Cilician Vehapar currently recognizing the big cheese in Etchmiadzin as the Catholicos of *All* Armenians. In 1920, the Genocide forced the Cilician See to Antelias, a small suburb outside of Beirut, where it has served worshipers of Lebanon, Syria, Cyprus, and, since 1957, the Tashnags of America.

"There are so few Armenian Americans," I confessed to Father Khntoun, "it's hard for me to understand why the church is separated into two factions. I don't want to upset anyone by writing about Archbishop's murder, but I think it's important to look at our history, however ugly."

The day before, I had called my parents and asked them about the murder. They didn't know that much about it, but naturally my mother had an opinion.

"Why are you writing about that? I don't think it's very nice. No one wants that wound to be opened."

Now as I confessed my aims for investigating the murder to Khntoun,

---

[10] Another word for the Cathdicostate, the spiritual and administrative center of the Armenian Apostiolic Church.

I expected him to hold similar disdain. Instead his eyes opened wide and he exclaimed, "Oh, you have the true Armenian spirit. I can tell. It is very nice Armenian spirit!"

Along with his approval, Khntoun also bestowed upon me a commemorative book that the Holy Cross Church published in 1979 to mark their fiftieth anniversary. There were black and white pictures of choirs filled with saddle-shoed young women, antsy Sunday school kids, smiling grandmas making *yalanchee* at church picnics, and congratulatory letters from Jimmy Carter and Ed Koch; there was no mention of the Archbishop's murder.

There was, however, a picture of my old priest, the Der Hayr, Father Dikran Hovanessian, just as he looked when I took communion from him as an eleven-year-old child; I shuddered. He wrote a letter that stated he had begun his pastoral duties at Holy Cross twenty-two years before and now wished them sincere best wishes for many more years of continued success. I looked at the photo carefully, detecting the faintest trace of a smile across his lips.

It was my intention to go back to Holy Cross to see and meet the parish, but I woke Sunday morning feeling anxious. In the past fifteen years, I had gone to church once a year at Christmas, if that much, since I was still stricken by the memory of Sts. Sahag and Mesrob's service of indecipherable Classical Armenian, incessant, depressing music and women participating on the altar only to sing in the choir.

"Oh you should definitely go, Nancy," my mother said when I called her for support. "Armenians always welcome new people to church."

I put on a button-down sweater and pleated pants and modest makeup and took the subway to the 191st Street stop and walked four blocks down the hill, past the Dominican bodega and the empanada cart and the abandoned Greek Orthodox church on Broadway, turned left on 187th, passed a couple of Armenian men in Soviet-style crewneck sweaters under suit jackets hanging out in front of Holy Cross, and strode into the vestibule at 10:40.

The organ was going full blast and an unseen lady was singing a minor-key Armenian church song in a soprano warble. Incense filled my nose and dried out the back of my throat, a familiar smell from forever: frankincense. There were only two people in the congregation—an old lady in a navy suit in the last row of pews, and a curly-haired fortyish man loitering by the candle stand. I stepped into a pew on my right, three rows from the back.

When the soprano lady stopped singing, one of the deacons, wearing the standard white robe with pink panels, pulled the curtain on the altar. It made a clacking noise and Father Khntoun appeared, wearing a glittery brocade robe and matching hat. He reminded me of a little girl playing dress up. The organ music started again, and Khntoun descended the steps of the altar and floated to the corner of the church, stage right, chanting in Armenian and making the sign of the cross; he was trailed by an elderly priest in a black robe and a deacon who thrice swung a brass shaker which jingled as it released incense: a trio of men, young, middle-aged and old.

I was witnessing the blessing of the four corners of the church, something I had only heard about because my family always got to church a half an hour before the service was over. We couldn't stand sitting through the whole entire thing. Even a half-hour seemed like an eternity of sitting and standing and the priest making the sign of the cross at you, and you making the sign of the cross back at him, and the singing and the chanting and the sitting and the standing, and no one knowing exactly when to sit or stand so half the people would be up, half down, and a baby crying.

Father Khntoun and his entourage progressed down the stage right aisle of the church to the far corner, blessed that, then loomed towards me and I started to panic. Just then, the old lady in the navy suit moved into the center aisle and kissed a bejeweled gold cross that Khntoun was holding in a lace hanky. He actually came out of the procession to hold the cross to me, and I kissed it too, trying not to get lipstick on it. *Not very sanitary, that cross,* I thought as I let out a deep breath, relieved that I hadn't flubbed a ritual.

I saw the Divine Liturgy book in the pew pocket in front of me so I took it out. On the left-hand page were the Armenian words, on the right, the English translation. It suddenly hit me that this was the first time that I had come to church by myself, that I was in control of my worship, that I could actually try to figure out what the service was about. I was searching for the words the deacons were chanting, when the old lady walked over to me and pointed to the spot. "Thank you," I mouthed to her.

Now that I could read Armenian letters again from my classes, I was able to follow the Armenian side of the page. I could even understand some of the words without checking the right side, the heavy curtain of somberly chanted Classical Armenian now actually moveable, meaningful.

More people wandered in; the bulk of the people arrived at 11:30, an hour late. It got kind of noisy by the front door and people turned around to shush the latecomers. They took their time parading in: everyone looked slightly bedraggled, like they were sick or tired or smoked too much. A girl in her twenties was wearing tight checked pants. A lady in a flowered rayon dress carried a baby. The baby cried. No one knew when to stand or sit. Sometimes half the people were up and half were down.

I realized I had never prayed in Armenian church before, and since I had been going through a tough time lately with the breakup, I felt I could use some spiritual sustenance. Over the years, I had developed a patchwork religion that was based on my own personal beliefs, whatever I picked up in L.A. from New Age trends like Marianne Williamson and *A Course in*

Miracles, and the twelve-step theory I had learned from the few times I had attended Al-Anon with friends. Now I tried hard to find some comfort from the Divine Liturgy. The words mainly expressed how great God was and how pathetic we were, but there was one part that made me cry; it had something to do with God watching us and witnessing us, in all our strengths and weaknesses.

As he strode into the basement auditorium, Father Khntoun made a dramatic entrance, wearing a flowing black robe with a matching pointy hat like the men on the walls in the room off the vestibule. He was obviously proud of the wardrobe change, and I felt my gaydar go off. *No wonder I like him so much.* Khntoun greeted everyone who had been waiting for him to bless the food for the coffee hour, and then he approached me and swelled up with a smile. "Hello, Nancy! I'm so glad you came!"

Father Khntoun introduced me to Edie, a friendly woman in her forties with a New York accent and a slightly triangular hairdo. "Nancy is Armenian American," Father Khntoun said.

"I'm Armenian American too," Edie said. "Do you speak Armenian?" she asked.

"No, but I'm taking classes now," I told her. I asked her if she grew up in this neighborhood. She said yes, but that her family had moved away long ago. "We still come to church here though, since we're attached to the place."

Edie introduced me to a few people. An old lady lacking eyebrows and wearing a tan felt hat said, "She looks Armenian."

"Yes, she's Armenian but she doesn't speak the language," Edie explained. "She's learning."

"Are you half Armenian?" the old lady asked.

"No, both my parents are Armenian."

"Why don't you speak the language?" she asked, her waxen face twisting into a question mark.

"My parents didn't speak it in the house. They were born here too."

"Why didn't they teach you? I'm half Portuguese and I taught my children and grandchildren how to speak Armenian."

I couldn't believe I was encountering the "why don't you speak Armenian?" issue of yore when I was actually making the effort to learn it. I looked down at the sallow old woman; she appeared to be ill. "Where are you from?" I asked.

"Brazil," she said.

The curly-haired man who had been loitering by the candle stand now loomed by Edie's shoulder and looked at her expectantly. "Nancy, this is Sevag," she said with an unnerved frown. Sevag had cracked, chapped lips and a gummy smile. He didn't say a word but stared at me hungrily like I was a piece of *lokhum*. Somehow I had time-traveled back to my grand-mother's village and was being considered for marriage by the lowly *ghent*.

I was relieved when Edie asked, "Did you meet the Yeghitzee and the Yeghitzeegeen?" and we turned around to face the elderly priest who had been on the altar and the old lady in the navy suit. I knew from Armenian class that *yeghitzee* meant holy and *geen* meant woman. She was the priest's wife.

"Yes, we met already," the Yeghitzeegeen said and winked at me. But when I smiled and shook the old priest's hand, his face turned as if he had swallowed an olive pit. Another faux pas, apparently.

Father Khntoun blessed the table and it was time to eat. I piled a plate with choreg, lentil pilaf and boreg and sat next to Melineh, a zaftig woman in her fifties with thick red hair and black liner encircling her eyes. She told me she was from the former Soviet Armenia and that she had just become an American citizen. She introduced me to her son Viken, a very handsome twenty-something wearing close-cropped hair and a smart gray suit.

Across from me sat a staid, depressive older couple, staring at me. I smiled at them and asked where they were from. "Turkey," the woman answered. Before I could ask another question, she asked, "So you don't speak any Armenian?" She proceeded to interrogate me with practically the same questions of the Brazilian-Armenian woman, shaking her head and tsk-tsking my answers. This really pissed me off, but I was oddly satis-fied, her judgment serving as actual proof of why I had exiled myself from Armenians for so long.

Melineh announced to Father Khntoun, "I would like to recite my poem now, Hayr Soorp." I noted her form of address, the term for a celibate priest.[11] Melineh walked to the middle of the room, and began delivering her lines in Armenian, projecting her voice and arching her arms for added grandeur. Luckily, the Yeghitzeegeen was sitting next to me and whispered a translation into my ear. It was the seventeen hundredth anniversary of Armenia's mass conversion, and the poem was celebrating St. Gregory the Illuminator for bringing Christianity to Armenians in 301 A.D.

According to the ancient Roman historian Agathangelos, Gregory was a member of King Trdat's court. When he converted to Christianity and refused to sacrifice to Anahid, a pagan fertility goddess, the Armenian king imprisoned him in a snake pit for thirteen years. Trdat spent those years per-secuting Christians, including a beautiful nun. He was in love with her, but she refused his advances, so he had her killed. As punishment, God changed Trdat into a boar. (Yes, you read that correctly. A boar.)

Meanwhile, Gregory was surviving with the help of a widow who had a dream that she should throw a loaf of bread into the snake pit every day. Trdat's sister, receiving a message in one of her dreams that if she released

---

[11] A Hayr Soorp rises higher in church hierarchy than a non-celibate priest, called Der Hayr.

Gregory, her brother would return to human form, sprung Greg from the snake pit. Upon his release, Gregory commenced to teach the porcine king about Christianity for sixty-five days. On the sixty-sixth day, he told Trdat about a dream *he* had that they should build a big church with chapels for the martyred nun. King Trdat constructed the chapels with his bare hooves and then he was transformed back into a man. Gregory and Trdat then set out to rid the land of pagan temples, and presumably, pagans. The largest temple to Anahid was razed to the ground and replaced with the Cathedral at Etchmiadzin.

The credibility of a human being turning into a boar wasn't my only problem with the conversion story. I wasn't impressed with the tendency of the plot to move forward only if someone had a dream—*Come on, Agathangelos, couldn't you come up with a couple other literary devices?*—not to mention the sexism: the nun, Trdat's sister and the bread-tossing widow all received second billing, not to mention violent treatment from the men. Armenian Christians destroyed Anahid, personal guardian of the Armenians, and banished her fire rituals, replacing them with a hierarchy of men in robes: the Catholicos, the Patriarchs, the Archbishops, the Bishops, the Hayr Soorps, and finally the lowly Der Hayrs, possessing less prestige in the church for sexually commingling with women.

After the poem, I struck up a conversation with the Yeghitzeegeen.

"I'm from Worcester," she told me, launching into her life story. She grew up in a ghetto ("We didn't *know* it was a ghetto") where everyone was an immigrant—from Poland, Germany, Lithuania. Her father insisted she learn Armenian. "I wasn't happy about it, of course," she said. "But later I was." Armenian girls didn't leave their families until they married, but she joined the service without telling her father, working as a secretary in intelligence overseas during WWII. After the war, she married the Der Hayr.

The Archbishop told her that as a Yeghitzeegeen she wasn't allowed to dance or wear any color but black. "I ignored him. We broke all the rules," she said in her 1940s Judy Garland cadence. "We were the link between the generation from the old country and the new generation in America. We introduced ideas to our parents, however difficult it was for them to accept, that were *modern*."

I was really starting to like this Yeghitzeegeen, even if her title was completely unpronounceable. "My father was so upset that I went into the service, but there was nothing he could do. I was very independent. My parents were worried that I wouldn't find someone to marry. No one thought I'd become a Der Hayr's wife. I certainly didn't." I suspected the Yeghitzeegeen was telling me her story to illustrate that an independent woman like me belonged to the church too.

At this point, people were gathering up their things to leave. Father Khntoun said goodbye to the Yeghitzeegeen and me, and she and I walked

across the auditorium to the entrance. As Viken caught my eye and we nodded goodbye to each other, I felt transported back to my mother's Armenian
church hall of the Fifties, shyly returning a young man's gaze under the
protection of the Yeghitzeegeen.

I recalled that I had a habit of thinking people were attracted to me
when in fact it was I who was attracted to them. It occurred to me now that
the Holy Cross parish may not have been reacting to me in the multitude
of ways that I had experienced—judgment, rejection, desire, identification.
Perhaps I was just seeing their actions the way I wanted to, and my mother
was right; Khntoun, Edie and the Yeghitzeegeen were welcoming a new
young person to join their flock. Even the ladies who had shriveled their
lips at me when I told them I didn't speak Armenian were embracing a wayward ewe the only way they knew how—with the same criticism they had
probably received for being half Portuguese or from Turkey.

The question now was whether I wanted to belong.

18. HISTORICALLY PERSONAL

The Zohrab Center, a location for Armenian scholarship and study,
was located in a stone building between Saint Vartan's Cathedral at 34th
and 2nd Avenue, with its resplendent gold conical dome, and the exhaust-
encrusted entrance to the Queens Midtown Tunnel. When I was inside, the
Zohrab Center didn't feel like it was at the center of anything though; it
was more like some forgotten closet or unused bathroom below the stairs;
the windows were tiny inside. I went to the Zohrab Center to find out the
story of Tourian's murder and the split of the Armenian Apostolic Church
of America, but I was having trouble concentrating. The librarian, Harut
Zilelian, wearing a sweater with golfing figures knitted into the design, had
retrieved for me a pile of books he thought would help, and I had actually
been excited to read all the intricacies of Armenian-American church history. But now, after a few hours, I needed a break from the blurry words in
the dim light.

Here's a little summary: From what I gathered from the historians' as-
sertions, politics had long been intertwined with Armenian church history.
Basically, the Church maintained an Armenian national identity while the
country possessed no formal home of its own during the dark period, the

fifteenth to nineteenth centuries. And in the late nineteenth century, both clergy and parish often supported or belonged to the emerging political parties—the Armenakan, a socialist party called the Hunchags, and eventually our pals in question, the federation of revolutionary organizations, a.k.a. the Tashnags.

I read that the founding of the first Armenian church in America was actually suggested by a revolutionary. In 1888, Mgrditch Portukalian, who had helped found the Armenakan, visited Worcester, Massachusetts, the first Armenian community in America; he suggested to the 250 Armenian men living there, mostly mill and foundry workers, that a church would help keep the flame of mother Armenia alive. I'm sure they'd thought of it themselves already though, and this Armenakan guy was receiving undue credit: the Armenian expats had been renting out a local Protestant church for their services, but they often faced racial and religious discrimination from the WASPs. The Church of Our Saviour, the first Armenian Apostolic Church in America, thus was built in 1891.

Not long after the consecration, there was trouble between the priest and the revolutionaries. A conservative from Constantinople, the priest didn't want copies of *Hunchag,* the newspaper of the party by the same name, kept in the church library. When the priest refused to allow the library's committee, composed mainly of Hunchags, some of whom were Protestant, to gather at the church, a brawl broke out. The story made it into the *Worcester Daily Telegram,* purporting that the priest handed out chair legs to his defenders.

I continued reading about other altercations, infighting and disagreements, not just between the church and the political parties, but between priests and their parish councils and among priests vying to become the Primate of America. At one point, I simply stopped reading and flipped to random pages in the book in front of me. Wherever I landed, I found some sort of dispute: it became clear that divisiveness was prevalent at every level and stage of development of the Armenian Church of America.

I looked up from my book at the Zohrab Center at the outdated computers and copy machine and the receptionist behind the desk with her big red hair; I clutched my sweater around me in this cold tomb of a room, exhausted from reading about a people who couldn't reconcile their differences. It reminded me of the way my parents fought. Instead of seeking resolution, they would sulk at each other for days until they couldn't remember what it was they were mad about. It was their fault, I was convinced, that I didn't know what a healthy relationship looked like and that I was single now, at the age of thirty-four, depressed and confused, sitting in a cold library, studying the petty differences of a tiny tribe of insignificant people.

As I fell further into my miasma of Armenian blame and despair, the door opened to the Zohrab Center and I turned to see my cousin Malcolm, who was studying to become a Der Hayr, standing in the door, smiling.

Grammy and Malcolm's grandfather had been first cousins. I hadn't been close to Malcolm when I was growing up; he usually called me Valerie. Still, I was happy to see my big, friendly cousin.

"Hey, what are you doing here?" he asked in a Rhode Island accent similar to my mother's. He sat down next to me at the study table. Even in his priest's collar, he still resembled Fred Flintstone—a likeness that Leo had once noted in our childhood.

"I'm researching the split in the Armenian church."

"We just studied that at seminary. Wanna know what the cause of it was? In a word?"

"What?" I asked.

"Communism," he said.

"Communism," he said again when I hadn't responded. He gestured to my notebook.

"Oh," I said, scribbling the word down.

We chatted a while. It turned out Malcolm was in town for the weekend from the Westchester seminary to help with Easter services at the Cathedral. His wife and kids were coming down from Providence to visit. Malcolm asked me if my brother lived in New York too—he'd seen us at a festival at the church. I told him no, that my brother lived in Boston and he was looking for a job. "He's in transition," I said.

"We're all in transition," Malcolm said and laughed. Then he turned around and left without saying goodbye.

I continued reading to verify Malcolm's claim. Here's the deal: Understandably, Eastern Armenia was caught in great upheaval after the Genocide. When the Bolsheviks and Lenin came to power, the little former province joined with Georgia and Azerbaijan to form a Transcaucasian provisional government. But then Georgia and Azerbaijan individually decided it would be better to be independent, so Eastern Armenia was forced to become a nation too, officially on May 18, 1918. Tashnags held four of ten cabinet positions of the vulnerable new Republic.

Things started to look up for Armenia when Turkey and Germany surrendered and World War I ended in November, 1918. The Allies worked out a plan for Turkey, dividing it up amongst themselves, and for Armenia, carving out a country, specified in the Treaty of Sèvres, that would include much of both Western and Eastern Armenia. But in order for it to exist alongside Turkey, Armenia would need protection in the form of a mandate. President Wilson was favorable towards a U.S. mandate, but he needed approval from Congress; they eventually rejected the idea in 1920.

This left the door open for Atatürk, a former Young Turk rising from the ashes of the Ottoman Empire, to make a move. He negotiated with the Bolsheviks: if they could convince Georgia to join the Soviet Union, then he would persuade the Azeris to also go Soviet. He could then rid Eastern Armenia of Armenians and do with it as he wished. The Turkish-Soviet pact was signed on August 24, 1920 and by the end of September, Ataturk attacked the enfeebled Republic of Armenia, still in a shambles from the effects of war and genocide. With no help from Europe or America, and facing further annihilation, Armenia chose the lesser of two evils and became a republic of the Soviet Union.

During the transition to Soviet leadership, Armenian government officials, who by now were mostly Tashnags, were arrested or driven out of the country by the Communists.

Clergy were also persecuted and churches were confiscated and destroyed because the Catholicos, Kevork V, refused to recognize the Soviets. After he finally gave in to their pressure, he started signing his name as "Kevork the Sorrowful." The history books didn't give an explanation of his new name—had he gone a little nuts from the persecution, or was this some sort of admirable last form of protest, or did he want to acknowledge his guilt to the rest of the world? In any case, after sad Kevork died in 1930, the Soviets wouldn't allow an election of a new Catholicos for another two years.

Since only seven of seventy-two delegates who voted for the new Catholicos, Khoren I, were from outside the U.S.S.R., it seemed to Tashnags in America that he was hand-selected by the Soviets. They feared Soviet use of the Vehapar's influence in the diaspora to support the Communist regime, and that they would lose their dream of a free and independent homeland.

The Ramgavars believed the situation in the Soviet Union, although not ideal, was the only chance for the survival of an Armenian homeland; they supported the Catholicos, who they thought was doing the best he could under grave circumstances.

So Malcolm was right. In a word, Communism.

On the morning of December 24, 1933, an altar boy led a procession through a packed-to-capacity Holy Cross Church. Behind him shuffled several boys and girls holding candles, the Bishop of Holy Cross, and between a pair of deacons, Archbishop Tourian.

Tourian had requested police protection in front of the church and a bodyguard loomed behind him; he feared a reprise of the previous August when he'd been beaten up at a church picnic in Worcester by a gang of Tashnags. Ever since he had been elected Archbishop in 1931, Tourian had faced the ire of Tashnags, suspicious of his connections to Soviet-controlled Etchmiadzin. It hadn't helped Tourian that he dutifully obeyed Catholicosan orders not to do anything that might be seen as defiant to the Soviet Union: he told clergy not to partake in any non-church sanctioned (i.e. Tashnag) April 24th commemorations, and he refused to speak under an Armenian tri-color flag (which he saw as pro-Tashnag) at the Chicago World's Fair. In September, he'd been re-elected Archbishop, but amid much drama; the Diocesan Assembly actually split when Tourian's supporters up and left, voting for him at a local hotel, while the remaining group at the church voted against him. Naturally, the Catholicos in Soviet Armenia brokered the tie by deeming that Tourian should remain in his position. To Tashnags, who had seen the Soviets betray them and subsume their broken homeland, and now suspected them to be gaining even greater control over Armenians in the diaspora, the situation must have seemed dire.

As Tourian now made his way down the aisle on Christmas Eve, his attending bodyguard, thinking he would be safe during the short walk towards the altar, stopped at the back of the center aisle. When Tourian reached the fifth row of pews, a man dropped to his knees and grabbed the Archbishop's hands, as if in religious ecstasy. From the fifth and sixth rows, several men silently nudged the deacons out of the way, surrounding Tourian on all sides. He suddenly groaned and slumped forward onto his scepter, the force of his six-foot-four body collapsing it, his hat tumbling from his head. He had been stabbed several times in the gut. Sprawled in the aisle, his head near the altar, he died in the next instant, his last words, "I am fallen."

The men surrounding Tourian dispersed, running into the street, but two of them were snatched by the crowd and attacked with umbrellas and canes. A policeman arrested the two men, Matios Leylegian and Nishan Sarkisian.

A squad from Homicide arrived and brought many of the traumatized congregation to the local precinct for questioning. No one had seen who wielded the murder weapon, which had been found on the altar: a butcher knife with an eight-inch blade, covered in blood and wrapped in newspaper. Churchgoers blamed the murder on the Tashnags, but many witnesses were afraid to identify suspects, fearing the wrath of those brazen or crazy enough to assassinate an archbishop in a crowded church. Detectives soon questioned Tashnag members and charged five men with the murder, including Leylegian and Sarkisian.

A few days later, detectives brought witnesses back to Holy Cross and recreated the murder in order to determine if there were more suspects. They asked neighbors and friends of the witnesses to serve as translators, also planting in the church their own NYPD translators incognito to overhear what the witnesses were *really* saying.

Eventually nine men were charged, all Tashnags.

The *Herald Tribune* reported that when witnesses were called to court to identify Leylegian as the leader of the attack, one woman clamped her hand down on his shoulder and said *Ays mart eh.* This is the man.

> She was so nervous she had to be helped back to the stand by a courtroom guard. Thomas I. Sheridan, who with Joab H. Banton, former District Attorney, is leading the defense, requested that no subsequent witness be permitted to touch a defendant. He was afraid hot-tempered Armenians—witnesses and defendants alike—would forget themselves. Judge Joseph E. Corrigan granted the request.

Leylegian, identified as the knife-man, and Sarkisian, who held Tourian's hands, were sentenced to death. The remaining seven Tashnags were given ten to twenty in Sing Sing. Leylegian's and Sarkisian's sentences were later commuted to life imprisonment seventy-two hours before they were to be executed.

I found myself staring at old newspaper photos of the defendants, of Armenian men in '30s-era pinstriped suits and fedoras, similar to men I had seen in my family's photo albums, in community magazines, and hanging on the walls of churches; now they were scandalous subjects of a sensationalistic crime, handcuffed together on a train to Sing Sing.

Juan Gonzales Tchalcikian, a member of the guilty party, was only twenty-eight; he had been tracked down through a laundry tag on a bloody shirt he had left behind in a store after the murder. He was from Panama, hence his Spanish first name. He had a thick pompadour of shiny black hair and big eyes. When questioned, he said that he was at the church, but had not taken part in the murder and had yelled to the crowd, "We are Armenians, we shouldn't do anything like this!"

I found out this last part from reading an article in *Master Detective* from 1936, written by the Assistant District Attorney and prosecutor on the case, Alexander H. Kaminsky, who reported Tchalcikian's experience of the Genocide:

> At an early age he was taken [from Panama] to Armenia where his parents settled. During one of the many massacres the Turks inflicted on these people, his father and mother had been killed and at the age of eight he was sold into slavery. Seven years later an American missionary, going through a Mohammedan country, noticed a youth making a sign of the cross. His curiosity aroused, he made a few inquiries and learned the boy's story. He was instrumental in having him released, and aided him in sending him to America.

If Tchalcikian was twenty-eight in 1933, then he was born in 1905, the same year my grandmother thought she was born. And the story of his rescue sounded a little like the Mairam Chavoush story. In his picture on the train, all his older cohorts are sitting opposite the aisle from him; they are turned towards the camera, but Juan looks sadly at his fellow, and significantly older, Tashnags.

The last line of the *Master Detective* article read:

I did and do feel that the verdict of the jury is an object lesson to those who come to our shores from foreign lands; teaching them that they must forget those political and religious differences that might lead them to the extreme of assassination; and that they must respect the institution of the country of their adoption, by a careful observance of our laws.

Even though I recognized a patronizing tone towards immigrants here and in the *Herald Tribune*'s statement about "hot-tempered Armenians," I also saw embarrassing aspects of Armenianness caught and processed through the filter of a bewildered American press and legal system—the insularity of speaking their private language in front of the *odar* authorities, the melodrama of the murder itself, and the naiveté, or guilt, represented by Tchalcikian's exclamation, "We're Armenians, we shouldn't do anything like this!"

Historical accounts from both the Diocese and the Prelacy echoed this sentiment. Though one side blamed the Tashnags, and the other claimed that the convicted men were actually Bolsheviks set out to destroy Armenian identity, they were united in stating that the murder brought shame on all Armenians.

It seemed to me that it would be easy to dismiss the few Tashnags convicted of killing Tourian as a bunch of nuts. The admitted embarrassment seemed to suggest that the murder was not the action of a few misguided extremists, but that there was something inherently Armenian about it. Both sides, Prelacy and Diocese, Tashnag and Ramgavar, were acknowledging my thesis, the driving force behind my investigation: Armenians divide into factions because they are unreasonable lunatics.

Hold on a second! I had been depending on the Armenian establishment to resist my resentful attacks. Apparently, my self-loathing was not so unique.

By 1933, ten years after the end of the killings in the Ottoman Empire and the new Turkish Republic under Atatürk, it must have become clear to much of the Armenian-American community that there would be no returning to the homeland. A generation had been born which felt more allegiance to America. There was a desperate need for many genocide survivors to know their culture would not be destroyed. American assimilation and the Soviet regime must have seemed like grave threats to Armenian survival. A free Armenian homeland was important to Tashnags because they wouldn't have to let go of the idea of their home, their identity. But for the Ramgavars, the idea of a free homeland did not seem realistic; the fight for such a place might lead to more annihilation.

While I had been studying the split, I tended to side with the logical compromise of the Ramgavars, that Armenia needed protection from a greater power in order to get on her feet again. Now I tried to consider both sides from a purely philosophical view, and found myself siding with the Tashnags; I admired their drive towards independence and fearlessness. But I couldn't get around the fact that both sides seemed overwhelmingly convinced that if they didn't act in certain ways, their homeland may no longer exist.

Now at the Zohrab Center, I stared into space, recalling how hard it had been for me to be independent at various times in my life, how I was naturally drawn to strong figures such as Louise and Bee whom I thought would take better care of me than I could. But at some point in such a relationship (like the one that just dissolved), I bridled against what I sensed was my partner's power in order to prove myself. Now I was having trouble belonging to various groups—at school, at the AGLA, at church—not just because my identity defied categories, but because I was scared that if I belonged, I would lose myself, I would no longer exist.

I followed Auntie Agnes into ALMA, the Armenian Library and Museum of America in Watertown Square. I was visiting for the weekend, and we decided to stop in. I found myself standing in front of a group portrait: A Hunchag picnic in Milford, Massachusetts, August, 1930. As I stood staring at the faces, one stood out at me from the back row: Grammy. With black hair, smooth skin and a staunch frown.

I called out to Agnes. As she tried to confirm the face in the back row was her mother's, I found Agnes and Aunt Sherrie, little girls with pageboy haircuts, sitting together in the front row.

"There you are," I cried.

"Holy smokes, there I am," Agnes said, smiling at me. "And there's my aunt Araxie."

Sitting on the ground by the two girls was a woman with black hair and a gaunt face. She reminded me of that Dorothea Lange portrait of a Dust Bowl Okie, with some of her teeth missing from a strained smile. Here was the woman who lost her two children in the genocide and renamed her later children after them, who sold my grandmother to the Arabs so that they both might survive.

"There's Ruth," I cried out, noticing a little girl with black Shirley Temple curls.

"And grandma is holding her." A husky woman with a wide square face, white hair and dark eyebrows, Marta looked pretty mannish; Daddy told me she used to work on the farm as much as the men. I wondered if my sister inherited some of her butch genes.

"Do you recognize anyone else?" I asked.

"*Gunkamayr!*" Agnes cried. That would be Zarouhie, my father's godmother (and my godfather's mother). I had visited her in assisted living recently to find out her story. "You're too late," she had told me, lying on her side. In the photo she is standing next to Grammy, but her face is slightly blurry.

"Oh and there's Noyemzar," Tina, Lucy and Lora's mother, with the brush head of hair.

The funny thing was that none of the men of the family were in the photo.

"Why were you there?" I asked Agnes.

"It was probably more social than anything, although my father sympathized with the Hunchags."

"Was Grammy a Hunchag?"

"No, not really."

I couldn't help feeling awed by my grandmother's image. The photograph was taken through the process in which you must stay still while the shutter is opened for an extended period or your visage will come out blurry, as many faces did. Grammy must have been standing completely stock-still because her face was crystal clear.

She had lost her parents and sister fifteen years prior. She was twenty-five, and she had five children. Her husband had quit his job and built a house against her will and now they were poor, they had no money. There were people who did not want her to exist, and they almost had succeeded.

And now she was getting her picture taken, as an Armenian woman. Her act of self-determination—an expression of unhappiness, recorded for posterity: a frown.

Standing in a pew in St. Vartan's Cathedral on a Sunday before Easter, I felt a warm rush all over, a jittery attraction. Next to me: prominent, swerving nose; shoulder-length messy brown hair; greenish eyes and asymmetrical eyebrows. All I wanted to do was kiss her, to swish my lips and tongue around hers.

What was I thinking, inviting her here? "Do you want to go to Armenian church with me?" I had blurted out as we were sipping mint tea on our first date. Tabitha was originally from Oregon and had put herself through college by working in the logging industry. She never had much contact with the Armenian community, but her paternal grandfather was Armenian, so she had an -ian at the end of her name. She was also a visual artist and I thought she would find the highly ritualistic Armenian mass interesting.

My cousin Malcolm was one of several clergy men officiating on the altar, and there were hardly any people in the vast, open space of the brightly lit cathedral. I hoped Malcolm wouldn't be able to figure out I was on a date, but it seemed pretty obvious. Tab and I were sharing a liturgy book, standing close and giddily smiling at each other.

"There are snakes inside the priest's slippers so that he stamps out evil every time he makes a step," I whispered to her. I'd learned this fact from the Lenten classes I had been taking in St. Vartan's basement. The priest went out of his way to stress that Communion was not merely symbolic. "During the Badarak," he had said, "the holy spirit transforms the bread and the wine so that we are actually eating Jesus' flesshh." He said the word flesh with a lot of mouth and saliva, as if he were about to bite into a juicy steak, a rare piece of Jesus meat.

"Actual snakes?" Tab asked.

"No, they're embroidered," I whispered.

"Oh," she laughed and touched my arm with the back of her hand playfully.

Doesn't she know flirting is not allowed in church? I was appalled for a moment, till I recalled that Tab hadn't been indoctrinated like me to completely shut down all feelings of joy in a liturgical setting. Luckily, a young couple with rambunctious twin boys sat down in front of us, distracting any holy men who might have caught on to our lesbian courtship.

A young guy in a plaid shirt came around to give the kiss of peace. Into my right ear he said, *Kreesdos ee mech mer haydnetsav.* Christ is revealed among us. He was kindly hesitant, about to walk away if I signaled that I didn't know the response, but I deftly switched my mouth to his left ear and said into it, *Ornyal eh haydnootiunun Kreesdosee.* Blessed is the revelation of Christ. I smiled at my achievement and the man smiled back.

I was discovering that there was a theme of oneness to the Badarak. We take communion so that we can be united with Christ's love in our stomachs. Christ is revealed among us and we kiss, we whisper the news ear to ear. Because the rituals had always been a mystery to me, because their stern, solemn performance failed to reveal their loving spirit, I'd never realized before that church was about inclusiveness and unity. Not to mention wrought with so much sexual tension.

"I think we should go now," I whispered to Tab.

Tab stood up from the bench where she was sitting and lay down on the ground next to me. After church we'd taken a drive to the Rockaways with her dog Goose. We had walked along the beach for a while, then followed a path inland to a little pond in a marshy clearing. I'd been fantasizing about our first kiss all day; I wanted to initiate it. Suddenly, I put my arm over her waist. *This is it.* I leaned in and put my lips to her mouth and softly puckered up, like I was tasting a candy from a foreign country.

Our teeth clanked. Not sensuous at all. She wouldn't move her lips.

"Some straight kids are coming," she said. I looked up and saw, over the rise of a hill, a cavalry of three kids running towards us, followed by their parents.

Later, when we were saying goodbye, sitting in her Cutlass Supreme, Tab leaned in and put her hand under the base of my skull, through my hair, and kissed me with her lips. I caught my breath and sighed and she swirled her tongue around the nape of my neck. A consummation of what I had wanted to do in church with her.

Afterwards, I walked through the East Village to the West Village, not knowing where I was going, dizzy and wet. I had kissed a woman. I knew it shouldn't be such a big deal. I had always claimed that it was the person, not their gender, that I was attracted to. Still, everything seemed so different, like my life had shifted to another continent.

Tab was lying on her back on her couch, and I was straddling her, her thighs propped behind me. I was holding her hand, telling her about my gay brother, lesbian sister and homophobic parents, when she said, "Families are funny, aren't they?"

Tonight was our third date. We had met for tea at an Italian bakery in the East Village after my Armenian language class at St. Vartan's Cathedral. Then we went back to her place and we listened to an old Dolly Parton album. The one with "Jolene" on it.

"This record always makes me sad," she said.

"Why?"

"My dad really liked it. He died when I was twenty-four."

"What did he die from?"

"Lung cancer. He smoked a carton of Pall Malls a day. I'm so glad that when I was eighteen I decided to get to know him. He lived in a trailer park outside of town."

I was thinking of someone I had dated a long time ago in L.A.; he had grown up in a trailer park and seemed to have a lot of shame about it.

"That's weird," she said. "Your eyes were the same as my father's, for just a second, just then. I never saw that before."

We talked and cuddled for a while, and then decided it was too late for me to leave. Tab gave me a pair of her men's pajamas to wear. I watched as she undressed, surprised to see that under her khaki workmen's shirt were full breasts. She put on a wife-beater and men's pajama bottoms and we fooled around a little bit, tentatively. Her body was wiry and strong, but she could also be soft like a girl. I was laying down and she grazed her fingertips up and down my body; it was such a gentle and sweet stimulation. "No one's every touched me that way before," I told her. Then she lay down and I pushed her wife-beater up and wrapped my mouth around her breasts a little bit, but she abruptly pulled the shirt down and propped herself up on one elbow. As I was pulling in to kiss her, my face in hers, I caught a glimpse of something—a mix of anger, sadness, strength, determination and resignation—that reminded me of my grandmother.

The morning after Tab and I had sex for the first time, I wrote in my journal:

> It was so intense. We were naked and she was so incredibly beautiful. I can't even describe. She's perfect and different and new and feminine and totally curvy and beautiful… but then she changed, became distant and went on automatic. Like she was a guy plowing into me.

It was ironic that I thought of Tab as if she were my grandmother. Yes, she had the big nose, and the survivor's temperament. But I also found myself totally unnerved most of the time we were dating; I was constantly worried that I had done or said something wrong and our connection would go up in smoke. Grammy never made me feel this way; the dynamic was more akin to the fear I had of losing my mom's approval.

"Why is she sitting with you?" Tab asked when we were each lying on our own double bed at the Holiday Inn in Cincinnati; Goose was sitting on mine and not hers. I felt like telling her Goose was trying to make up for the road trip from hell. We were driving across country together—she was on her way to Oregon to work for the summer; I wanted to spend as much time with her as I could. But it didn't seem to be the best plan, now.

After a long day of driving through Pennsylvania, West Virginia and Ohio, I asked, "How are you doing, Tab?"

"I have a lot on my mind."

"Like what?"

"Like the next four months of my life!" she retorted.

"Are you anxious to get to Oregon?" I asked. She had expressed some concern about going home and spending time with her mother.

"Anxious? I don't know. I don't want to talk about it. Here, *Seinfeld* is on."

I turned my back to her and wrote in my journal everything she had just said. The therapist I had been seeing, a waspy blond woman with an office on the upper West Side with ergonomically-designed black leather chairs, paid for by my school health insurance, had advised me to be brave and not ask reassurance from Tab. "Was there a relationship in your childhood in which you felt accepted?" she had asked.

"My grandmother," I answered.

"Well, why don't you imagine that type of dynamic when you're with Tab?"

But now I'd had enough of being brave and not talking. I turned over and in the glow of the blue TV light, I asked, "Tab, is there something you want to tell me?"

"Yes," she said. "It's about the sex."

Gulp. "What about the sex?"

"There's an imbalance. You need to be with someone who is gentle.

I'm rough. I don't think I'm the right person for you."

For some reason, I hadn't accounted for someone to be as sensitive as I was about sex. "I don't mind the roughness," I told her, realizing how bad that sounded as I said it. "It just felt like you weren't really there."

"I don't think we should have sex," she said. "It's too intense and we can't go back to our own apartments. We should just have fun and laugh and be together on this trip. When I get back in the fall, we can see, we can try things out."

I tried to be the way Grammy had been to me, to not ask anything of Tab, to be accepting and give her space. So as we drove through the bottoms of Illinois and Indiana, I wondered how I could be more rough. In Missouri, I wished I weren't so middle-class that I needed to stay in safe-looking motels and not in the car at a rest stop. In Oakley, Kansas, we visited the Fick Fossil Museum and I got depressed from walking through a sod house and viewing Depression-era photos of rabbits clubbed to death, but then Tab ruffled my hair, put her arm around me and asked, "How are you doing Agabian?" In Rocky Mountain National Park, I drank Scotch and got stoned with her and tried to be rough when she had sex with me. But she kept pinning my hands down whenever I tried to touch her. I finally figured it out—she didn't want me to be rough. She wanted to be the one who was rough, and for me to be passive.

I was embarrassed that it took this long to understand what was going on, that I couldn't see who Tab was.

After we made it across the country, we parted ways for the summer, and I never saw her again.

When I got back to New York, the therapist said that it was no wonder I felt insecure, with Tab being so uncommunicative. Then she asked me what I could have done in order to speak up about my feelings more.

"I wanted to ask her what was wrong, but I was trying to give her space. I was trying to be like my grandmother and not my mother."

The therapist apologized. "Nancy, you didn't listen to your instincts because of something I had said."

"It's so stupid because my grandmother never would have acted like that. If she had been in that car with Tab treating her the way she had treated me, she would have screamed at her to pull over."

"But Nancy, your great strength is how flexible and adaptable you can be. It wouldn't have been like you to make a scene," the therapist offered to make me feel better.

This was cause for pause. In effect, the therapist was saying that if I acted as my grandmother would have in that situation, I wouldn't be loving someone well. The truth was Grammy had managed to do both with me—be herself and love me unconditionally.

I'd somehow never mastered such a balance. Speaking up for myself might be misconstrued as rejection, as it often was with my mother. It was safer to love by staying silent and subordinate to someone, even if I feared that I wasn't existing. Flexible and adaptable—that was me.

I'd been so flexible and adaptable with my therapist, apparently, that I'd taken her entire load of crappy advice. Instead of trusting myself, I'd trusted someone else with my decisions. As always.

Something shifted then, when the therapist apologized.

I'm the only one here, I thought. *It's just me.*

19. ARMENIAN REALITY

Armenian's allege [*sic*] that the previous Turkish Ottoman Empire without reason killed large numbers of Armenians during 1885-1915. However they fail to note that Armenians had sided with their religious breatren [*sic*] the Russians betraying the Ottoman Empire which they were a citizen of [*sic*]. This uprising grew with the inclusion of Armenians into Russian, French and their own armed groups resulting in a wide scale civil war where both sides suffered terrible losses. Armenian fanatics have called this a massacre instead of a civil war ignoring the larger losses suffered by the none [*sic*] Armenian populations of the empire.

My research into the murder of Tourian had temporarily deposited me onto an internet site called Turkish Forum. The words "Armenian Question" appeared in large black letters over a blood red background, with the above text below it. I'd stumbled upon Genocide denial, and I could not turn away. As I clicked on a suggested link, called Armenian Reality, my blood boiled—a page with bright red letters on a gray alligator print background announced: "The Turkish Genocide by Armenians." A photo depicting corpses on the ground was captioned, "Turks massacred by Armenians." Posed, professional photographs of men in uniforms, holding rifles, were labeled "Armenian gangs" or identified as Hunchags or Tashnags. The site claimed that Armenians were deported because they had staged rebellions, and their caravans were attacked by Turkish villagers who had been assaulted in the past by these Armenian gangs.

Why haven't I heard about Armenian aggression in my readings or studies? I thought. Then I remembered the Armenakan, the *fedayees,* and the revolutionaries who fled across the border to join the Russian army. Surely they had killed Turks in the name of vengeance. Still, I didn't see how such isolated incidents would justify the mass execution of a people, nor its denial.

Maybe Armenians conspired with Russians for a homeland more than I thought? But women and children in traditional Armenian culture weren't exactly taught to be warriors—that was left to the men, and those men who didn't flee to the border were wiped out. If the events had been civil war, why hadn't there been more reports of fighting?

Although I could counter the claims, I felt confused and sick and unnerved and I couldn't help wondering if Armenians were partly responsible for their undoing. It didn't make sense, but perhaps there was some truth to the denial.

No, I thought as I shut down my computer. *It's all lies.*

I felt guilty, like I was betraying my grandmother.

"The Balkan War of 1912 set the stage for the emergence of more conservative Young Turks," Harut Zilelian stated. He was the librarian who had helped me at the Zohrab Center, and he was giving a lecture, at the invitation of the Ottoman Studies department, entitled "Nationality Politics of the Young Turks." I walked into a fluorescent-lit, windowless seminar room a half-hour late. As I located a seat a row in front of Lori, my Armenian teacher, she gave me a weary smile. I pulled out my notebook to write.

According to Harut, the Young Turks felt they were faced with three options to shape, strengthen and revive the empire: Ottomanism, which would give more autonomy to the varied ethnic groups within the remaining empire; Islamism, which would connect the country to all the various Muslim people in the world; and Pan-Turkism, which would unite the people of the Turkish race. Ottomanism had lost favor with the conservative Young Turks and Islamism could pose a problem further along the line due to the divisions between Sunni and Shi'ite. That left Pan-Turkism, which could unite all regional Turkic peoples (such as the Azeris) linguistically and ethnically to someday create one large Turkish nation. When Turkey entered World War I, the Young Turks made a statement that reflected their Pan-Turkism aims: "Our participation in the world war represents the vindication of our national ideal. The ideal of our nation and people leads us towards the destruction of our Muscovite enemy, in order to obtain thereby a natural frontier to our empire, which should include and unite all branches or our race."

Harut spoke of WWI Ottoman deportations of all those who were not Turkic: Jews, Greeks, Assyrians, Syrians and Arabs. "But the most extreme case was of the Armenians," he said. He also said that before 1915, there were about two million Armenians in the land that's now Turkey, and today there were only fifty thousand.

At this point, a man sitting on the aisle wearing a dirty Planet Hollywood sweatshirt with a large tattered plastic shopping bag by his feet said out loud, "I'm getting upset. I gotta leave." He walked out of the room, loudly crumpling his shopping bag. I couldn't figure out if he was an Armenian, a Turk, a Jew, a Greek, an Assyrian, a Syrian, an Arab, or what.

Harut didn't notice. He proceeded to discuss what happened in the region post-1915. Decomposing bodies spread disease to Turkish and Kurdish villagers, who also suffered from famine. The Russian Army advanced into Anatolia in 1916, and Russian Armenian soldiers possibly killed tens of thousands of Turks in retaliation of the genocide. The Young Turks fled at the end of the war, so there was no formal retribution. Armenians assassinated the Young Turk masterminds of the Genocide—Talaat Pasha, the Minister of the Interior, Enver Pasha, the Minister of War, and Military Governor of Constantinople, Jemal Pasha. Harut concluded that Turkey made a big mistake by entering World War I because it caused the deaths of millions, Muslims and non-Muslims alike, "which sowed seeds of enmity."

It was easier for me to now hear and understand the suffering and deaths of the Turks, since Harut had placed the events into the context of the Young Turk political climate. In contrast, the denialist websites had overlooked this history, choosing instead to solely blame Armenians for their deaths in mass numbers. Knowingly or unknowingly, Armenian historians must have downplayed Turkish deaths as a way to completely avoid the possibility that Armenians might be seen as complicit in their own genocide. I'd certainly never heard of any retaliation killings of Turks by Armenians or Turkish collateral losses as a child in Armenian school.

At the end of the lecture there was a question and answer session. A hand went up in the front of the room and a voice with a Turkish accent asked, "If there was genocide, what would be the reasons? Because there was no genocide."

My chest tightened; I heard Lori sigh.

Harut maintained his calm demeanor. He said in a good-natured tone, "I kinda went through all the reasons," and then he summed them up again. "The Ottoman Empire was collapsing. When Armenians called for reforms and international intervention, there was a fear that the Empire would lose more territory."

"Okay it was collapse," the voice said. "So something be done. The Ottomans didn't kill, they relocate."

Harut stared blankly.

"The Armenians were killing the Turks," the voice insisted.

I sighed. The voice was not listening. The voice sounded like the attitude on Turkish Forum and Armenian Reality. Tension was rising in the room, grumbling and sighs. I feverishly wrote in my journal to avoid being present.

"We can talk afterwards," Harut said. "The bulk of documentation from Turkish allies prove that the deportations were not just simple deportations, but a premeditated plan to rid the Empire of Armenians."

A young woman sitting in front of me, wearing a green shirt, black skirt and a little barrette in her hair was raising her hand up high, as high as she could. *She's getting poised to spew some denial,* I thought.

Harut called on her. "Yes, the reason there was nationalism was because French, English and Italian invade Turkey and why the people in certain territories in the Empire were relocated has to do with this—"

"The Allies occupied Turkey *after* World War I," Harut said.

"Englishmen, Frenchmen and Italians," the girl persisted "came in order to remove Ottoman Empire. The only thing to do was this solution. You talk as if there was no reason."

"If you recall, I spoke from the Balkan War," Harut said.

"But there was a lot of violence too. It was an invasion. It wasn't an occupation and there was violence inside. There was a war going on; there was no genocide."

I hate her, I scrawled in my journal.

"If you look at the documentation and look at the definition of genocide—" Harut said.

"I understand the definition. I thought you open it up so I understand why what happened to the Armenians was a genocide."

Again, Harut gave the calm incredulous look with his intent blue eyes and said, "Well, that was pretty much the topic of my lecture."

When I saw Harut the next week while I was doing research at the Zohrab Center, I told him, "I was really impressed with how calm you were when the Turkish students were interrogating you. I was getting so angry that they weren't listening."

"Well, it was the first time many of them have heard this history," he replied. Just as some difficult Armenian history had been kept from me, Turkey's ugly history regarding the Armenians had been kept from the Turkish students, but on a much larger scale. "So it's normal they should react that way," Harut continued. "You just have to be firm, and maybe someday they'll be able to hear what you are saying. This was a good start; I know it got them thinking."

"Oh," I replied, dumbstruck. It had never occurred to me that the point of the lecture was to educate Turks. I thought the only way to deal with Turks was to get angry at them for denying the Genocide.

I was late again, rushing into the School of International and Public Affairs building at Columbia at midday. Sukru Elekdag, the former Turkish Ambassador to the U.S., who wrote a column for the Turkish newspaper *Milliyet,* was speaking at the Middle East Institute brown bag lunch series on April 17, 2001. It was a week before April 24, the date in 1915 when Armenian intellectuals were rounded up in Istanbul and killed, the date that Armenians now commemorate the Genocide every year.

The Armenian Club had launched a letter-writing campaign to the director of the Institute, Davis Poore, calling for the lecture to be canceled. Davis Poore responded in an email that the brown bag lunch series had hosted many controversial speakers, including a senior representative of the Taliban discussing women's issues, and the Consul General of Israel on Palestine. "We feel it is our responsibility to provide a forum for a wide diversity of views, and we believe that a non-violent exchange on issues of great controversy and great moment is a legitimate academic enterprise..."

In the hallways of the Middle East Institute offices I encountered a Columbia security guard and a man in a suit with a wire spiraling down from his ear to the inside of his jacket. "We can't let you in," the Columbia guard said. "The room's full."

"What are you talking about?" I asked. I didn't want to be here in the first place, to protest a Genocide denier. And now I was being turned away?

"You're welcome to wait and if someone leaves, you can go in," the wired man said.

"Who are you?" I asked. He was wearing a lapel pin with the initials S.S. "What does that stand for?" I interrogated, pointing to the pin. *Secret Service* I realized as the words came out of his mouth.

My adrenaline was surging. "What are you doing here?" I asked, irritated that the Secret Service was called in to stave off Armenians. *What, are we gonna kill the diplomat or something?*

"I'm here to protect the Ambassador," S.S. said gruffly and walked away.

Sitting on a couch in a hallway, I caught my breath. I was (and still am) generally a big wimp, unable to stand up for myself in most situations, from the registrar to the grocery checkout. It wasn't like me to be so forceful with officials, but the circumstances had somehow made me forget myself. I looked around the room, at other latecomers, who could have been Turkish, could have been Armenian, but there was practically no way for me to identify friend or foe, which was eerie. This mistrust felt familiar, a buzz always in the background of my daily life, but never so blatant and confusing as today. Finally, a man left the panel and the security guard let me in.

Ten or fifteen people were standing in two doorways to a small conference room. I peered into one of the doors to see the former Turkish Ambassador, a man about seventy with jet black hair, tan skin and large glasses sitting about twenty feet from me, at the head of the table, the countenance of a slick, aged, Hollywood producer. He was speaking nervously with a thick accent. Davis Poore, a tall, thin man, with enormous glasses and stiff gray hair that resembled a toupee, asked if there were any questions.

A woman raised her hand. "You said in your introduction that you are seeking dialogue between Armenians and Turks in order to reach a rapprochement between the two countries. That is a nice sentiment, but there cannot be a dialogue when Turks deny the Armenian Genocide. If you treat it as fact, then we can talk about what to do about it."

"No," Elekdag said firmly. "The Genocide is not fact, we cannot discuss it as such. There was a civil war; just as many Turks were killed as Armenians."

The crowd erupted in response, some laughing nervously.

Another woman stated, "I think it's very disingenuous of you to say that you don't represent the Turkish government, when everything you have said reflects all their views."

"No, I do not represent the Turkish government," Elekdag said. "I only represent myself."

"If you aren't covering up what your government did, then why are the Turkish archives closed?"

"No, now see. It is very embarrassing, but the archives are in such poor condition, that many of the materials are much much much too fragile for people to look at."

And so it continued, with people challenging and Elekdag denying. People often spoke to him in heightened emotion, and he frequently responded in a belligerent staccato.

The meeting ended with Poore: "Thank you for being a peaceful crowd."

As I was lingering in the hallway, not quite knowing what to do with myself, I overheard a woman say, "I feel sorry for these Armenian students. They're just blindly holding onto all their grandparents' anger. It's really pathetic." She had it all wrong and I wanted to say something but I thought if I opened my mouth, I would release a flood of anger, proving her statement. Walking out of the building, I felt dismayed, worthless.

Lori was sitting on the front steps of SIPA with a tall man, who she introduced as her friend Eric, one of her private Armenian language students. He'd been a student at Columbia Law School a couple of years ago. They looked about as disgusted as me.

"What did you think?" I asked.

"I wish I could shove a rifle up that old fuck's asshole," Eric said. I was taken aback by his reaction, which seemed overly violent. But at the same time, I understood where his rage was coming from, and I stayed on, talking to him and Lori. "I think we should go back up there and give that Poore prick a piece of our minds."

Not knowing where else to go with my feelings, I followed Lori and Eric upstairs where we encountered a few other Armenian students gathered in the hallway. We introduced ourselves and told each other how upsetting this all was, insulting the memories of our survivor grandparents; I was feeling a little better.

Then a small man in khakis with gray hair approached me and asked, "Are you Armenian?"

"Yes," I answered.

"I'm Azeri," he said. "From Karabagh. Armenians deported my people." He was my height, and he turned to me, as if expecting an apology. I knew the situation between Armenia and Azerbaijan had been horrible; during the war between 1989 and 1994, the Azeris had lost twenty-five thousand people, the Armenians five thousand. I sympathized, but I didn't know what to say.

"Well, you shouldn't have massacred us in the first place," Eric broke in. Massacres of Armenians in Sumgait, Azerbaijan had prompted the war. "What, were we supposed to let you fuck us over?"

The little Azeri man immediately scuttled away. "Oh my God, Eric," Lori laughed.

"What? I have to put up with this bullshit?" Eric said. The man was still in earshot. "They were killing Armenians and they expected them to do nothing?"

Something wasn't right about what had just happened, but I wasn't sure what it was—Eric or the Azeri or me. Before I had a moment to think, react or respond, Davis Poore's office door opened, and we all filed in. There were five of us in the tiny, bookshelved space. A few students took turns telling him what an offense the event had been.

"I understand your disappointment. But let me explain the brown bag lecture series to you. We have had other highly controversial speakers, it's really not unusual."

"But this was like inviting a Holocaust denier to speak," one woman said.

"No one invited him. He approached us because he had a tour of U.S. universities planned, and he originally wanted to come on April 24."

"So he was going to come here on our day of commemoration to spread propaganda of the Turkish state," Eric said. "And you basically let him."

"We're not in the position to limit free speech," Poore said.

"This wasn't free speech, it was *hate* speech," Lori countered.

"I thought that he might change his mind about the Genocide," Poore said. "For example, he used to be very hard line about the Kurds, but he has since softened. Also, he wanted to come here and just read a lecture, and I convinced him to respond to people." Poore was telling us he was just trying to open up dialogue. Then he said, "You know, there were a lot of Kurds killed in Iran, but Human Rights Watch has refrained from calling it a genocide because there isn't enough proper proof—"

It seemed Poore was about to tell us we didn't have documentation either.

"It's been proven!" Eric interrupted. "We shouldn't have to be put in a position to prove the Genocide happened AGAIN!"

"The problem here," Eric continued, "is that your institute provided a forum for denial. You would never do this with a known Holocaust denier, and it's because the Jews at Columbia wouldn't stand for it and would pull all their money out of the place. The Armenians are a small minority and we don't have the power to prevent this from happening, but I'm telling you, if you do this again, I'm going to come down here and personally kick your fucking ass."

Davis Poore looked sick. Pale and scared. Judging from the "non-violent exchange" phrase in his email, the small room he'd chosen, and the security detail, it was obvious Poore had been worried about violence. It was ironic, then, that violence—the threat of an ass-kicking—was the only thing that got him to listen. It *seemed* he was listening, anyway; he sat quietly, looking at us with wide eyes, his mouth set in a short line.

A few more students reiterated how harmful it was for us, as grand-children of survivors, to have to listen to Elekdag. I was pretty sure Poore would be more careful the next time a Turkish official wanted to talk about the Armenian Genocide. As we filed out of his office, I turned around and looked at him seated at his desk.

I saw a thin, frail, frightened old man.

That night, the voices of Elekdag, Poore, the Azeri man and Eric stayed with me. I thought of the woman's words of the Armenian students, "blindly holding onto their grandparents' anger." I felt disgusting, like I'd descended into hell, like I needed to take ten showers.

The Poore-Elekdag incident shook me hard; I started wondering about the rest of the world's perception of current-day conflict between Turks and Armenians. So I decided to read a book called *The Crescent and Star,* on Atatürk's founding of modern Turkey, by Stephen Kinzer, *The New York Times* bureau chief in Istanbul for many years. *The New York Times,* which had reported news of Armenians being systematically annihilated by Turks on their front page in 1915, had a recent history of presenting the Genocide as a disputed event with an "Armenian side" and a "Turkish side." In line with the policies of the U.S. government, *The Times* refrained from any acknowledgment of the Genocide in an effort to pacify the Turks, an important Middle Eastern ally.

In his book, Kinzer portrays Atatürk as a dictator who forced Western ideals on his people in order to create his vision of a modern, secular nation. Given this context, Kinzer explains the current situation—of the military ultimately ruling over the parliament and the press acting as a mouthpiece for the government—by comparing Turkish citizens to overgrown children and their government as an overprotective parent. "Something about the concept of diversity frightens Turkey's ruling elite. It triggers the deep insecurity that has gripped Turkish rulers since the Republic was founded in 1923, an insecurity that today prevents Turkey from taking its proper place in the modern world." This insecurity is also responsible for Turkey failing to recognize and atone for past human rights abuses, a requirement to join the European Union.

In a chapter titled "Ghosts" about Armenians, Kinzer visits Van and meets Kurds who tell him that in 1915, Turkish gendarmes paid their grandfathers a silver piece for every head of an Armenian. Then he states, "Armenians may bear some blame for the tragedy of 1915, and some undoubtedly killed Turks during that tragic year. But this is far from the whole truth. Huge numbers of innocent Armenians were horribly victimized by armed bands operating with the sanction of the Ottoman authorities, and no individual or nation who denies it can honorably claim the mantle of truth." Kinzer then attempts to explain what was behind the massacres:

> In the spring of 1915, Armenians in this region made common cause with their Orthodox cousins in Russia, who hoped to seize eastern Anatolia and turn it into a Russian-Armenian province. The Ottoman authorities, understandably alarmed, ordered the deportation of populations "suspected of being guilty of treason or espionage". Soon bands of Ottoman soldiers and Kurdish tribesmen were storming through Armenian towns, forcing their citizens to flee the land of their forefathers and killing hundreds of thousands of them in an orgy of ethnic violence.

Kinzer was reiterating the usual Turkish stand: Armenians collaborated with Russians. Though he admitted the mass killings, there was no acknowledgment that they were the premeditated actions of the Young Turks to exterminate the Armenian and other populations. Unnerved, I read on.

> Successive Turkish governments have resisted the campaign aimed at forcing them to acknowledge Ottoman atrocities against Armenians, which is waged not from Armenia itself but from Armenian communities abroad... [where] anti-Turkish feeling burns with passionate intensity. Some leaders of Armenian communities in the U.S. and elsewhere have become more nationalistic than most Armenians in Armenia. More than a few are driven by a desire not to shed light on the truth of 1915 but to bring modern Turkey to its knees as a form of long-delayed revenge. Once Turkey is forced to acknowledge the slaughter of 1915, these radicals say, Armenians must demand compensation for their losses and, ultimately, return of their lands and all of Eastern Anatolia to Armenian rule.

I was coming to terms with the diaspora's "anti-Turkish feeling," but I found it misleading of Kinzer to present it within the context of radical nationalists. I assumed he was talking about the Tashnags, so I looked up their manifesto online. I was dismayed to find their goals indeed included a united Eastern and Western Armenia with borders specified by the Allies in the Treaty of Sèvres of 1920, an arrangement I found completely unrealistic when Armenia could barely survive on the land they currently occupied, and the possibility would surely require aggression and bloodshed.

Still, by portraying "more than a few" Armenian leaders who want to "bring Turkey to its knees," Kinzer was casting all diasporan Armenians in the paranoid light of the Turkish government. I certainly didn't want to bring Turkey to its knees—I just wanted an acknowledgment of history.

The Armenian Assembly echoed these sentiments, informing me in an email that they wanted "at least recognition and apology from Turkey," but they had no position on compensation or restoration of lands. I knew this was an official position; it could be that some people at the Assembly actually want the same as the Tashnags, but to own up to it would hurt their efforts at acknowledgment.

In any case, when I conducted an informal email survey of diasporan Armenian individuals with roots in both Eastern and Western Armenia, entitled "What Armenians want," I found widely varying answers among just seventeen responses. Most wanted some sort of acknowledgment of the Genocide and an apology, very few wanted land returned, some wanted monetary reparations to survivors and their families, others wanted reparations made to Armenia, still others wanted the reparation to be in the form of change within Turkey—to restore Armenian landmarks, to revise history books with the truth, to establish a monument or museum to the Genocide, and/or to form committees on the current treatment of minorities.

There was also a desire expressed to open the border between Turkey and Armenia, to improve relations with Turkey and with Azerbaijan. Lori, my Armenian teacher, stated she wanted the development of a close relationship. "I feel we are part of each other, the two people having lived together for so many centuries, and that the current psychological and political rupture is very painful to say the least."

A week or so after I read Kinzer's book, I was walking across 34th Street with Jennifer, a woman from my Armenian language class that I was taking at St. Vartan's Cathedral. She was talking about her son, who was about ten months old.

"What's his name?" I asked.

"Aram," she said.

"Oh, that's such an Armenian name," I told her.

"No it's not," she said, "it's Assyrian." Jennifer's husband was Armenian, but she was Assyrian, an ancient rival of the Armenians. There are about three and a half million Assyrians worldwide; more than half of them live in Iraq. An estimated three quarters of a million Assyrians lost their lives during 1915, about 75 percent of the Ottoman Assyrian population, which is actually much worse than the percentage of the Armenian losses. Many Pontic Greeks also lost their lives during the same time, but somehow, Armenians often exclude them too when discussing the Genocide, and when seeking recognition, which doesn't make sense. For one thing, it's practically genocidal to not mention all the lives that were intentionally destroyed, no matter what ethnicity they were. And for another, it would only make a stronger case in getting Turkey to admit the wrongdoing of the Young Turks if all the victims were united. The insistence to refer to it only as "The Armenian Genocide" was probably the major reason why I hadn't encountered many Assyrians in my adventures through the Armenian community of New York.

Now I was providing another. "Aram is a very common Armenian name," I told Jennifer. "I didn't know it was Assyrian." I was actually kind of shocked by this fact.

"Just because a lot of Armenians use it, doesn't mean it's Armenian. It's an Aramaic word. Aramaic was the Assyrian language. In fact, Syria used to be called Aram. This was before the Arabs took it over."

"I didn't know that," I said, still a little disoriented.

"Armenians are always claiming things as Armenian that aren't," she said. "For example, Mesrob Mashdots," the man who invented the Armenian alphabet, "was probably Assyrian because his name wasn't Armenian. The Armenian alphabet derives from Aramaic."

"I haven't heard of anyone from another culture having the name Aram," I suddenly announced, trying to explain why I was having trouble understanding Jennifer's claim.

"Well, I'm Assyrian and my uncle's name is Aram," Jennifer countered.

Now I was being offensive. "I'm just trying to explain why it's hard for Armenians"—i.e. me—"to accept Aram isn't an Armenian name. It's just like, a really common name. Maybe it's because of William Saroyan's book, *My Name is Aram*."

"He's half Assyrian."

"Who?"

"Saroyan."

"No."

"Yes. It's a little known fact."

Now she was annoying me. Everything that I thought was Armenian was suddenly Assyrian. *Who is she to tell me?*

At the same time, I felt like the Turkish girl in the green shirt and little barrette who couldn't take in anything at Harut's lecture.

Suddenly the insecurity of the Turks—that deep-seated fear of diversity that Kinzer had likened to the worry of controlling, overprotective parents—became clear. It was the same insecurity as that of the Armenians, the same as my own. We're all so concerned that someone will take advantage of us, or overlook us, that we overcompensate with self-aggrandizement. Turks to Europeans, Armenians to Turks, me to my parents or anyone I'm in a relationship with: we all want to avoid being swallowed up, we fear not having an identity of our own, we are terrified we may no longer exist.

"Nancy, I have to tell you this story," Mumma said on the phone.

She and my father had just made a trip to Maine where my father had an appraisal job. Mumma had trouble finding a motel at the last minute, until she contacted a place in a tiny town. "The man on the phone sounded a bit strange," she said.

They arrived late and Dad dropped off Mumma at the office. She checked in with the man who had spoken with her on the phone, then came back outside and said to my father, "He might be Turk."

"Why do you say that?" my father asked.

"He looks Middle Eastern," Mumma said.

"Just because he looks Middle Eastern doesn't mean he's Turkish."

"I have a feeling," Mumma said.

"Well, what are you gonna do," Dad said. He drove over to the machine company and went to work.

The next morning, while my parents were choosing their continental breakfast in the motel lobby overlooking Penobscot Bay, my mother said to the man, "You sound like you have an accent. Where are you from?"

"Turkey," he said.

"Oh, I'm Armenian," she said, smiling sweetly. "We can't be friends."

"Why not?" the man asked.

By now Daddy had approached and was standing behind Mumma and said, "You know what happened to the Armenians in 1915."

"Oh, yes, but it happened such a long time ago," the man said. "You have to forget those things and move on."

"Yes it did happen a long time ago," my mother said. "Those were different times then. My grandparents were from Istanbul, and they had to leave because conditions were bad for them."

The man didn't say anything. "So I just left it," Mumma told me. "But, I was discussing it with your father, because I didn't want to not say anything like a soft soap. So when we were checking out, your father asked him, 'Where in Turkey are you from?'"

"North Central Turkey," the man said.

"Do you know where Sivas is?" Dad asked. Imagining my father saying this caused me to choke up a little bit.

"Yes, in fact my family is from the next town over from Sivas," the man said.

"My family owned farmland there," my father said, "and livestock.

They had a livelihood, but they were forced to leave, like many other Armenians. My mother's family was killed. That's why we have hard feelings for the Turkish people."

"Listen," the man said. "I've been in this country for thirty years, and I went to a demonstration for the Armenian Genocide in Cochituate when I first got here. And at that time they said one hundred thousand Armenians were killed. And now every year they say it's more and more until one and a half million. My family took in Armenians. In fact, Armenians used to visit my grandfather and thank him for helping them."

"Yes," my father said. "We know there were some Turks who helped Armenians."

"When I was sixteen"—Daddy estimated the man must have been about fifty—"an Armenian man in our neighborhood died, and when we went into his house we found ammunition boxes in the rafters filled with Russian rubles. He was a spy for the Russians."

Mumma couldn't take it anymore. "Have you heard of Henry Morgenthau? He was the U.S. Ambassador to Turkey, and he compiled statistics on how many Armenians there were; after 1915 they were all gone."

"How could there be one and a half million Armenians when there were eighteen million people in the country?" the man asked.

"The country wasn't all Turks. There were other ethnic minorities there. You don't know because there is nothing in the Turkish history books about them or the Genocide," Daddy informed.

"That's because the government doesn't want people to feel badly and not be friends."

Finally Daddy said, "You can deny it all you want, but the government has to admit what they've done, hopefully in my lifetime, just like the Germans, and then they can go on. Until then, they'll never move forward."

Mumma and Daddy made their exit. My mother said she could still hear the man ranting and raving to his wife as they slipped into their car.

"So we left with a little hard feelings," Dad joked. "Your mother didn't want to go away mousy, she wanted to have her say. But I'll tell you, if we really wanted to make a stand, we should've just not stayed at his motel for three nights."

"He knew we were Armenian, because when I told him, he said 'I thought so by your name.' He wasn't going to say anything. We made our point," Mumma said.

I wondered if it was futile for my parents to cast their anger at the Turkish government onto a Turkish-American motel owner, searching for acknowledgment from someone who would never give it. It was like they were being like me when I demanded that they accept me and acknowledge my bisexuality. When would I be able to separate my reality from theirs? It was ironic that I was now learning from them, though: their action had served to inform the man, and I admired them for not hiding themselves, instead choosing to reveal who they were, to tell the truth, to speak their piece.

20. My Peace

"Did you hear him say, 'She won't let me have Taco Bell'?" Mumma asked.

She was referring to my father. I had just come home for Easter, and my parents had picked me up at the train station. On the way home, we passed Taco Bell; the franchise had opened a branch near the Walpole Mall two years before and every time Dad drove past it, he said he hadn't eaten there. This last time, he blamed it on my mother.

Dad walked into the living room. "Oh, I'm sorry I said you wouldn't let me eat at Taco Bell!" he announced in a whiny, mocking voice.

"You're as aggravating as hell," Mumma muttered.

Dad went back into the kitchen to mash the potatoes for dinner. He had a special way of sautéing onions in butter and milk and mixing it in with them.

"If I had known he was this aggravating, I wouldn't have married him," Mumma said.

"How long were you engaged?" I asked.

"A year and a half. Because when I met him, my grandmother was very sick. It was after my mother and grandfather died, and I was in no shape to marry him then. I was calling doctors in the middle of the night to take care of my grandmother. And then she *and* my father were both putting pressure on me to get married."

"Why?"

"My father thought I'd be out of the way and he wouldn't have to worry about me and my grandmother was just old-fashioned."

After dinner she poked her head into the room where I was watching TV and said, "You got to ask me about my life, so now I get to ask you. Are you dating anyone, or are you going to stay celibate forever?"

That's not a very nice way of wording things. "I'm not going to answer that," I said.

"Are you dating any males?"

"I've told you before, I'm going to date whomever I want to date."

"I don't like that."

"You were just talking about family and societal pressure. Now you're doing it to me."

"I'm just telling you because my heart will be broken if you have children and I'm not around."

I wanted to snap back that if she wasn't around, she wouldn't have a heart to be broken. But then she said, "It's been my biggest heartache that my mother never got to meet my children."

Here was the memory of her mother. It was tough to argue with her but I took a deep breath, softened my voice and said, "Mumma, wouldn't you rather I live my life the way I want and be happy, than live my life the way *you* want and *not* be happy? You always told me not to care about what other people think. I've always been true to myself and true to my heart. I've had a good relationship and I intend to have more and if anyone significant comes around I'll let you know."

"Move your leg, Agnes!" Mel yelled impatiently.

Agnes was stalled at her walker. Mel stood close to her, holding her by the armpit, and Ruth behind, holding a chair behind her in case Agnes's legs gave way. They were on their way from the den to the bathroom at their home in Watertown.

Agnes had been diagnosed with Parkinson's disease the previous February. She deteriorated very quickly after the diagnosis. She could barely walk, and Mel and Ruth had to install a chair lift which wound around the back staircase to the second floor.

"Why aren't you moving your legs Agnes?!"

"I'm trying!" Agnes said.

"If you're not going to walk then sit down!"

"I'm fine!" Agnes said, and then she plopped back into the chair. Ruth and Mel exchanged frustrated looks.

I knew they were fearful of Agnes falling to the floor. The last time she fell, they couldn't lift her and had to call the paramedics to help them. She had fractured a spinal disc and landed in the hospital, recovering for a few weeks until she was just recently discharged home.

I was visiting the aunts with my parents a couple of days after Christmas. Things seemed mighty grim, but they brightened up once Hamast, a recently widowed lady from their church, came to visit. "You've traveled all over the world!" Hamast said to Agnes. "At least you can feel good about the places you've seen. I haven't gone anywhere."

"Did you see Agnes's reaction," Mumma asked later, back in Walpole, "when Hamast told her, 'you've traveled all over the world'?"

"She didn't mean it as a criticism," Dad said.

"No, I know she didn't, but Agnes didn't have any response. She just sat there like it didn't register." I was about to tell her that the frozen face was a symptom of Parkinson's and that Agnes had told me several months ago, when she had given me the camera she had taken all around the world, "At least I got to travel a lot when I could."

But before I could reply, Dad said, "Agnes could have said the same thing to Hamast. 'You've been married and had a family all these years and you can say you've done that.'"

"Well, I think being married and having a family is hard work," Mumma said. "It's not like doing whatever you want to do."

"Like you," Daddy laughed, intimating that he was the one in their relationship who did all the work.

"And the other two," Mumma went on. "They've never had children, and now that they actually have to take care of somebody, they're beside themselves."

"They took care of Grammy," I said.

"Your grandmother was very healthy and never suffered a long illness."

"Auntie Ruth lived her whole life with Grammy. She took care of her."

"No, Nancy. It wasn't unusual for people to live with their parents in those days."

"But Agnes and Mel lived on their own. Ruth never left. I think she felt responsible for her mother."

"I don't think so," Mumma said.

I was angry at her for not understanding that there were a multitude of ways daughters could feel towards their mothers. But she was angry, obviously, that no one had seemed to recognize the sacrifices she had made as a mother. I certainly hadn't. It was then that I realized that my view, of a daughter taking care of a mother by obeying her wishes, by adhering to her expectations, was absolute too.

"Little Juan?" the librarian asked me. I was at the Bloomingdale branch of the New York Public Library, on 100th Street between Amsterdam and Columbus.

"No, *Little One.* O-N-E," I spelled.

I stood at the librarian's desk as she searched the catalog on her computer, noticing she had long, straight, gray hair, parted down the middle. "Oh, here it is," she said. "It's actually *Little 1.* Take this slip upstairs and they'll help you find it."

The entire second floor of the Bloomingdale branch library was the children's section. With its yellow walls, it looked like it hadn't been renovated since around the time I started checking out books from the Walpole children's library, circa 1974.

I felt awkward, a single woman wandering through the picture book section as a storytelling period with moms and kids was underway. I scanned the section called Stories, but I couldn't find it.

"This is in storage; it's not in circulation," the librarian said grimly. She was a woman about my age with wide-set rheumy eyes and flaking eyelids. "You can't check it out."

"That's okay, I just want to look at it," I said.

"Okay, I'll go get it." She stood up from her desk, grabbed a cane and walked around me, her body in a crooked line leaning, one lame leg arching out. I followed her awkward walk. When she arrived at a door on the other side of the room, she said, "Stay back, you're not allowed in." I peered into the slightly open door—the room was tiny and dark, with books piled in teetering columns.

I stood to the side while the librarian rummaged around. Suddenly she appeared, holding it up to me. "Is this it?" she asked.

There was **1**, in the middle of the cover. He looked different from how I had remembered. The porkpie hat was actually a triangular red cap. He was also wearing a string tie under his chin.

"That's the one," I said.

Little 1 was written by Ann and Paul Rand. I opened the book to find Little **1** frowning in the middle of a hopscotch pattern: "Little **1** had very small feet and a little red hat that sat on the tip of his head. He could hop and skip and spin, but he never had much fun, because he was only **1**."

I turned the page. "'I'd like to be a **2** like you,' Little **1** said, smiling at **2** yellow pears that lay in a dish. 'Go away,' said the pears. '**2** is company, but **2** plus **1** is three, and that would be a crowd.'"

The plot was basically the same as I had remembered: **1** searches for friends but he can't find any. The only difference was that those who spurn him are not numerals, but objects: three teddy bears, four bees, five umbrellas, six ants, seven mice, eight books and nine goldfish. The illustrations reminded me of early-sixties mod; Paul Rand used a three-color process: red, yellow and green.

The **0** was surprisingly gender neutral. "Little **1** was half ready to cry when a bright red hoop came looping by. 'Hi!' cried the hoop with a smile. 'Come and play for a while.'"

"'But I'm only **1**' said Little **1**."

"'Oh no, that's not so,' cried the hoop. 'Don't you know a circle that's empty inside is the same as zero?'"

Little **1** and the hoop formed the number **10** and lived happily ever, blissfully tripping out in the shadow of a steam engine and the Eiffel Tower. **1**'s hat is askew, his eyes closed, a satisfied smile on his face, while the **0** rolls around upside down.

But there was a final page I had also forgotten: **1** falling asleep inside a crescent moon, a tiny u of a smile on his face, an individual at peace.

Tina Marie was sitting on Uncle Tony's lap. She was two and a half. The daughter of my first cousin Jake, Tina Marie was the youngest, and arguably the cutest, of Auntie Sherrie's grandchildren. I was in an Italian restaurant on Long Island with my family, after Sherrie's funeral. She had died after a long battle with breast cancer.

At the wake, I saw a photograph taken of the Agabian family, circa 1946, on the occasion of Zanik and Jacob's twenty-fifth wedding anniversary. My father was around seventeen, with a full head of hair, wearing a suit and a shirt with an open collar, seated between his mother and father, and the four aunts, all so uniquely different and beautiful, in their early twenties, stood behind. I took a glance at Grammy, seated on the left. She was smiling.

At the church, I had been overcome, thinking about my aunt's link to my grandmother. Aunt Sherrie had told me in her interview how much she valued the family life her parents had given her. And then she went on to have a family, four children, who each in turn had their own children. Her daughter Julianne had eulogized her by saying how she hadn't been a stern mother, but that she led with grace and a strong gentleness. It seemed to me that Sherrie's spirit was a continuation of some part of Grammy—less of her resentment and anger, and more of her love and care. I thought of the four sisters sharing the two beds, laughing at night to the sound of the whippoorwills. My mother was sitting next to me, and I felt her put her soft hand over mine.

At the restaurant, I watched Tina Marie with her high brown ponytails and ultra-feminine cuteness. All her cousins and aunts and uncles wanted her attention; they kissed her full on the face and hugged her repeatedly. But she was sitting with Tony now, and it struck me that maybe he would be fine, after suffering this huge loss, this woman that he loved for so long. There was his granddaughter, this little spirit of love, that was going to comfort him.

As we were leaving, I was saying goodbye to Tina Marie's mom, and then I kneeled down to say goodbye to Tina Marie. She stared at me blankly, her tiny mouth set in a line.

"Kiss Nancy goodbye, Tina Marie," her mom said and she gently nudged her towards me. I kissed a bewildered Tina Marie on her chubby cheek.

"People used to make me do that too," I told her.

Now it doesn't seem like such a bad thing to have been—a little one to make up for all the death and nothingness—for my mother, for the Armenian culture. Zero is the emptiness inside my own circle, the

inheritance of loss from my mother and grandmother. They told their stories to me, but I don't have a child, so I told my stories to you. In the process
of writing this book, after pushing and relating and struggling and loving,
I learned to be on my own. I learned to understand my history, my self,
and how to be a bit more whole. When I need strength now, I think of my
mother and grandmother, of the lessons I learned from their lives.

In the time it has taken me to write this book, to go back in time to become myself again and again and again, my friends have started and ended
relationships, people have been born and people have died. September 11
happened and there is a war in Iraq, an occupation of troops, and a genocide in Sudan to which the world community has been slow to respond, a
continuing cycle of violence and indifference.

I could have kept these histories, these personal stories, some might
say selfish, self-centered stories to myself, solid in the knowledge that I had
grown. But then I would be betraying another inheritance from my mother
and grandmother: to speak the truth, not merely for the satisfaction of one's
self, but because it is the right thing to do.

AFTERWORD: THE HER I WAS THEN

The subtitle of this book is "True stories of an Armenian daughter." I would now like to acknowledge that I have discovered there's actually no truth, or just little multiple versions of it, and though this belief can drive people crazy sometimes ("Can't you just have an opinion for once?"), I do think it's, ahem, true.

I said earlier in chapter nine when my twenty-three-year-old self caught up with my twenty-three-year-old self, that I was actually forty. This is true: As I write these very words to you right now, I am forty. Some people will read them, ask me to change them or correct the mistakes, and then I will be a little older, but still, you get the idea. When I wrote the other words in this book, and re-wrote them, I was somewhere between the ages of thirty-one and forty. It's a long story (no pun intended) on how this book came into being. It involves my inability to write it in a succinct manner (at one point it was roughly one thousand pages) and the long road on the way to finding the right publisher, but what you mainly need to know is that I felt compelled to write it.

I realize how many stories are compelled to be told. I'm a teacher and have encountered thousands of stories over the years. The other night, I was confiding in a friend that I loved to hear my students' stories because I am lonely, because something delights me in the fact that a person would trust me with her or his story. There is some joy that someone is doing something I know is meaningful and important to her, that the story is no longer untold, but told. But there is also this small girl inside of me, delighted to be let in on the grown up world, to get to stay up late and really hear what people are revealing. To feel close to them.

It is no wonder I feel this way, since my mother and grandmother chose at various points in their lives to tell me their stories. Though I have often suggested within these pages that it was a burden to be a listener, now I realize how much closer I wanted to be to Mumma and Grammy, how many more stories I would have loved to have heard, about their true core and essence, and for the process to liberate them even more.

There is a scene that has been cut which appeared late in this book, in the last chapter, wherein my mother tells me that I am too free. We were having an argument, because she thought I should be doing something I wasn't (i.e. being straight), and I was telling her I had more choices now in my life, and she told me I was too free. And the chapter ended like that. On the words, "that's right, that's your problem, you're too free."

If the person reading such a line were a stereotypical American, with few links to past and ancestry, she might think, "Hmm. Agabian didn't seem that free to me. In fact, her lack of freedom seemed to be her problem." If the person were someone else from another culture with great duties to his family, he might have thought, "Yeah, she was too free. She had too many choices and it confused her. She should have been guided more by rules and family duty."

It is this conundrum of the Armenian American, or any traditional ethnic person living in the U.S., that I want to address now. Recently I lived in Armenia for a year, and my young students, who were in their early twenties, living with their extended families, studying English and the culture of the English-speaking person in America, understood the difference between their lives and the lives of Americans. They knew that Americans valued leading independent lives, making their own decisions, expressing themselves freely. But with this freedom came a price: a lack of connection to family support—the sense of security, generosity and sacrifice that a family can provide, which is valued in Armenia.

Here were my mother and grandmother, trying to find a way to be themselves at a time when Armenians were exterminated and women were oppressed. Here were my mother and grandmother, taking care of me, wanting me to stay close to them as they told me their stories of loss: of those they loved, of the choices they wanted in their lives.

Here am I at forty, still confused by this dynamic of freedom and connection.

But I suppose the difference between who I am now, and the her that I was then, is that instead of seeing myself as a completely unliberated daughter, needing to be liberated, I now think of myself as someone trying to balance my individuality and my need for collective identity.

Here I am now, writing to you from my childhood bedroom. I live in New York City, but I needed to get away for the weekend, and I wanted to see my parents. Lately, I have been spending as much time with them as I can, because they are getting older and more precious to me. They are downstairs in the living room: I don't usually write at home with them around, but I told them I had important work to do, and they have been surprisingly accommodating. They are not the same people you read about in this book. Sure, someone will get testy now and again, but they are small and gray and gentle and frail. I suppose with the knowledge of their eventual loss, I have revised some of my feelings towards them.

I also find myself in another relationship, this time with a much younger man from Armenia. It seems like I'm always looking for a relationship formula that will make sense to my particular balance of freedom and connectiveness. I suspect that this will remain unchanging throughout my life.

What will also remain the same: the fact of my family. Though I felt beholden to their expectations throughout my life, I now realize that they provided me with a unique sense of freedom. Nowhere else in the world, except for maybe here in these pages, could my expression of humor and rage be so allowed. My mother made sure to expose me to as much art as she could when I was a child, certain that it could only do good. And not everyone is made aware at a young age of how important it is to protest injustice.

Here I am, in the room where my mother rocked me as an infant. Here I am, where I looked out the window, wishing to get away. Here I am, again.

GLOSSARY (All terms are Armenian unless otherwise noted.)

abrees: Good job; literally, "you live."

aman: (Turkish) Interjection similar to "my God!"

Badarak: Liturgy; church service.

bastekh: A dried fruit delicacy which comes in a thin round sheet.

boereg: Phyllo dough around various mixtures of cheeses, meats and/or vegetables.

bulghur: Cracked wheat.

choreg: A diamond-shaped or knot-shaped sweet roll sprinkled with anise and sesame seeds.

dahn deegeen: Head wife of an Armenian village family.

Deegeen: The form of address for a lady or a married woman.

Eench?: What?

Eench genes?: What are you doing?

Eench goozes?: What do you want?

Eenchoo?: Why?

Etchmiadzin: City in Armenia where the patriarch of the Armenian Apostolic Church, the Catholicos, resides.

fasoolyah: (Turkish) Green beans cooked in olive oil, onions and tomatoes.

gamavor: Volunteer.

geeneg: Diminutive of wife or woman.

Gunkamayr: Godmother.

ghent: Idiot; crazy person.

Hantes: Show or presentation.

hanum: (Turkish) Master's wife; female head of house.

hars: Wife; bride or daughter-in-law. According to tradition, a new hars moved into the home of her husband, was beholden to her mother-in-law's wishes and wasn't allowed to speak unless spoken to first or in the presence of only little children, for a full year after her wedding.

Hayr Mer: Lord's Prayer in Armenian.

Hrammetsek: You are welcome, usually said to encourage guests to eat.

keet: Nose.

Kery: Uncle.

lahmejun: A pizza of ground lamb or hamburger, vegetables and spices on a thin crust.

lebne: (Arabic) Strained yogurt.

lokhum: (Turkish) Candy made of juice and nuts.

madzoon: Yogurt.

Mairig: Diminutive or term of endearment for "Mother."

miaseragan: Homosexual or gay.

moogovchee: Nosy and intrusive like a mouse.

odar: Other, outsider, non-Armenian person.

oosh: Late.

paghach: A sweet bread.

panjar abour: Barley, yogurt and spinach soup.

parev: Hello.

shnorhagalutiun: Thanks, thank you.

tahn: Yogurt drink.

tavloo: Backgammon.

tonir: Clay oven set into a hole in the ground.

tsoog: Fish.

undaneek: Family.

Vay yavroum: (Turkish) An exclamation, like "Oh dear!" or "My dear!"

Vehapar: The Catholicos or patriarch of the Armenian Apostolic Church.

yalanchee: Stuffed grape leaves.

yoghan: A quilt filled with sheep's wool.

SOURCES

Ashjian, Arcbishop Mesrob. *The Armenian Church in America*. New York: Armenian Prelacy, 1995.

Bedoukian, Kerop. *Some of Us Survived: The Story of an Armenian Boy*. New York: Farrar Straus Giroux, 1979.

Bournoutian, George A. *A History of the Armenian People*. 2 vols. Costa Mesa, CA: Mazda Publishers, 1994.

Dadrian, Vahakn N. *Warrant for Genocide: Key Elements of Turko-Armenian Conflict*. New Brunswick, NJ: Transaction, 1999.

Diocese of the Armenian Church of America. *Documents on the Schism in the Armenian Church of America*. New York: Diocese of the Armenian Church of America, 1993.

—. *The First Armenian Church in America: An Outline and Documents*. New York: Diocese of the Armenian Church of America. 1991.

Dzeron, Manoog B. *The Village of Parchanj: General History 1600-1937*. Trans. by Arra S. Avakian. Fresno: Panorama West Books, 1984. (Translated from the Armenian edition, Boston: Baikar Press, 1938.)

Findikyan, V. Rev. Fr. Daniel. *A Walk Through the Divine Liturgy of the Armenian Church: A Guide to the Badarak*. Illus. by Lilit Amirchanian. New York: Diocese of the Armenian Church of America, 2001.

Hambardzumean, Vahan. *Village World (Kiughashkharh): An Historical and Cultural Study of Govdoon*. Trans. Murad A. Meneshian. Providence, RI: Govdoon Youth of America, 2001. (Originally published Paris: Daron Publishing House, 1927.)

Hovannisian, Richard G., ed. *The Armenian People from Ancient to Modern Times*. 2 vols. New York: St. Martin's Press, 1997.

Kaminsky, Alexander H., as told to Michael Stern. "The Murder of the Archbishop." *Master Detective*. July 1935: 5-15, 65-70.

Kinzer, Stephen. *Crescent and Star: Turkey Between Two Worlds*. New York: Farrar, Straus and Giroux, 2001.

Laub, Dori, M.D., "Bearing Witness, or the Vicissitudes of Listening." *Testimony: Crises of Witnessing in Literature, Psychoanalysis, and History*. Ed. Shoshana Felman and Dori Laub, M.D. New York: Routledge, 1992. 57-74.

—. "An Event Without a Witness: Truth, Testimony and Survival." *Testimony: Crises of Witnessing in Literature, Psychoanalysis, and History*. Ed. Shoshana Felman and Dori Laub, M.D. New York: Routledge, 1992. 75-92.

Maksoudian, Father Krikor Vardapet. *Chosen of God: The Election of the Catholicos of All Armenians From the Fourth Century to the Present*. Ed. Christopher H. Zakian. New York: St. Vartan Press, 1995.

Mandeville, John. *Globetrotter Travel Guide: Turkey.* London: New Holland Publishers (UK) Ltd., 1997.

Miller, Donald E., and Lorna Touryan Miller. *Survivors: An Oral History of the Armenian Genocide.* Berkeley and Los Angeles: University of California Press, 1993.

Minassian, Reverend Oshagan. *A History of the Armenian Holy Apostolic Church in the United States, 1888-1944.* Diss. Boston University School of Theology, 1974.

Nersoyan, Archbishop Tiran. *Armenian Church Historical Studies: Matters of Doctrine and Administration.* New York: St. Vartan Press, 1996.

Nichanian, Marc. *Writers of Disaster: Armenian Literature in the Twentieth Century. Vol. 1.* Princeton and London: Gomidas Institute, 2002.

Nisan, Mordechai. *Minorities in the Middle East : A History of Struggle and Self-Expression.* Jefferson, NC: McFarland & Co., 2002.

Rand, Ann and Paul. *Little 1.* New York: Harcourt, Brace & World, Inc., 1962.

Terjimanian, Hagop. *California Armenians: Celebrating the First 100 Years, 1878-1997.* Los Angeles: Abril Bookstore, 1997.

Villa, Susie Hoogasian, and Mary Kilbourne Matossian. *Armenian Village Life Before 1914.* Detroit: Wayne State University Press, 1982.

Walker, Christopher J. *Armenia: The Survival of a Nation.* New York: St. Martin's Press, 1980.

Zahirsky, Valerie Goekjian. *The Conversion of Armenia to Christianity: A Retelling of Agathangelos' History.* Illus. Siran Kaprielian Pirani. New York: Diocese of the Armenian Church of America, 2001.

Zakian, Christopher Hagop, ed. *The Torch was Passed: the Centennial History of the Armenian Church of America.* New York: St. Vartan Press, 1998.

ACKNOWLEDGMENTS

Many grateful and humble thanks to:

My family for their cooperation, love, and understanding.

The Columbia University MFA Writing Program, including Lis Harris, Richard Locke, and Patty O'Toole for recognizing I had a book in me, and Lawrence Weschler for giving fertile ground to experiment with nonfiction stories.

The Armenian General Benevolent Union for their educational loan, and the Dolores Zohrab Liebmann Fund for paying most of my educational expenses and for providing a generous stipend to write.

The writing group Six Degrees—Laura Carden, Catherine Kapphahn, Brenda Lin, Elizabeth Seay and Jen Uscher—for their sisterhood, support, and ideal readership while helping to develop a first draft.

Aram Arkun for crucial research assistance. Lee Messerlian for sharing his kindred spirit and knowledge of our family tree. Marc Nichanian for teaching me about witnessing and Catastrophe. Lena Takvorian for her thoughtful, heartfelt and painstaking translations.

David Ciminello, Michelle T. Clinton, David Dratewka, Gigi McCreery, and Rene Vasicek: dear friends and writers who read early or partial drafts and offered insightful comments that stuck with me throughout my revisions.

Friends who rooted for me through a myriad of unique and special ways, including artistic kinship: Christopher Atamian, Shushan Avagyan, Heti Baker, Ahimsa Timoteo Bodhran, Chiqui Cartagena and K. Jennifer Knight, Haig Chahinian and Peter Simmons, Fred Cisterna, Mahru Elahi, Thea Farhadian, Ryan Hill, Ronna Magy, Laura Meyers, Shadi Nahvi, Yvette Perez and Mitra Rastegar.

Nada Taib and Ramzi Moufarej of Ziryab at the Cornelia Street Café for providing a vibrant audience and community of writers for which it was an honor to read work-in-progress.

Richard Abate for believing in this book throughout its long process into being.

Anahid Kassabian for her brilliance and foresight in guiding me towards Aunt Lute.

Arman Martirosyan for not letting me give up hope.

Aunt Lute Books: for enthusiasm and advocacy from everyone, including Riah Gouvea for her eagle eye, and Shay Brawn for her patience and her deep attention to changes.